D0122086

The New Rules of Measurement

What Every Psychologist and Educator Should Know

The New Rules of Measurement

What Every Psychologist and Educator Should Know

Edited by

Susan E. Embretson
University of Kansas

Scott L. Hershberger
California State University, Long Beach

IEA LAWRENCE ERLBAUM ASSOCIATES, PUBLISHERS
1999   Mahwah, New Jersey   London

Lawrence Erlbaum Associates, Inc., Publishers
10 Industrial Avenue
Mahwah, NJ 07430

Cover design by Kathryn Houghtaling Lacey

Library of Congress Cataloging-in-Publication Data

The new rules of measurement : what every
psychologist and educator should know / edited by
Susan Embretson and Scott Hershberger.
    p. cm.
Papers originally presented at a conference held at the
University of Kansas, February 21–22, 1997.
    Includes bibliographical references and indexes.
    ISBN 0-8058-2860-5 (alk. paper)
1. Psychometrics—Congresses.   2. Psychological
tests—Congresses. I. Embretson, Susan E.
II. Hershberger, Scott L.
BF39.N44 1998
150'.28'7—dc21   98–24513
                                                    CIP

Books published by Lawrence Erlbaum Associates are
printed on acid-free paper, and their bindings are chosen for
strength and durability.

Printed in the United States of America
10   9   8   7   6   5   4   3   2

Contents

Preface

Psychologists and educators today are faced with a dazzling array of new tests. Many new constructs are assessed by these tests, such as Attention Deficit Disorder, Simultaneous and Successive Processing, Big-5 Personality Factors, Mood, and so forth. Other new tests are revised versions of old tests; however, these tests often differ substantially from their predecessors. An obvious difference is that many tests are now computerized. The Graduate Record Examination, the Differential Ability Test, and MMPI-2 are just a few of the current computerized tests. Although the mere computerization of a test does not necessarily involve new measurement principles, many new computerized tests are administered in adaptive form. Examinees are administered only those items that are particularly informative about their trait level; consequently, different examinees receive different tests. How can performance be compared between examinees? Less obvious changes in some new tests is the system behind scoring and score interpretation. For example, the Exner system for the scoring and interpreting the Rorschach differs substantially from the old system, which has led to increased psychometric properties. Similarly, the familiar Stanford–Binet test has also been based partly on some new principles.

Despite the changes in the new generation of tests, with few exceptions neither measurement textbooks nor most test manuals have changed much from earlier versions. Most testing and measurement textbooks still emphasize classical test theory. Test manuals still report mostly classical test theory statistics. The technical details of test development are reported in appendices or omitted entirely. It is easy to conclude that the changes in tests are superficial; the same principles of measurement apply to the new tests as to the old tests. However, that conclusion would be erroneous. Measurement principles have indeed changed. Rather, testing reference sources have not kept pace with the changes.

What are the new measurement principles? Perhaps the most neglected topic is the role of item response theory (IRT) in all phases of test development. IRT is the method that makes adaptive testing practically feasible. Furthermore, IRT has important applications in calibrating items and measuring an individual. IRT is also very important in the construct development phase of measurement. Explicating the nature of the latent constructs underlying performance, establishing the applicability of the constructs to varying groups of people (e.g., racial–ethnic groups, gender groups, clinical populations, nonnative speakers), and establishing scalability are important issues in construct development. IRT is increasingly employed in construct development due to its many advantages over classical test theory approaches.

The use of generalizability theory to support the psychometric properties of measurements is also underemphasized in textbooks. Traditional textbooks mainly emphasize specialized reliability coefficients, such as stability, equivalence, rater, and internal consistency indices. Rather than report many separate reliability indices, generalizability theory can simultaneously analyze the effects of several varying conditions on performance.

Effective validation methods for free response measurements have received virtually no attention in standardized textbooks. Instead, free response tests such as projective tests are described as clinical interview tools rather than as tests. Yet, some important new developments have permitted supportive reliability and validity data to be observed for projective tests, such as the Rorshach.

This edited volume will bridge the gap between modern measurement concepts and testing practice by having prominent scholars from psychology and education describe how these new rules of measurement work and how they differ from the old rules. Several contributors have been involved in the recent construction or revision of a major test, whereas others are well known for their theoretical contributions to measurement. Our goal is to provide an integrated yet comprehensive reference source concerned with contemporary issues and approaches in testing and measurement.

This book supplements contemporary textbooks on measurement and testing by explicating some neglected topics. Although there are a number of textbooks on measurement and testing available, to our knowledge all are deficient in examining the contemporary psychometric methods that underlie the development of the current generation of tests.

Because the new generation of tests has changed so fundamentally from the old generation, it is impossible to cover all changes in a single edited book.

This book is intended for (a) graduate courses on measurement and testing, (b) applied psychologists and educators who work with tests—clinical, industrial, counseling, school, educational, (c) researchers in psychology and related areas. The book is also intended for the next generation of measurement and testing textbook authors. It is hoped that the topics covered here become routinely included in such future textbooks.

The chapters in this edited volume are based on presentations given at a conference organized by the editors of this volume held at the University of Kansas, February 21 and 22, 1997. The conference entitled "The New Rules of Measurement: What Every Psychologist and Educator Should Know" included eight invited presentations, several selected speakers, and many posters. This book includes seven of the eight invited presentations as well as an extended version of a selected presentation. We thank Continuing Education at the University of Kansas for their extensive support and organization of the conference. Special thanks to Karen Wilson for her attention to the many practical arrangements that made the conference successful. The editors also thank the Center of Measurement and Evaluation for their support.

—Susan E. Embretson
—Scott L. Hershberger

CHAPTER ONE

Issues in the Measurement of Cognitive Abilities

Susan E. Embretson
University of Kansas

The valid construction and interpretation of tests are two critically important activities for psychologists and educators, yet an apparent gap exists between the modern methods of measurement available and their use by applied workers. Many important tests have been constructed or revised by measurement principles that differ qualitatively from classical measurement concepts. Yet these principles are not well understood by test users and even many measurement specialists. However, available textbooks on measurement and testing provide only rudimentary coverage of some new principles and then fail to cover other important principles entirely.

In cognitive ability testing, computerization is the most salient change in the new generation of tests. Computerized presentation of items, immediate scoring, and report generation are attractive features of many revised tests. Computerized testing also has made adaptive testing feasible. In the adaptive testing, tests no longer have fixed-item content. Items are selected online for an examinee, depending on their responses to preceeding items. Thus, examinees no longer are exposed to items that are far above or below their performance level. Test forms are optimally selected for each person from the test item bank.

Another salient change in cognitive ability testing is increased flexibility for administering and interpreting individualized tests, such as the Differential Ability Scales (Elliot, 1990), the Woodcock–Johnson Psycho-Educational Battery (Woodcock & Johnson, 1977), and several others. Special procedures for missing data in testing (e.g., persons measured out of level or omitted

1

items) are available so that ability may be estimated without bias. Furthermore, some individual cognitive tests also provide ability estimates that do not depend on a norm-referenced standard for meaning. The ability estimates have optimal scale properties that permit comparisons directly to abilities obtained earlier or to abilities at another developmental level. The abilities may be used to measure developmental change or distance from some developmental standard.

Item response theory (IRT) is the set of measurement principles that have made adaptive testing and increased flexibility for individualized tests practically feasible. Yet IRT has not been given sufficient coverage in graduate educations. Worse, psychologists and educators are often unaware of its application on specific tests. Test manuals do not elaborate how IRT is implemented. Often IRT is, at best, discussed only in an appendix. Why? Test publishers are sensitive to the preparation of test users. Because test users typically are not adequately trained in IRT, they would not understand it as a basis for the test. Of course, because the test actually is based on IRT principles, test users are deprived of knowledge that is crucial to test expertise. In addition, test users are not motivated to understand IRT because its application is not made sufficiently explicit.

IRT is also useful in the construct development phase of testing. IRT now includes a vast array of models that postulate qualitatively different types of underlying constructs. Comparative fit indices for different IRT models can provide interpretations about the constructs that are measured. For example, inconsistent findings about the number and nature of constructs involved in specific tests result, in part, from applying methods that are inappropriate for item-level data. Applying multidimensional IRT models to item level data results in more valid findings. Furthermore, it is often suspected that some test items are population-specific; that is, performance may differ qualitatively over different groups of persons. Sometimes the populations are intrinsic to the measure, such as employing different strategies to solve the items. Other times the populations differ in background, such as defined by gender, racial–ethnic background, native language, or clinical status (e.g., handicaps, etc.). IRT models are available not only to assess these differences, but their application can provide solutions.

IRT also has many practical advantages for test development. Unlike classical test theory, IRT item parameters are not biased by the population ability distribution. In contrast, the classical test theory indices for item difficulty and discrimination (i.e., p values and biserial correlations) are directly influenced by ability distributions. Furthermore, greater flexibility in test calibration, using item subsets with varying groups, is possible because IRT readily handles missing data problems.

Unfortunately, textbooks do not elaborate how applying IRT fundamentally changes testing concepts and results. In fact, most general measurement and testing textbooks still emphasize classical test theory. Although texts are available that are exclusively devoted to IRT, many such textbooks are inaccessible due to their statistically oriented presentation. A notable exception is Hambleton, Swaminathan, and Roger's (1989) textbook, which is quite readable without advanced statistical knowledge. However, the topics covered are pertinent mainly to large scale ability or achievement tests. Yet IRT has important applications to individual ability tests, personality traits, and psychopathology and clinical tests as well as to behavioral rating scales. Unfortunately, prototypic applications to these areas are available only in the specialized journals or readings.

Particularly neglected in readily available intellectual resources is coverage of the special IRT scores that do not require norm referencing for meaningful interpretation. However, descriptions of these scores, and the alternative standards, often are available only in the technical manual (or an appendix of the manual) of specific tests or in isolated technical studies.

Last, but not least, the importance of measurement scale properties in interpreting individual differences in constructs has been mentioned only in passing in most textbooks. Although the importance of obtaining interval-level measurements are mentioned in passing, the potential for IRT scaling to obtain fundamental measurements is inadequately elaborated.

IRT is not the only significant change in the new generation of tests. Generalizability theory is increasingly applied to organize results on the accuracy of measurements over varying conditions. Generalizability theory is readily applicable to both cognitive and personality tests. One could argue that pedological resources for generalizability theory are even fewer for IRT. Not only has generalizability theory received insufficient attention in many textbooks, but also fewer scientific papers are available. Generalizability theory represents a major extension of classical test theory. Traditionally, generalizability theory has been used to analyze the effects of different measurement conditions on the psychometric properties of tests. In most applications of IRT, the impact of varying measurement conditions on trait level is not estimated. Thus, generalizability theory addresses psychometric issues that are not included in IRT and that are important in the new generation of tests.

CHAPTERS AND AUTHORS

Four chapters in the cognitive ability measurement section concern IRT and its role in testing. Robert M. Thorndike examines the future of IRT in the context of its historical origins. Thorndike has unique resources to examine the context in which psychometric methods were developed and applied. His grandfather, E. L. Thorndike, was the pioneering force behind the earliest standardized tests, which required decisions about measurement methods. Further, his father, R. L. Thorndike, is well known for his contributions to ability testing. R. M. Thorndike has authored several books on measurement and statistics, including *A Century of Ability Testing* (1990). Furthermore, he has published numerous papers and monographs on measurement and multivariate methods. For the last 7 years, he has worked with Riverside Publishing Company in capacities related to the Stanford–Binet.

Daniel elaborates how IRT was applied in some popular individualized cognitive tests, the Kaufmann Adult Intelligence Scale (KAIT; Kaufman & Kaufman, 1993) and the Differential Ability Scales (DAS; Elliot, 1990). Daniel has been actively involved in applying IRT to develop major tests. Currently, Daniel is senior scientist in test development at American Guidance Service (AGS). He has also worked in test development at the Psychological Corporation. Daniel has directed psychometric developments on ability tests (e.g., DAS, KAIT), behavior rating scales, neuropsychological tests, and other instruments.

Wright examines some fundamental measurement issues and how applying a special IRT model, the Rasch model, results in person measurements that have scale properties. Wright is particularly able to comment on measurement scale issues because he is well known for making the family of Rasch models available and meaningful in American psychometrics. Wright has conducted numerous workshops on the Rasch model and directed 70 doctoral students, many of whom are now contemporary leaders in psychometrics. As a former student of both Thurstone and the Danish mathematician Rasch, Wright has published extensively on Rasch measurement models, including nearly 150 scientific papers, 12 books (including *Best Test Design*, Wright & Stone, 1979, and *Rating Scale Analysis*, Wright & Masters, 1982), and 2 computer programs for Rasch models, BIGSTEPS (Wright & Linacre, 1997) and FACETS (Linacre & Wright, 1977).

Woodcock shows how indices based on Rasch measurement models can enhance interpretations of a person's performance. Woodcock is particularly able to comment on how these indices aid score interpretations because he pioneered the application of Rasch measurement models in American testing. Woodcock has authored several tests, including Woodcock–Johnson Psycho-Educational Battery (1977), the Woodcock Reading Mastery Tests (1973), the Woodcock Language Proficiency Battery (1991), and the Woodcock–Munoz Language Survey (Woodcock & Munoz-Sandoval, 1993).

The last chapter in the cognitive measurement section concerns generalizability theory. Marcoulides describes how generalizability theory picks up where IRT (e.g., the Rasch model) leaves off. Marcoulides is especially able to elucidate how generalizability can contribute to testing because he has published extensively on design optimization issues and on the variance component estimation procedures in generalizability theory. Marcoulides is very actively involved in measurement and statistical scholarship, including serving as review editor of *Structural Equation Modeling* and on several editorial boards. In addition to his regular teaching position, he also serves as president of the Western Decision Sciences Institute.

A VERY BRIEF INTRODUCTION TO IRT

In the remaining space, a very brief introduction to IRT is given. IRT is a major topic in the cognitive measurement chapters. Although most psychologists are familiar with classical test theory, IRT is relatively unfamiliar. IRT provides a qualitatively different basis for the selection of items for a test and for the basis by which to interpret scores. Furthermore, many intuitions about tests and measurement that were developed from classical test theory no longer apply. The rules of measurement are indeed different. To illustrate these differences, some rules of measurement under IRT are contrasted to some rules of measurment under classical test theory.

Measurement Models: IRT Versus Classical Test Theory

In testing, one is interested in assessing a latent variable (i.e., a trait, disposition, or syndrome from a sample of behavior). A measurement model relates performance on the behavior sample (i.e., test) to the latent variable. Figure 1.1 shows two versions of how a latent variable relates to behavior. The upper panel shows how latent variables relate to behavior in classical test theory. The behaviors observed are test scores, whereas the independent variables are the latent variable and error. The classical test theory model is often represented like this in structural equation modeling studies. Thus, the independent variables are the latent variable score and error score and the dependent variable is observed test score. For each test form, the familiar equation may be derived, as follows:

$$\text{Observed Score} = \text{True Score} + \text{Error} \qquad (1.1)$$

Applying the classical test theory model requires several assumptions about error distributions; namely, errors are normally and uniformly distributed in persons, have an expected value of zero, and are uncorrelated with all other variables.

The classical test theory model is limited in several ways. First, true score applies only to items on a specific test or to items on a test with equivalent item properties. That is, because no provision for possibly varying item parameters are included in the classical test theory model, they must be regarded as fixed on a particular test. Second, although the model specifies two separate independent variables for a person, these independent variables are not really separable for an individual score. When combined with other

CLASSICAL TEST THEORY

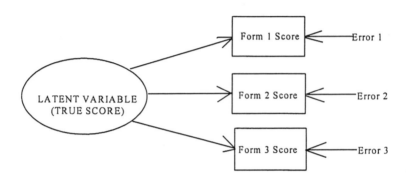

ITEM RESPONSE THEORY

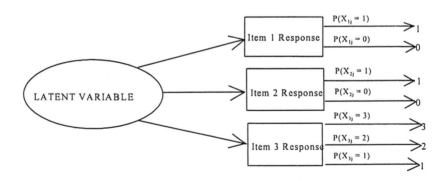

FIG. 1.1. Two versions of the relationship of a latent variable to behavior. (Reprinted with permission from Embretson, S. E., & Reise, S. R. (in press). *Item response theory for psychologists.* Mahwah, NJ: Lawrence Erlbaum Associates.)

assumptions (e.g., error distributions), the model is used to justify estimates of population statistics such as true variance and error variance. Third, item properties are not linked to behavior. The omission of item properties from the model requires that they be justified elsewhere, such as by their impact on various group statistics such as variances and reliabilities.

The lower panel of Fig. 1.1 shows how the latent variable relates to behavior in IRT. Here, the observed behavior is individual item responses (e.g., 0 or 1). The latent variable influences the probabilities of the responses to the items (shown as $P(X_{ij} = 1)$, etc.). Notice that the number of response options varies across items. This representation corresponds to the mathematical models of IRT.

The IRT model, then, applies to individual item response. The probability that a person will pass or endorse a particular item depends on their trait level and on the difficulty of the item, as follows:

$$PROB(ItemPassed) = FUNCTION \ [(TraitLevel) - (ItemDifficulty)] \quad (1.2)$$

It can be seen that trait level and item difficulty combine additively, according to some (unspecified) function, to produce the probability that the item is endorsed or passed.

Extending this equation to symbols, the independent variables are the person's trait level, θ_j, and the item's difficulty level, b_i.

$$P(X_{ij} = 1) = FUNCTION \ (\theta_j - b_i) \quad (1.3)$$

The Rasch IRT model is a simple logistic function of trait level and item difficulty, as follows:

$$P(X_{ij} = 1 \mid \theta_j, b_i) = \frac{\exp (\theta_j - b_i)}{1 + \exp (\theta_j - b_i)} \quad (1.4)$$

where θ_j and b_i are defined as previously shown. Equation 1.4 is also sometimes presented as the one-parameter logistic (1PL) measurement model due to its exponential form in predicting probabilities and the inclusion of one item parameter (i.e., item difficulty) to represent differences in items.

Several features of the simple Rasch model contrast directly to the classical test theory model. First, the meaning of trait level applies to any item for which difficulty is known. For a given trait level, the odds of success can be given for any calibrated item. The simple Rasch model includes item difficulty in determining relationship to performance. In contrast, because the classical test theory model does not include item properties, the trait score applies to the items on a particular test or its equivalent. Other item properties, such as discrimination, guessing, the nature of the alternatives, and even substantive features of items, are included as independent variables in more complex IRT models. Second, item properties, as well as trait levels, are linked to behavior. IRT provides a full model of behavior because separate parameters are included for both persons and items. Third, trait level and item properties are independent variables that may be estimated separately. The separability of these parameters is essential for an important property in measurement theory; namely, specific objectivity, which will be further discussed later in this chapter.

Two other major advantages that result from the more complete IRT model are: (a) Person trait level estimates are controlled for the properties of the items that were administered and (b) item difficulty estimates are controlled for the trait levels of the particular persons in the calibration sample. In this sense, item-free person estimates and population-free item estimates are obtained.

Item Characteristics Curves (ICC).   The IRT models individual item responses. Equation 1.3 will produce a probability of passing or endorsing the item for a person at any trait level. An ICC regresses changes in response probability on trait level. Figure 1.2 shows ICCs for four dichotomous items as specified from the two-parameter logistic model. First, these ICCs are S-

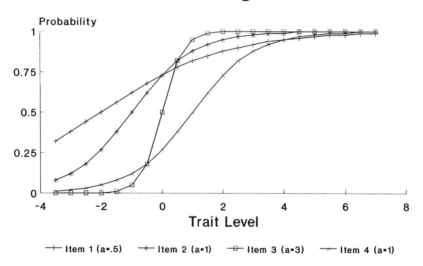

FIG. 1.2.   Item characteristics for four items from the two-parameter logistic model.

shaped; in the middle of the curve, small changes in trait level imply large changes in item-solving probability. At the extremes, large changes in trait level lead to small changes in the probabilities. Second, although all three ICCs have the same general shape, they differ in both location and slope. Location corresponds to item difficulty in CTT; however, location is directly linked to trait level. For example, the trait level that yields an item-solving probability of .50 is much lower for Item 1 than for Item 2 or Item 3. Thus, Item 1 is easier. Slope corresponds to item discrimination. It describes how rapidly the probabilities change with trait level. For Item 2, the change is much slower. Thus, Item 2 is less discriminating because item response probabilities are less responsive to changes in trait level. Third, the ICCs have upper and lower bounds. For the example in Fig. 1.2, the item response probabilities range from .00 to 1.00. In some IRT models, however, a more restricted range of probabilities is specified to accommodate features like guessing.

Another way to view the ICCs is to interpret the meaning of a particular trait level. Given a trait level such as 2.00, the probabilities that specific items are passed or endorsed may be given exactly.

Estimating Trait Levels and Item Difficulties

IRT: Item Responses as Symptoms. Estimating a person's trait level is fundamentally different in IRT than in classical test theory. Under classical test theory, trait levels are estimated by summing responses across items and then converting the sum into a standard score. However, in IRT, determining the person's trait level is not a question of how to add up the item responses. In a sense, the IRT process of estimating trait levels is analogous to the clinical inference process. Latent variables (or syndromes) must be inferred from presenting behaviors (including test item responses). Given the behaviors that the clinician was able to observe and knowledge of the likelihood of these behaviors under certain syndromes, what diagnosis best explains the presenting behaviors? Analogously, trait levels are estimated in IRT by addressing the following question: Given the properties of the items and knowledge of how item properties in influence behavior (i.e., the IRT model), what is the most likely trait level to explain the person's responses?

Intuitively, if a person passes most items on a very hard test, this behavior is not very likely if a person has a low trait level. This behavior is somewhat more likely if the person has a moderate trait level; but, of course, the behavior is more likely if the person has a high trait level. Estimating the IRT trait level that corresponds to a response pattern requires a search process rather than a scoring procedure. That is, the trait level under which the response pattern has the highest likelihood is sought.

In IRT, estimating trait levels from response patterns depends on (a) the IRT model and (b) the properties of the items that were administered. Trait levels typically are estimated by a maximum likelihood method; specifically, the estimated trait level for person j maximizes the likelihood of his or her response pattern given the item properties. To find the appropriate trait level, one must (a) compute the likelihoods of a response pattern under various trait levels and (b) conduct a search process that yields the trait level that gives the highest likelihood.

To illustrate a brute force search method, suppose that a test with five items was administered. Assume that item difficulties are known to be $(-2,-1,0,1,2)$. Suppose further that a person passed the first four items and failed the last item; thus the response pattern for person j is $(1,1,1,1,0)$. Now, if the person's trait level were known, the probability of passing (or failing) each item, in turn, could be computed from the IRT model, such as Equation 1.4. The likelihood of the whole response pattern is just the product of the individual item responses

$$L_j = P_{1j}P_{2j}P_{3j}P_{4j}(1 - P_{5j}) \qquad (1.5)$$

Now, the latent trait value for the response pattern is exactly what we do not know. But, like clinical inference, we can consider hypothetical conditions on the latent variable for implications. The likelihood of the response pattern under different hypothetical trait levels can be compared. The goal for an IRT search process is finding the trait level for which the likelihood is highest.

In Fig. 1.3, the likelihoods for 22 different hypothetical trait levels are computed in the range from -3.5 to 7, at intervals of .5, for the response pattern $(1,1,1,1,0)$, shown as Pattern 1. Notice that the trait level that yields the highest likelihood for the pattern is 2.00. Based on our brute force method, then, this would be the estimated trait level. Of course, the greatest accuracy for this brute force method would be obtained by increasing the number of calculations (but this rapidly becomes computationally burdensome). Methods for numerical analysis, however, may be applied to more efficiently search for the point of maximum likelihood (beyond this introduction).

Figure 1.3 also shows the likelihood for three other response patterns. For Pattern 2, only three items are passed. For this pattern, the best estimate of trait level is $-.50$. For Pattern 3, only the easiest item is solved, so high trait levels are not likely. The maximum likelihood was calculated for the trait level of -2.0. Pattern 4, which has the same total score as Pattern 1, reaches the highest calculated likelihood at the same point (i.e., 2.0), but the whole pattern is less likely (a harder item was solved while an easier item was missed).

The calculations for Fig. 1.3 employ the Rasch model. Here, individuals with the same total score will have the same estimated trait level. However, for other IRT models, such as the 2PL model, the likelihoods for the various trait levels depends on which items were passed.

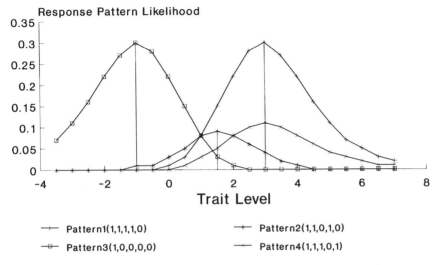

Brute Force Estimation
with Item Difficulties(-1,0,1,2,3)

FIG. 1.3. The likelihood of four response patterns at varying levels of ability.

IRT: The New Rules of Measurement

How much difference does IRT make for the principles of measurement? Consider Table 1.1, which contains some old rules of measurement based on classical test theory and associated test development practices. These rules represent either direct derivations or common heuristics in testing. Few would disagree with these rules.

Now consider the new rules in Table 1.1 from IRT. These rules conflict directly with corresponding old rules. Let us consider a few of these, in turn.

Rule 1: The Standard Error of Measurement

Old Rule 1. The standard error of measurement applies to all scores in a particular population.

New Rule 1. The standard error of measurement differs between persons with different response patterns but generalizes across populations.

In classical test theory, the standard error of measurement is based on a reliability coefficient that is calculated for a particular population. It is computed by taking the square root of 1 minus reliability times the standard deviation of the test ($SE_{Msmt} = (1 - r_{tt})^{1/2} \sigma$). The standard error of measurement is useful to provide confidence intervals for individual scores, assuming that

TABLE 1.1
Comparing Some Rules of Measurement

The Old Rules

Rule 1. The standard error of measurement applies to all scores in a particular population.
Rule 2. Longer tests are more reliable than shorter tests.
Rule 3. Comparing test scores across multiple forms depends on test parallelism or test equating.
Rule 4. Unbiased assessment of item properties depends on representative samples from the population.

The New Rules

Rule 1. The standard error of measurement differs between persons with different response patterns but generalizes across populations.
Rule 2. Shorter tests can be more reliable than longer tests.
Rule 3. Comparing test scores across multiple forms is optimal when test difficulty levels vary across persons.
Rule 4. Unbiased estimates of item properties may be obtained from unrepresentative samples.

measurement error is distributed normally and equally for all score levels. However, it is well known that reliabilities vary between populations, so that the SE_{Msmt} may vary as well.

New Rule 1 conflicts with both aspects of Old Rule 1. First, the standard error of measurement does not apply to all scores as it differs between score levels. The standard error of measurement in IRT depends on the appropriateness of the items for each particular trait level. Therefore, the standard error of measurement is usually highest for extreme scores. Second, the standard error of measurement generalizes across populations. That is, the same trait level has the same standard error of measurement, regardless of the population. Unlike classical test theory, the standard error of measurement does not depend on population true and error variances, which can vary across populations.

Rule 2: Test Length and Reliability

Old Rule 2. Longer tests are more reliable than shorter tests.
New Rule 2. Shorter tests can be more reliable than longer tests.

The old rule is based on a well-known axiom in classical test theory; namely, the Spearman–Brown prophesy formula. This formula shows that if a test is lengthened by a factor of *n* parallel parts, true variance increases more rapidly than error variance (Guilford, 1954, presents the classic proof). In contrast, if a test is shortened, true variance decreases more rapidly than error variance. Longer tests have proportionately less error variance; therefore, longer tests are more reliable than shorter tests.

The new rule asserts that under some conditions, short tests can be more reliable. Because the standard error of measurement is specific to each trait level, minimizing these errors leads to greater reliability for a group as a whole. This may be readily accomplished by adaptive testing, in which the most appropriate items are selected from the item bank for each examinee. Because the standard error is smallest when the most appropriate items are administered, short tests can be quite reliable. Thus, for example, it can be shown that an adaptive test of 20 items can be more reliable, on the average, than a fixed content test of 30 items (see Embretson, 1995).

Rule 3: Interchangeable Test Forms

Old Rule 3. Comparing test scores across multiple forms depends on test parallelism or test equating.

New Rule 3. Comparing test scores across multiple forms is optimal when test difficulty levels vary between persons.

In classical test theory, strict conditions for test parallelism were defined, which included the equality of means, variances, and covariances across test forms (Gulliksen, 1950). If test forms meet Gulliksen's statistical conditions for parallelism, scores may be regarded as comparable across forms. When tests are not parallel, comparable scores between test forms are established by techniques such as linear equating and equipercentile equating (see Holland & Rubin, 1982). However, not all tests can be adequately equated. Test forms with low reliabilities and dissimilar score distributions will be least adequately equated.

The new rule has a somewhat different focus. It can be restated as meaning that the most accurate assessment of trait level is obtained when tests are administered adaptively. Parallel test forms, although yielding similar patterns of standard errors, do not produce the most accurate ability assessments. Most important, better estimation of trait score is obtained by nonparallel test forms, selected optimally for each person. That is, each adaptive test is a separate test form that differs substantially, and deliberately, in difficulty level from other forms.

Rule 4: Unbiased Assessment of Item Properties

Old Rule 4. Unbiased assessment of item properties depends on representative samples from the target population.

New Rule 4. Unbiased estimates of item properties may be obtained from unrepresentative samples.

The classical item statistics, item difficulty (i.e., p values as the proportion passing) and item discrimination (i.e., item-total correlations) are clearly biased by the distribution of trait level in the population. For example, a p

value from a population with many low trait levels will be much smaller than a p value from a population with many high trait levels. Similarly, item–total correlations also depend on population level and variance.

In contrast, the inclusion of a person's trait level in an IRT model implicitly controls the item parameter estimates for trait level. That is, prediction is made at the individual data level; the probability that each person passes each item is modeled. The model is a complete model for the data, unlike classical test theory, because it includes both person and item parameters. Consequently, the same item difficulty and discrimination values will be estimated regardless of the trait distribution. A skeptic might study this directly. In fact, initially a skeptic of these invariance properties, I studied the empirical equivalence of item parameter estimates by systematically varying features of the test and the population. Nearly identical estimates of item difficulty were obtained (Whitely[1] & Dawis, 1976). Of course, if the data fit the model, theoretical proofs of these effects are also available.

New Rules, Old Rules

An extended discussion of these rules is given by Embretson (1995). The rules presented here are only some of the differences between classical test theory and IRT. A much larger set of rule comparisons can given by Embretson and Reise (in press).

The old rules represent common knowledge or practice among psychologists who are trained in classical test theory. These rules have guided the development of many, but certainly not all, published psychological tests. Large-scale testing corporations (e.g., ETS) have developed non-IRT procedures that circumvented the limitations of some old rules. That is, nonlinear test equating (see Holland & Rubin, 1982) and population-free item indices, such as the delta index used by ETS (see Gulliksen, 1950) were developed to counter Old Rule 3 and Old Rule 4, respectively. However, these techniques are not well known nor widely applied outside large-scale testing programs. Thus, the old rules characterize traditional testing practices.

The new rules contrast rather sharply with the old rules. Although, in fact, classical test theory principles may be derived from IRT (by specifying special conditions, constraints, and so forth), IRT is substantially more flexible. Testing practices differ greatly as a consequence.

CONCLUSION

The topics in the chapters on cognitive measurement were selected to give the reader some examples of how IRT and generalizability principles can make a real difference in testing and measurement. Each chapter is self-con-

---

[1]Susan E. Embretson has also published as Susan E. Whitely.

tained; no necessary sequence is needed to understand their content. IRT will be described again in some chapters and, although seemingly redundant, different aspects are highlighted. Furthermore, the particular testing context also should help extend the reader's knowledge.

REFERENCES

Elliot, C. D. (1990). *Differential ability scales.* San Antonio, TX: The Psychological Corporation.

Embretson, S. E. (1995). The new rules of measurement. *Psychological Assessment, 8,* 341–349.

Embretson, S. E., & Reise, S. (in press). *Item response theory for psychologists.* Mahwah, NJ: Lawrence Erlbaum Associates.

Guilford, J. P. (1954). *Psychometric methods.* New York: McGraw-Hill.

Gulliksen, H. (1950). *Theory of mental tests.* New York: McGraw-Hill.

Hambleton, R. K., Swaminathan, H., & Rogers, H. J. (1989). *Fundamentals of item response theory.* Newbury Park, CA: Sage.

Holland, P., & Rubin, D. (1982). *Test equating.* New York: Academic Press.

Kaufman, A. S., & Kaufman, N. L. (1993). *Kaufman adolescent and adult intelligence test.* Circle Pines, MN: American Guidance Service.

Linacre, J. M., & Wright, B. D. (1997). *FACETS: Many-faceted Rasch analysis.* Chicago: MESA Press.

Thorndike, R. M. (1990). *A century of ability testing.* Chicago: Riverside.

Whitely, S. E., & Dawis, R. V. (1976). The influence of test context on item difficulty. *Educational and Psychological Measurement, 36,* 329–337.

Woodcock, R. W. (1973). *Woodcock reading mastery tests.* Circle Pines, MN: American Guidance Service.

Woodcock, R. W. (1991). *Woodcock language proficiency battery—revised.* Chicago: Riverside.

Woodcock, R. W., & Johnson, M. B. (1977). *Woodcock–Johnson psycho-educational battery.* Chicago: Riverside.

Woodcock, R. W., & Munoz-Sandoval, A. F. (1993). *Woodcock–Munoz language survey—English form.* Chicago: Riverside.

Wright, B. D., & Linacre, J. M. (1997). *BIGSTEPS: Rasch computer program for all two facet problems.* Chicago: MESA Press.

Wright, B. D., & Masters, G. N. (1982). *Rating scale analysis: Rasch measurement.* Chicago: MESA Press.

Wright, B. D., & Stone, M. H. (1979). *Best test design: Rasch measurement.* Chicago: MESA Press.

CHAPTER TWO

IRT and Intelligence Testing: Past, Present, and Future

Robert M. Thorndike

Western Washington University

The psychometric model that has come to be called Item Response Theory (IRT) and that has developed out of the work Rasch first published in 1960 did not spring from nothing. Quantitative psychologists, particularly L. L. Thurstone and E. L. Thorndike, had been working with similar models as early as the 1920s. In fact, Thorndike had published a test based on the same foundational logic that underlies IRT as early as 1926 (E. L. Thorndike, Bregman, Cobb, & Woodyard, 1926). Great strides have been made in the quantitative theory supporting measurement in the last 35 years, but the fundamental logic of psychological measurement remains essentially as Thurstone described it over 70 years ago (Thurstone, 1925).

This chapter begins with a short historical journey to see where the ideas underlying the IRT model came from. Then, how these ideas were applied to one contemporary test, the Fourth Edition of the Stanford–Binet Intelligence Scale (R. L. Thorndike, Hagen, & Sattler, 1986a, 1986b) is discussed. The chapter concludes with some speculations about where IRT and psychological measurement might go from here. What might measurement be like, particularly the measurement of human abilities, in the 21st century, and how do IRT and currently available technology fit in the picture?

My interest in the history of measurement is no accident. Most psychologists and educational researchers probably have heard the phrase, "Whatever exists at all exists in some quantity. To know it thoroughly involves knowing its quantity as well as its quality." The author of that phrase was my grandfather, Edward Lee Thorndike (E. L. Thorndike, 1918; ELT for short). ELT brought an ardent belief in the quantifiability of human experience, a belief which he probably had learned from James McKeen Cattell, to all his work in psychology and education. By 1903, 2 years before the presentation of Alfred Binet's famous test, ELT had reported similar and successful efforts to measure individual differences in human cognitive abilities in a study carried out by one of his students, Naomi Norsworthy (E. L. Thorndike, 1903). Binet (Binet & Simon, 1905, 1908) achieved his success by relating his items to another scale that was already well accepted, the scale of normal human development with age. But ELT believed one could scale the items independently of age. Throughout the first third of this century, he and his students worked to create scales for quantifying aspects of human performance and experience as diverse as handwriting, cognitive ability, and aesthetics. The fundamental premise was that there is a single continuum underlying both the stimuli and the individuals. If one could place the stimuli correctly on the underlying or latent continuum, then the responses of an individual to those scaled stimuli could be used to locate the person on the continuum as well.

Most of the formal mathematical work for developing scales to represent latent traits was done by L. L. Thurstone, starting in the early 1920s. In a brilliant series of papers, Thurstone (1925, 1927, 1928) showed how one could use probability logic from the cumulative normal distribution to scale the stimuli. An example will help clarify what Thurstone was talking about.

Consider the words *sleepy, somnolent,* and *oscitant.* The words are synonyms, but as elements of vocabulary they are quite different. Most children know what the word sleepy means by the time they are 2 or 3. Perhaps half of high school seniors know the definition of the word somnolent, and probably not one college graduate in a hundred knows the definition of oscitant. If one thinks of a continuum of vocabulary knowledge, each of these three words might be placed on that continuum as shown in Fig. 2.1. A word that reflects only a little of the trait shows up on the left; words requiring a moderate amount of the trait are in the middle, and those making the greatest demands on vocabulary knowledge are at the right. The question is, how does one find the correct order for the words and their exact locations along the continuum?

Both Binet and E. L. Thorndike came to the straightforward conclusion that tasks requiring higher levels of the trait would be solved correctly by fewer people. That is, finding the order of the tasks is easy. Binet related

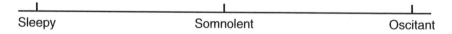

Sleepy   Somnolent   Oscitant

FIG. 2.1. Three words can be located at positions along a latent continuum of word knowledge depending on the amount of the trait required to know the definition of each word.

task level to age. Tasks a 10-year-old could perform that an 8-year-old could not were more difficult than those the average 8-year-old could do, so they were placed higher on the scale. For ELT, the order might be found by the simple expedient of using judges, as in the case of his scales of handwriting samples, or people with higher levels of education might be considered as those with higher levels of ability development. The essential and more difficult problem was to find a common unit, to produce at least an interval scale of measurement.

This is where Thurstone (1925) came in (see Thurstone, 1959, for a collection of papers from this period applying similar methods to the measurement of attitudes). What Thurstone realized was that the farther apart two stimuli were on the continuum, the less likely it was that there would be inconsistent responses to them. For example, the three words sleepy, somnolent, and oscitant are so far apart on the word knowledge continuum that there is zero probability that someone who knows what oscitant means would fail to correctly define the other two terms; furthermore, anyone who knows somnolent would certainly know sleepy. Order is known, but not distance.

Now consider the term lethargic. Lethargic is close in meaning and probably fairly close in difficulty to the word somnolent, but not all people who know one word could necessarily define the other. There would be inconsistency. It is this feature that allows the scaling of the stimuli in terms of distances. The closer two terms are to each other in amount of the trait they require, the greater will be the inconsistency in responding to them. This is true regardless of whether the stimuli are statements of attitudes such as those used by Thurstone (1959), tasks measuring human abilities such as concerned Thorndike (E. L. Thorndike et al., 1926) or statements reflecting psychopathology. If there is no inconsistency in responding to the statements by at least some respondents, it is possible to establish an order for the stimuli but not the distances between them.

THE ITEM TRACE LINE OR CHARACTERISTIC CURVE

From here on, the discussion will be restricted to human ability measurement, but the same basic principles apply to the measurement of other psychological characteristics. Ability measurement allows a simplifying assumption and makes it possible to use some convenient graphs.

The simplifying assumption is that as people possess more ability, they are more likely to be able to complete successfully a task requiring that ability. This feature is known as monotonicity. A relationship is monotonic if it always goes in the same direction, either always upward or always downward. Positive monotonicity is generally true of the ability domain, but it does not necessarily characterize measures of typical performance such as personality and attitude measures.

The relationship that is assumed to be monotonic and positive is the relationship between a person's level on the trait in question and their probability of succeeding in a task. Probability, of course, can range from zero to one. There is probably not a single 3-year-old in the country who knows the meaning of the word somnolent, so a person at this level on the trait has a zero chance of succeeding with this item. By the time we reach 12-year-olds, there are probably a few who know the term because there will be some who have reached the required level on the trait. The farther up the trait continuum we go, the greater is the likelihood that a person will know the word.

The graph of the relationship between probability of success on a specific task or test item and ability level is known as the item characteristic curve or item trace line. A typical trace line might look like the one in Fig. 2.2. The trait continuum is represented on the abscissa and the probability of correct response is on the ordinate. Notice that at low levels of the trait the probability of success is zero, at moderate levels the line is rising as the probability of success increases, and at high levels of the trait the curve peaks at 100%. Any test item has a trace line that describes its relationship to the underlying trait continuum in terms of the probability of a correct response, and the curve generally approximates the cumulative normal distribution (for reasons that need not concern this discussion, IRT generally uses an exponential function that closely approximates the cumulative normal distribution).

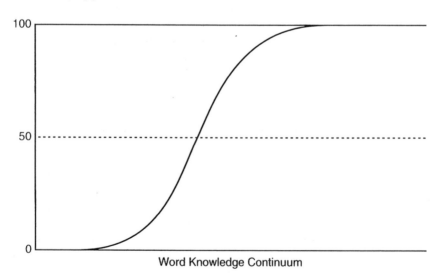

FIG. 2.2. An item trace line shows the relationship between position on the underlying continuum and probability of answering the item correctly.

An item trace line has two important features: its location relative to the trait continuum and the rate at which it rises. The first feature reflects the item's difficulty. The difficulty of an item is defined as the ability level required to have a probability of 50% of succeeding at the task. More difficult items require a higher level of ability to achieve a 50% chance of success, as is shown in Fig. 2.3.

The second important feature of the trace line is the rate at which the probability of success changes with ability level. This is known as item discrimination and indicates the ability of the item to differentiate those with more of the trait from those with less. It is equivalent to the slope of the trace line. The steeper the slope, the more rapid the change in probability of a correct answer and the more sharply the item differentiates between people at different points on the ability continuum. Two items that have the same difficulty but differ in discrimination are shown in Fig. 2.4. The ability of an item to discriminate is greatest at the center of its range of functioning and decreases for lower and higher ability levels.

Note that an item can differentiate between people with different levels of the trait only in the range where there is some uncertainty whether they will succeed on the item. Items that everyone in an examinee group gets correct or everyone misses cannot differentiate between members of the group. For example, both person A and person B in Fig. 2.4 have a 100% probability of passing item 1. Therefore it gives us no information about their relative or absolute abilities (other than that they both exceed the ability requirements of this item). However, a test made up of items like number

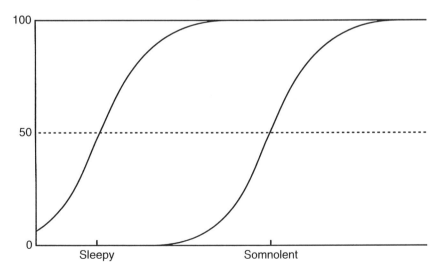

FIG. 2.3. Trace lines for two items of different difficulty. The difficulty of an item determines its location on the latent trait continuum.

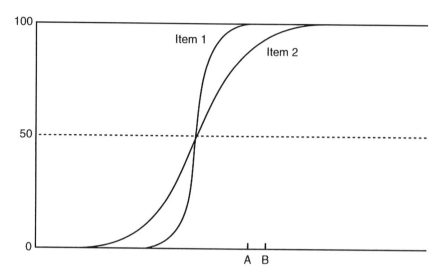

FIG. 2.4. Trace lines for two items of different discrimination. The slope of the trace line reflects the item's discrimination.

2 would reveal their relative positions because B has a higher probability of succeeding on items like this and would, on average, earn a higher score on a test composed of such items. Of course, if the people are far apart, almost any item can differentiate between them, but a test probably would not be needed under those circumstances.

The two properties of an item just described are called the first and second or *b* and *a* parameters in IRT vernacular. The first item parameter, which is called *b*, is the item's difficulty, its location on the trait continuum; the second is its discrimination, the rate at which the probability of a correct response changes. There is also a third parameter, *c*, that can be applied to select response or multiple choice ability items. This is the probability that an examinee can get the item correct by guessing. The three characteristics of a trace line are shown in Fig. 2.5.

IRT models that estimate only the first parameter in fitting an empirical set of data, assuming that the value of the second is equal for all items and that the value of the third is zero, are called Rasch models (see Wright, this volume). Two-parameter models estimate both difficulty and slope to fit the data, and three-parameter models estimate all three. The one-parameter model is quite restrictive due to its equal slope assumption, but requires less data than the other two to obtain stable estimates.

Consider now how a person is measured by a set of test items. Figure 2.6 shows two test items and two examinees arrayed on the trait continuum. The height of an item's trace line above the base line at the point that corresponds to an individual shows the probability that a person with that

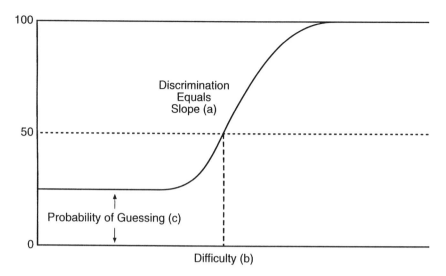

FIG. 2.5. An item can have up to three parameters. The first parameter is the difficulty (*b*), the second is discrimination (*a*), and the third is the probability of a successful guess (*c*).

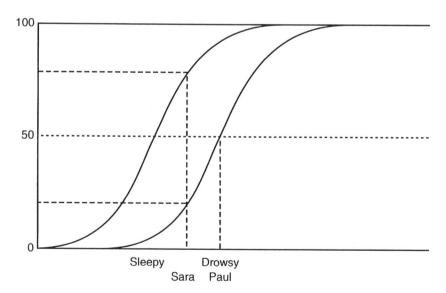

Sleepy   Drowsy
Sara   Paul

FIG. 2.6. Persons can also be placed on the trait continuum. The height of an item's trace line above a person's location is the probability that this person will successfully answer this item.

level of ability will succeed on that item. For example, Sara has a low level of word knowledge. The probability is about 80% that she will know the definition of the word sleepy and other words of this difficulty. If she were given a test with 100 words, all of which had exactly the same difficulty as sleepy, she would be expected to get 80% of them correct. Viewed another way, 80% of people with exactly Sara's level of ability would get this item correct. These same people would have a success rate of about 20% with the word drowsy.

Now consider Paul. Paul and the word drowsy are at exactly the same place on the trait continuum, which means that Paul has a 50% probability of being able to define drowsy and other words at this difficulty level. It is this feature that provides the measurement of Paul's ability. That is, the difficulty level of an item, its scale value, is defined as the point on the continuum where respondents in the calibration sample had a 50% probability of getting the item correct. Likewise, a person's position on the trait continuum is defined as corresponding to the scale value of the items they have a 50% chance of answering correctly. Once the difficulty levels of the items in a test, their positions on the latent continuum, are determined, that information provides a scale of ability that is the same for all future examinees. By the same token, given a group of people whose ability levels cover the entire trait continuum, the order of the items and the distances between them can be determined, and these properties of the items do not depend on the properties of the particular group of examinees so long as the entire trait continuum is covered. The key is to have a group of stimuli that are distributed over the entire continuum and a group of examinees, necessarily quite large, whose abilities cover the same range.

It is not necessary to go into the details of how this miracle is accomplished. ELT gave the details of his method, which used the normal distribution, in 1926 (Thorndike et al., 1926) and any book on IRT, such as Lord (1980), can provide the logistic function equivalents used today. What is interesting is how this logic can be applied to practical testing problems. ELT's approach is reviewed first, then the Fourth Edition of the Stanford–Binet is examined.

THE CAVD

E. L. Thorndike believed that intelligence is a multifaceted property of organisms and that any test can measure only a selection of the possible intellective traits. He would, for example, speak of "Intellect *abcd. ... n*", meaning that the measuring device under consideration assessed the listed traits *a, b, c, d, ...* to *n*, a subset of the possible intellectual traits. In a 2-year program of research culminating in 1926, he and his coworkers

(Thorndike et al., 1926), one of whom was his son, my father, Robert L. Thorndike, constructed and tested out an instrument to measure the intellectual traits of Comprehension, Arithmetic, Vocabulary, and Direction Following abilities. The test was designed, in ELT's terminology, to measure intellect CAVD; therefore, that was the name given to the test.

Each of the four basic traits was measured by a series of 17 10-item short tests or testlets. The 10 items in any testlet were selected to be highly similar in difficulty. A uniform scale for the differences between the testlets was determined from the probable error of one group near the middle of the ability continuum (Thurstone, 1927, suggested using standard deviations instead) and provided a scale with 17 nearly equal steps ranging from the ability of a below-average 2-year-old up to the ability of a very superior adult. A given examinee would take only those items that were near his or her ability level, making the test relatively efficient by eliminating items where the examinee had a near perfect or essentially zero chance of success. An examinee's level on any one of the four traits was estimated as the point on the scale where they had a 50% chance of success, a point that might fall between two adjacent testlets.

An interesting feature of the CAVD was that it represented one of two attempts undertaken at about that time to define an absolute zero for intelligence. The other was by Thurstone (1928). By using a set of judges, all of whom were members of the American Psychological Association, ELT was able to estimate the intellectual requirements for various sets of behaviors appropriate for infrahuman organisms. The lowest point defined on the scale was the ability to differentiate a pleasurable stimulus from an unpleasurable one. Any organism that could not do this was assumed to have negligible intelligence. Comparative psychology could thus fix 0 intelligence as an ability level slightly below that of an earthworm. Twenty-three equal-appearing intervals were defined between this point and the bottom of the scale of human performance, resulting in a 40-step ratio scale. On this scale, a superior adult would have a little less than twice the intelligence of a 2-year-old.

Before one jumps to the conclusion that this statement is silly, it is important to remember that ELT believed intelligence was multifaceted and that as a global concept it was characterized by three properties: altitude, breadth, and speed. The CAVD was untimed, eliminating speed, and it was designed as a pure measure of altitude. What a person can do in the real world is a function of all three characteristics, and ELT saw the potential breadth of intellect as increasing with altitude. He argued that what we see as intelligent functioning is akin to the area of one's intellect, a composite of altitude, the most complex tasks a person can do, and breadth, the range of tasks one can perform at a given altitude. Because breadth was seen as increasing as a function of altitude, the potential for emitting intelligent behaviors, the area of intellect, might increase as the square or cube of altitude. Thus, the area of intellect of a superior adult might be 20 or 100 times that of a 2-year-old, although its altitude would be only twice as great.

THE STANFORD–BINET FOURTH EDITION

By 1926, Thorndike and his colleagues had produced a test in which the items, in the form of their testlets, were scaled on at least an interval scale of the underlying trait, a scale that did not depend on any specific norm group, and a person's standing on the trait was given by the scale value of the items they had a 50–50 chance of passing. But the test was too long and cumbersome for common use. The Stanford Revision of the Binet–Simon Scales, which Terman had published in 1916, was firmly entrenched as the test of choice for individual testing and a variety of group tests, some of which ELT had designed, were available for school and commercial use, so there was little market. ELT had too many other interests to get tied up with this test, and Thurstone soon turned his attention from scaling to factor analysis (Thurstone, 1931). With the exception of a few theoretical papers (for example, Lazarsfeld, 1959; Lord, 1953), little was done with what came to be known as latent trait theory, and the CAVD remained an interesting footnote in psychometric history.

By the early 1980s the Stanford–Binet had not had a meaningful revision for 50 years. Two rather feeble efforts had been made in 1960 (Terman & Merrill, 1960) and 1972 (Terman & Merrill, 1973), but the Stanford–Binet, through neglect, had lost its place of primacy as a measure of intelligence to the Wechsler tests. A decision was made to attempt to modernize the Stanford–Binet using contemporary test development procedures. Riverside Publishing Company, the publisher of the Stanford–Binet, also happened to be the publisher of a widely used group ability test, the Cognitive Abilities Test or CogAT (R. L. Thorndike & Hagen, 1986) whose senior author was the same 15-year-old, now past 70, who had worked with his father on the CAVD in the 1920s. Robert Ladd Thorndike, RLT for short, and his associate, Elizabeth Hagen, were asked to prepare a revision of the Stanford–Binet in company with Jerome Sattler, a well-known child clinical psychologist (R. L. Thorndike, Hagen, & Sattler, 1986a, 1986b).

The original Stanford–Binet (Terman, 1916; Terman & Merrill, 1937) was constructed in what has sometimes been called a spiral omnibus format, which is a more general term than age scale, the term usually associated with the Stanford–Binet. The test included several types of items at several levels of difficulty, but the items were arranged by difficulty rather than by content or cognitive function. At one level an examinee might confront vocabulary items, memory items, quantitative items, and comprehension items. At the next level of difficulty there might be more vocabulary items, then some absurdities items, and so on. The manifest content of the items changed from level to level. If one adopted ELT's notions about the nature of intellect, then the test measured different functions at different levels, but the instrument was scored to provide only a single global index of intellectual ability.

RLT and I had several conversations about the direction he planned to take with the revision of the Stanford–Binet, some before the fact, and some after. First, because this was a revision rather than a new test, there was an effort to retain updated versions of the best items from the original test. Second, his own group-administered intelligence test, the CogAT, was structured to provide separate scores for verbal, quantitative, and spatial or non-verbal abilities. The new Stanford–Binet Fourth Edition (SB–IV) would articulate better with the CogAT if it provided these three scales. Also, RLT was favorably impressed with Raymond Cattell's model of fluid and crystallized intelligence (Horn, 1985; Horn & Cattell, 1966) and felt the test should provide measures of these. Finally, memory, particularly short-term memory, had been an integral part of the Stanford–Binet from the beginning and also appeared in the later Cattell–Horn version of G_f–G_c theory, so memory subtests were included.

These considerations, plus the results obtained with various item types during tryouts, dictated the general structure of the test. It would contain items measuring 15 types of cognitive functions as shown in Fig. 2.7, and these were organized into subtests by content rather than into levels by difficulty to allow for separate scoring of the subtests. The subtest scores could then be combined to provide four area scores, three corresponding to the scales of the CogAT, and one for short-term memory. The quantitative and verbal scores could be combined to yield a score for G_c and the nonverbal score was seen as a measure of G_f. A global cognitive ability score similar to the IQ score of the earlier Stanford–Binets was produced by summing the four area scores.

IRT and the Stanford–Binet

IRT has little to say on the matter of the psychological theory underlying a test and general matters of test design. It is at the stage when one has a set of items and those items have been administered to a group of examinees that the methods of IRT come into play. Most applications of IRT assume that the items being analyzed fall along a single continuum like the ones discussed earlier. In the case of the Stanford–Binet, item tryout data for each subtest were used in a one-parameter or Rasch scaling model to determine the proper order of the items, and this is the limit of how IRT is used in most testing applications unless the test is administered by computer. This may be akin to using a hydraulic press to crack a peanut. That is, the practice of testing generally is unaffected by the statistical rigor of IRT. The end user

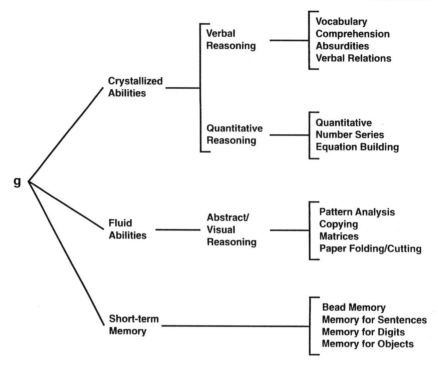

FIG. 2.7. Theoretical structure behind the Stanford–Binet: Fourth Edition.

sees only the order of the items, not their latent scale values, and scores are usually simply the sum of the items answered correctly. That certainly is the case for the SB–IV. After this discussion of the current version of the Stanford–Binet is finished, some suggestions are offered about how the situation might be improved.

The CAVD and the Stanford–Binet

Remember the structure of the CAVD? It had 17 10-item testlets with items of homogeneous content and difficulty for each of the four cognitive functions tested. The Stanford–Binet IV has exactly the same structure for each of its 15 subtests (although with different numbers of levels), and this fact is no accident. RLT explicitly borrowed this feature from ELT. The difference is that, as a concession to practicality, each testlet has 2 items rather than 10. Each item of a pair was intended to be of the same difficulty, and successive pairs were to differ in difficulty by a constant amount. Item selection and placement were based on a Rasch scaling, but because of a limited item pool and quite limited subject sample, some items were misplaced, a fact that was not discovered until after the normative data were collected and RLT, in order to have something to do in idle moments, rescored all 5,000 tests in the norm sample by hand and ran a Rasch analysis on the new data. A second consequence of this tour de force was that he found a disturbingly large number of scoring errors in the norm sample protocols. Other studies have found that errors are more the rule than the exception for individually administered tests, such as the Stanford–Binet and the Wechsler scales, that must be scored while testing is under way (see Kaufman, 1990, for a review of studies with the Wechsler scales).

So the fourth edition of the Stanford–Binet is a test that is nearly as much a modern CAVD as it is an updated Stanford–Binet. But there is one additional feature of the SB–IV that is unique, the use of a routing test as an attempt to adapt testing to the specific ability level of each examinee. RLT was very impressed with the work of David Weiss in the area of computer adaptive testing or CAT (Weiss, 1982), and he tried to incorporate some of this methodology into the new Stanford–Binet. Adaptive testing, selecting the next test item based on whether the examinee got the last one right or wrong, is almost impossible to carry out without a computer. What RLT used as an approximation was the routing test.

Remember that we obtain useful information about the ability level of a person only from items where he or she has a chance to succeed, but also a chance to fail. An untimed test of two-digit addition problems would give no information about the quantitative abilities of a group of college graduates. Most individual and group tests of cognitive ability use a starting point for testing that is based on the age or grade level of the examinees (grade level probably is better because it incorporates some information about prior accomplishments). This practice means that above-average students will waste time taking unnecessarily easy items and below-average students will start testing at a level where they cannot succeed, which results in frustration, negative affect for education, and various other potential ills.

In administering the SB–IV, one first gives the Vocabulary subtest. Raw score on this test, combined with age, is used to select the starting point for each of the other tests. That is, a brief estimate of verbal ability is used to adjust testing to eliminate items that are likely to be too easy or too hard for a particular examinee. The result is that more information is acquired per unit of testing time, but a greater skill demand is placed on the examiner to determine where to start testing with each subtest. RLT found errors in selecting the correct starting point to be fairly common in the norms data.

WHERE ARE WE GOING FROM HERE

Prediction is always somewhat perilous and should be attempted only with caution and restraint. However, one can detect some trends in psychological measurement that it may be reasonable to expect to continue.

First, and this should come as no surprise, computers will play an increasing role in all phases of testing, but particularly in test administration. People have been using computers for over three decades to analyze standardization data and prepare test norms. Elegant IRT programs are readily available to do sophisticated analyses of item data and to scale the items. Every year better software becomes available to aid in test interpretation and report writing (an ad in one recent professional newsletter announced that it produced reports ready for signature!), but in clinical test administration little progress has been made that affects common practice. The routing test found on the SB–IV is one of few clear examples.

Computer-Assisted Test Administration

Almost 10 years ago, I tried without success to interest Riverside Publishing Company in computer-assisted administration of the Stanford–Binet. What I envisioned was not an examinee sitting alone at a computer terminal or substituting the computer for the insightful judgment of an experienced clinician, but a computer program that would assist in recording and scoring examinee responses and, more important, suggesting the next item to be administered. For example, items in tests like Vocabulary, Comprehension, and particularly Equation Building from the Stanford–Binet can have multiple correct answers. Being able to decide quickly whether an atypical answer is correct can put a tremendous burden on the examiner (consider, for example, if somnolent were a vocabulary word to be defined and the person's response was oscitant), but it is a trivial task to put a wide range of admissible alternatives in a database and search for a match. Because the examiner records the answers verbatim on the test protocol anyway, entering them in a computer would be little or no added effort. The computer would score the answer as right or wrong, always leaving the examiner the option of overriding the program or probing the examinee for more detail, and store the scored response for future use.

One important task of the examiner with a test like the Stanford–Binet or one of the Wechsler scales is to keep track of how many items have been missed. When a particular criterion that differs from one instrument to another has been reached, no further items of that type are to be administered and the examiner moves on to the next subtest. One of the most common errors RLT found in test administration was that examiners had stopped testing at the wrong time, a mistake that resulted in erroneous test scores. This is a purely mechanical decision that could be left to a computer program, again with the option for the examiner to override the computer for specific clinical reasons. When the stopping criterion is reached, the computer prompts the examiner to begin the next subtest.

Computer-assisted test administration of this simple kind has several additional advantages. Of course, clerical scoring errors would be eliminated, but if the examiner is going to use test interpretation software, the labor of inputting the scores is also eliminated. Test protocols could be stored on disk to be printed later as needed, much as tax forms now are. Once such administration-assisting software became available, many other applications would quickly be found.

Computer-assisted test administration of the type just described can be implemented easily with existing tests, but this is only the beginning of the possibilities. Consider, for example, a test like the classic Stanford–Binet (Terman & Merrill, 1960). Many clinicians liked its spiral omnibus format, both because it gave them opportunities for clinical insights and because the rapid variation in item type was more interesting, particularly for younger or less able examinees. With the computer to assist in administration and scoring, there is no reason not to have the advantages of both a subtest format and a spiral omnibus item presentation arrangement in the same test. The items for a given level could be presented together in the spiral omnibus format, and the computer could score them as subtests or as an omnibus test at the choice of the clinician, the best of both worlds.

This program can be taken further. Suppose one were to apply truly adaptive testing methods to a spiral omnibus administration (see, for example, Wainer, 1990). The advantage of a truly adaptive approach is that testing focuses very quickly on items that are at the examinee's ability level, so the testing produces more information per item administered. Testing could also focus on areas that appear to be of particular concern. A clinician using today's methods might administer a WISC or WAIS to a client and suspect a memory deficit as a result of the pattern of scores. It would be necessary to administer a separate battery of memory tests to probe more deeply. But an adaptive test program could alert the clinician to the score discrepancy while the first test was being administered and recommend that auxiliary memory items, stored on the disk, be used immediately. There is a vast literature (Kaufman, 1990, 1994) on the interpretation of various score patterns on the Wechsler tests, such as Verbal-Performance discrepancies, and there are several whole atlases of scale patterns and their interpretations for the MMPI. Adaptive testing could detect indications of common clinical patterns early and suggest additional items to probe reasonable hypotheses or allow the clinician to suggest hypotheses. Because the items would be available in the program, the diagnostic testing would integrate seamlessly with the primary evaluation. More testing time would be spent on areas of clinical interest, yielding more precise measurement of those intellectual features of greatest diagnostic significance. Where a learning disability was suspected, for example, aptitude and achievement items tapping various cognitive functions could be blended into a single testing session.

These suggestions merely scratch the surface of what is possible. Computers, and moreso video games, have become such an integral part of the urban human experience that there is no reason not to present test stimuli on the screen and have the examinees touch a spot to indicate their answers. This would work well for tests such as the Absurdities subtest on the Stanford–Binet or on the Raven's Progressive Matrices. It might even be possible to administer Block Design or Pattern Analysis or Object Assembly tasks in this way if the examinee could move the images around on the screen with a mouse or a finger. Accurate timing of stimulus presentation and of client responses, always a problem with traditional test administration, then becomes trivial. Speech recognition software might make it possible to eliminate the need for manual recording of responses, even to tasks like Digit Span. Actively involving computers in test administration would also make it simple to incorporate working memory or information processing tasks, such as sentence verification, into standard intelligence measures, thereby linking cognitive psychology research with intelligence testing practice.

A New Scale of Ability

Perhaps one of the greatest public relations errors in the history of psychological testing was Terman's (1916) enthusiastic adoption of the concept of the intelligence quotient. Because it is explicitly normative, it conveys false and unpopular notions about human abilities to those who do not understand it, and it can be employed by people opposed to the use of tests to make incorrect but seemingly telling criticisms of testing. This next, and last, point is more a hope than a prediction, but psychological and educational measurement would be well served if traditional norm-referenced metrics for ability measurement were abandoned. Alfred Binet and E. L. Thorndike had the right idea, and now the psychometric theory is available to implement that idea in the form of IRT.

It was noted earlier that Binet solved the scaling problem for intelligence by relating test performance to age. For him, a particular test score corresponded to a mental level, the mental level of the average 3-year-old, for example. When expressed this way, growth from year to year became obvious because the person's mental level changed. An average child would have a mental level of three at age 3 and a mental level of ten at age 10, clearly indicating growth. In 1911, the year Binet died, Stern (1914) suggested that a measure of relative ability could be obtained by dividing the mental level score, which he called mental age, by the examinee's chronological age, resulting in an intelligence quotient. In this metric, the average person would have a score of 1 regardless of age. The average child's quotient would not change with age. In the 1920s the practice of multiplying the ratio by 100 to eliminate the decimal point was adopted, producing the now famous (or infamous) metric (R. M. Thorndike, 1990). Wechsler (1939) took the process one step further when he defined the mean for any reference group to be 100 and the probable error to be 10, resulting in the scale in common use today.

Although the intelligence quotient, or IQ, had the advantage of expressing in a single number the person's ability relative to others of the same age, it covered up the fact of growth. For most of this century people have had the idea that a constant value for one's IQ means that ability does not change. Unfortunately, Terman and others prominent in testing fostered some of these erroneous ideas (see R. M. Thorndike, 1990). The IQ metric has outlived whatever usefulness it ever had and should be abandoned in favor of the kind of metric that ELT suggested for the CAVD. Specifically, a test like the Stanford–Binet or the Wechsler scales should provide scores on a metric that is not norm referenced but latent-trait referenced. The application of one- or two-parameter IRT to items on a test like the Stanford–Binet can easily produce a scale where the average performance for 3-year-olds might be set arbitrarily at a number like 50. Suitable equal intervals could then be chosen so that the performance of the average adult might be a value like 200. It would be nice to make this a ratio scale if possible, but it may be impolitic to saddle any species with an intelligence of zero.

The biggest advantage that would accrue from such a change, in addition to unloading a large cargo of unwanted and unnecessary baggage, is that the scale would then have certain behavioral implications. For example, changes in ability with age, both positive in the growth years and negative in the declining years, would be directly reflected in ability score changes. If a score of 120 was typical of people just learning long division, then we might expect someone with a quantitative ability score of 130 to be able to do long division, regardless of their age. A person with a short-term memory score of 170 might be expected to be able to repeat 6 digits backward regardless of whether they were 10, 35, or 80.

Another problem with norm-referenced scores that would be reduced or eliminated with a latent-trait score is that norm-referenced scores are easily misinterpreted. A 7-year-old with an IQ of 200 is not thinking like a 14-year-old; he or she is unusually proficient at tasks that 7-, 8-, and 9-year-olds can do. Likewise, a 14-year-old with an IQ of 50 is not thinking like a 7-year-old. A latent-trait referenced scale would reduce tendencies for such misinterpretations.

A third benefit to eliminating the IQ metric might be a decreased tendency to reify the index. Psychological measurement is, by its nature, indirect, and buzz words lead to oversimplification. The response to a test item may be an indicator of some aspect of cognitive ability, but it is not the ability. RLT (R. L. Thorndike, 1985, 1994) would agree with Gottfredson (1997), Jensen, (1986), Ree and Earles (1992), Schmidt and Hunter (1992) and a host of others who argued that the vast majority of the predictive power of cognitive ability tests is found in the global score obtained from a diverse group of items, but that does not mean intelligence is not a multifaceted characteristic. It may be that a core construct such as the general efficiency of an individual's brain for processing information provides an overarching unity to intelligence, but no measurement procedure now available or likely to be developed in the foreseeable future can capture that unity. It would be well to remember that the days of positivism, when the measurement operation was a sufficient definition for a construct and Boring (1923) could define intelligence as what intelligence tests test, are now behind us.

Prognostication is always precarious. The first 30 years of the last century saw huge changes in the practice of psychology generally and psychometrics in particular, but at least two more recent commentators on the scene, Buros (1977) and Linn (1989), saw little progress affecting the practice of testing during the next 50 years. There is progress to be made, and some of it may occur in the directions outlined here before too many more years go by.

REFERENCES

Binet, A., & Simon, T. (1905). New methods for the diagnosis of the intellectual level of subnormals. *L'Année Psychologique, 11*, 191–244.
Binet, A., & Simon, T. (1908). The development of intelligence in the child. *L'Année Psychologique, 14*, 1–94.
Boring, E. G. (1923). Intelligence as the tests test it. *New Republic, 33*, 35–37.
Buros, O. K. (1977). Fifty years in testing: Some reminiscences, criticisms, and suggestions. *Educational Researcher, 6*(7), 9–15.
Gottfredson, L. S. (1997). Why *g* matters: The complexity of everyday life. *Intelligence, 24*, 79–132.
Horn, J. L. (1985). Remodeling old models of intelligence. In B. B. Wolman (Ed.), *Handbook of intelligence* (pp. 267–300). New York: Wiley.
Horn, J. L., & Cattell, R. B. (1966). Refinement and test of the theory of fluid and crystallized ability intelligences. *Journal of Educational Psychology, 57*, 253–270.
Jensen, A. R. (1986). *g*: Artifact or reality? *Journal of Vocational Behavior, 29*, 301–331.
Kaufman, A. S. (1990). *Assessing adolescent and adult intelligence.* Boston: Allyn & Bacon.
Kaufman, A. S. (1994). *Intelligent testing with the WISC-III.* New York: Wiley.
Lazarsfeld, P. F. (1959). Latent structure analysis. In S. Koch (Ed.), *Psychology: A study of a science* (Vol. 3, pp. 476–542). New York: McGraw Hill.
Linn, R. L. (1989). Current perspectives and future directions. In R. L. Linn (Ed.), *Educational measurement* (3rd ed., pp. 1–10). New York: Macmillan.
Lord, F. M. (1953). The relation of test score to the trait underlying the test. *Educational and Psychological Measurement, 13*, 517–548.
Lord, F. M. (1980). *Applications of item response theory to practical testing problems.* Hillsdale, NJ: Lawrence Erlbaum Associates.
Rasch, G. (1960). *Probabilistic models for some intelligence and attainment tests.* Copenhagen: Danish Institute for Educational Research.
Ree, M. J., & Earles, J. A. (1992). Intelligence is the best predictor of job performance. *Current Directions in Psychological Science 1*, 86–89.

Schmidt, F. L., & Hunter, J. E. (1992). Development of a causal model of processes determining job performance. *Current Directions in Psychological Science, 1*, 89–92.

Stern, W. (1914). *The psychological method of testing intelligence* (G. M. Whipple, Trans.). Baltimore: Warwick & York. (Original work published 1912)

Terman, L. M. (1916). *The measurement of intelligence.* Boston: Houghton Mifflin.

Terman, L. M., & Merrill, M. A. (1937). *Measuring intelligence: A guide to the administration of the new revised Stanford–Binet tests of intelligence.* Boston: Houghton Mifflin.

Terman, L. M., & Merrill, M. A. (1960). *The Stanford–Binet Intelligence Scale: Manual for the third edition. Form L–M.* Boston: Houghton Mifflin.

Terman, L. M., & Merrill, M. A. (1973). *The Stanford–Binet Intelligence Scale: 1973 Norms Edition.* Boston: Houghton Mifflin.

Thorndike, E. L. (1903). *Educational psychology.* New York: Science Press.

Thorndike, E. L. (1918). The nature, purposes, and general methods of measurement of educational products. In S. A. Courtis (Chr.), *The measurement of educational products* (17th Yearbook of the National Society for the Study of Education, Pt. 2, pp. 16–24). Bloomington, IL: Public School Publishing Company.

Thorndike, E. L., Bregman, E. O., Cobb, M. V., & Woodyard, E. (1926). *The measurement of intelligence.* New York: Teachers College Bureau of Publications.

Thorndike, R. L. (1985). The central role of general ability in prediction. *Multivariate Behavioral Research, 20*, 241–254.

Thorndike, R. L. (1994). g. *Intelligence, 19*, 145–156.

Thorndike, R. L., & Hagen, E. P. (1986). *Cognitive Abilities Test* (Form 4). Chicago: Riverside.

Thorndike, R. L., Hagen, E. P., & Sattler, J. M. (1986a). *The Stanford–Binet Intelligence Scale: Fourth Edition. Guide for Administration and Scoring.* Chicago: Riverside.

Thorndike, R. L., Hagen, E. P., & Sattler, J. M. (1986b). *The Stanford–Binet Intelligence Scale: Fourth Edition. Technical Manual.* Chicago: Riverside.

Thorndike, R. M. (1990). *A century of ability testing.* Chicago: Riverside.

Thurstone, L. L. (1925). A method of scaling psychological and educational tests. *Journal of Educational Psychology, 16*, 433–451.

Thurstone, L. L. (1927). The unit of measurement in educational scales. *Journal of Educational Psychology, 18*, 505–524.

Thurstone, L. L. (1928). The absolute zero in the measurement of intelligence. *Psychological Review, 35*, 175–197.

Thurstone, L. L. (1931). Multiple factor analysis. *Psychological Review, 38*, 406–427.

Thurstone, L. L. (1959). *The measurement of values.* Chicago: University of Chicago Press.

Wainer, H. (1990). *Computerized adaptive testing: A primer.* Hillsdale, NJ: Lawrence Erlbaum Associates.

Wechsler, D. (1939). *The measurement of adult intelligence.* Baltimore: Williams & Wilkins.

Weiss, D. J. (1982). Improving measurement quality and efficiency with adaptive testing. *Applied Psychological Measurement, 6*, 473–492.

CHAPTER THREE

Behind the Scenes:
Using New Measurement Methods
on the DAS and KAIT

Mark H. Daniel
American Guidance Service

Item response theory is by far the most significant technology to arise in applied measurement in recent years. In chapter 2, this volume, and in her 1996 article "The New Rules of Measurement," Embretson itemized some important ways in which test development, administration, and interpretation can be changed by IRT. Some areas of testing are far ahead of others in applying the possibilities offered by this new methodology. Multiple-choice achievement tests such as the GRE, for example, are being delivered on a large scale through adaptive computerized administration guided by IRT concepts of score accuracy and ability estimation. Somewhat surprisingly, individually administered tests, such as the cognitive and achievement measures used by clinicians, are among types of tests that have made the least use of IRT. Yet these tests, which have long utilized a simple form of adaptive administration, ought to be prime candidates for the application of IRT.

This chapter describes some ways in which new design and development methods are being applied to individually administered tests and how they might be used more extensively in the future. Methods based on IRT are the primary focus. Part of the chapter, however, discusses another methodological area, appropriate procedures for manipulating and interpreting normative scores. Although normative scores such as standard scores and percentiles are important to those who interpret tests, and constructing norms takes much time and effort for test developers, the statistical properties of these scores have received little attention in the measurement literature.

THE ROLE OF IRT IN DESIGNING AND DEVELOPING
INDIVIDUALLY ADMINISTERED TESTS

The tools and techniques provided by IRT have revolutionized how test developers do their work. IRT has become so fully assimilated into test development practice that it can now be thought of as a fixture. This thorough acceptance of IRT is due to its success in solving measurement problems that formerly were intractable. IRT solves problems by looking at tests from an alternative perspective, focusing on the interaction of persons with items. This perspective complements the classical model, which remains useful for some areas of application where IRT is relatively weak. Several widely used psychometric methods displaced by IRT-based procedures were not so much derivative of the classical model as they were straightforward, practical, atheoretical tools. One familiar example is the use of p, the proportion of examinees in a sample passing an item, as an index of item difficulty; another is using the correlation of an item with the total score on the scale of which it is a part as an index of how well the item measures the construct underlying the scale. These statistical indicators, the best available before IRT, have fundamental and serious weaknesses when applied to tests (such as individually administered tests) on which different examinees take different subsets of items. IRT provides far superior methods for evaluating the difficulty and validity of items on such tests, and so its difficulty and discrimination (or fit) indexes have largely displaced p values and item–total correlations. This does not, however, represent a rejection in principle of the basic equation of the classical model. The classical and IRT models are not exclusive and it is possible to take advantage of each model for solving different kinds of development problems.

Table 3.1 compares some pre-IRT and IRT methods of dealing with measurement issues, and depicts the organizational structure of this chapter. The

TABLE 3.1
Comparison of Some Pre-IRT and IRT Forms of Information About Tests

Information	Pre-IRT	IRT
Item difficulty	proportion passing (sample dependent)	location on scale of difficulty/ ability (sample free)
Item validity and accuracy	item–total correlation (sample dependent)	discrimination parameter or fit statistic (sample free)
Person ability*	raw score (test dependent)	location on scale of difficulty/ability (test free)
Score accuracy	reliability (sample dependent), *SEM* (usually averaged across ability levels)	*SE* of ability estimate (sample free, and specific to the ability level)
Population distribution (norms)	no difference between pre-IRT and IRT methods	

Ability is used generically to refer to any trait.

first section discusses the first two items in the table, illustrating how IRT has improved item analysis. Later sections cover person analysis (ability and person fit), score accuracy and reliability, and population distributions (i.e., norms).

Item Analysis With Missing Data

Most individually administered tests are adaptive, because different examinees are given different sets of items according to how they perform on the items already administered. Although their adaptivity is relatively crude compared with computer-adaptive administration, the goal in each case is broadly the same: to administer just enough appropriately difficult items to provide an accurate score while avoiding giving items that are extremely easy or difficult. When a professional is giving a test interactively, there is strong motivation to avoid spending time needlessly on items that are trivially easy or excessively difficult for the particular examinee.

During development as well as in the final instrument, it is typical for individually administered tests to provide some form of basal and ceiling rules that the examiner uses to adapt the test to the examinee. A basal is performance on a sequence of items that is sufficiently good to justify an assumption that all easier items would have been passed if they had been administered. An example might be passing five consecutive items. A ceiling is the converse: a series of item failures that allows one to predict failure on all more-difficult items.

When basal and ceiling rules are applied during administration of a tryout or standardization version of a test, the result is person-by-item matrices that look like Fig. 3.1. This is actual data from an individually administered reading comprehension test given to students in kindergarten through grade 12. The ceiling rule on this test is six consecutive failures, and the basal rule is six consecutive passes.

The harder items tend to be given only to the more able people and the easier items only to the less able. The proportion passing, then, cannot meaningfully be compared across items. As shown in the bottom row of the figure, the item p values do not decline systematically even though the items increase in difficulty from left to right. Items 10 and 50 each were passed by 67% of the examinees who attempted them, but they are not equal in difficulty; the people who took Item 50 were more able than those who took Item 10, so Item 50 is harder than Item 10. Prior to IRT there was no good way to quantify this fact. The best that could be done was to make assumptions about how examinees would have performed on the items they did not take; that is, to assume that each examinee would have passed all the items below their starting point and failed all the items above their stopping point. Filling in scores on the items not administered made it

						Item							
Person	5	10	15	20	25	30	35	40	45	50	55	60	65

```
 1   111101000000.....................................................
 2   111100001000000...................................................
 3   111111011111111111111001001000000.................................
 4   11101010100101111111001010100010010000000.........................
 5   ......111111111111111111111111111111011101000000..................
 6   ......11111111111111111111111111111100101110100010100000..........
 7   ...........11111101111100111111010000000..........................
 8   ...............1111111011111101010010001000000....................
 9   ................1111111111111000000...............................
10   ...............11111101100100000101000000.........................
11   ................111111111011101101100010000000....................
12   ..................1111111011000000................................
13   .................11111110111000000................................
14   ....................111111001110100010000000......................
15   ....................11111111111111011100011000010000000000.........
16   ....................111111111111111111111111011111111010000010110000
17   .......................111111111000000............................
18   .....................111111111111110110110111111110000000..........
19   ........................1111111111111101011110101010010011011
20   ...................111111101011111101111110001010100000000
```

| p: | .75 | .67 | .80 | 1.00 | .79 | .75 | .53 | .64 | .40 | .67 | .40 | .67 | .33 |

FIG. 3.1. Sample person-by-item score matrix for an individually administered reading comprehension test.

possible to compute p values for a set of items as if all had been given to the same set of examinees.

However, there was a weakness in this assumption: It was being made at a point in the development of the test at which good information often was not yet available about the difficulty of the items. It is likely that the items were not perfectly arranged in order of increasing difficulty. Thus, there may have been some items below a person's starting point that the person would have failed, and some items above the stopping point that the person would have passed. If a relatively hard item accidentally got placed early in the test, for example, and the assumption was made that all of the people who took a harder set of items would have passed that item, then that item's p value would be overestimated.

The extensive missing data typically present in datasets for individually administered tests caused even greater difficulties for evaluating the degree to which items accurately measure the same thing that the total test is measuring. Because items are taken by different sets of examinees, it is impossible to compute item–total correlations from the raw data without first filling in some of the missing data. The threat this posed to the validity of the results was serious. After all, the purpose of examining item–total correlations is to find out whether a particular item tends to be failed by people who are low in the ability and passed by people high in the ability. But filling in missing item responses assumed the very thing being investigated. This method tended to overestimate item discrimination and obscure item weaknesses, especially if the items were not well ordered in difficulty.

Thus, some of the most basic statistics in pre-IRT test development methodology had serious imperfections when applied to individually administered tests. The coming of IRT methods was a liberating event for developers of these sorts of tests, offering a method that cut through the Gordian knot of problems created by missing data.

In the IRT model, people have abilities along an ability scale and items have difficulties along a difficulty scale. These two scales are the same. An item's difficulty can be estimated by observing performance on that item by examinees of known ability. Missing data do not affect this estimation procedure. It does not matter whether the people who took Item A are different from the ones who took Item B. As long as the ability levels of the people in each set are known, and the items are reasonably appropriate in difficulty for those individuals, difficulties can be assigned to Items A and B.

IRT also permits the validity and accuracy of an item—that is, the degree to which it measures what the rest of the items measure—to be evaluated accurately even when there is extensive missing data. One useful way of doing this is to draw an item response curve, which is the plot of the proportion of examinees at different levels of ability passing the item. For example, Fig. 3.2 shows data for two items from the standardization edition of the Kaufman Adolescent and Adult Intelligence Test (KAIT; Kaufman & Kaufman, 1993). As ability increases from left to right along the horizontal axis, the proportion passing increases from 0 to 1. The steeper this curve, the better the item discriminates between high-ability and low-ability examinees. The slope of the curve is related, then, to the traditional item–total correlation. Figure 3.2 also shows the expected curves for these items according to the Rasch model, which represent the average shape of the curves for all of the items in the subtest. If the observed curve is flatter than the expected curve, as in Fig. 3.2b, then the item is doing a relatively poor job of discriminating and may be a candidate for revision or deletion. (This particular item was not included in the final edition.) In the Rasch model, the discrepancy between an item's observed and expected curves is reflected in a fit statistic, whereas other IRT models report the slope of each item's curve as one of the parameters characterizing the item.

The particular shape of a curve can sometimes help diagnose a problem in an item. For example, if the lower end of the curve flattens out at a proportion greater than 0, something in the item may be giving away the answer. If the upper end of the curve levels off or takes a downward turn before reaching 1, then high-ability people may be perceiving a more sophisticated answer that is correct but that the test developers did not anticipate. Such an item, also from the KAIT standardization, is illustrated in Fig.

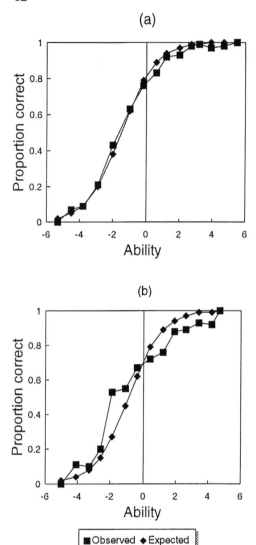

FIG. 3.2. Item response curves for two items from the KAIT stand-ardization edition.

3.2b. This is the kind of curve that would be shown by the SAT mathematics item that made headlines in 1997 because bright examinees, who realized that a variable in the problem could take on negative values, chose an answer that, although mathematically correct, was not given credit.

For the purpose of this discussion, the important feature of this type of item analysis is that there can be different groups of examinees contributing to the data points at different levels of ability. Thus, in the case of both item difficulty and discrimination, IRT techniques deal easily with what formerly were difficult development problems caused by extensive missing data. The solution of these problems rests on shifting from the traditional concepts of p value and raw score to the newer concepts of item difficulty and person ability.

Person Analysis

Person analysis is analogous to item analysis. Whereas item analysis is concerned with the columns of the person-by-item data matrix, person analysis is concerned with the rows. The analog of item difficulty is person ability. Just as item difficulty is estimated on the basis of the performance on the item by examinees whose abilities are known, person ability is estimated from the person's performance on a set of items of known difficulty. The concept of item discrimination (or item fit) has its analog in person fit, the degree to which the person's pattern of item scores conforms to the trend the IRT model would predict according to the person's ability and the items' difficulties.

Ability Estimation With Missing Data: Adaptive Testing. In the discussion of item analysis, missing data was treated as a problem to which IRT provides an effective solution. In the case of person analysis (and particularly ability measurement), missing data can instead be seen as a desirable outcome of efficient test administration, provided that IRT is used to transform raw data into ability estimates. Adaptive testing aims to obtain an accurate ability estimate with a maximum amount of missing data.

Although the phrase *adaptive testing* typically brings to mind computer administration, tests can be administered adaptively without computers. As noted earlier, the traditional basal and ceiling rules of most individually administered tests are adaptive because they are designed so that each examinee will take only a portion of the full range of items in a test or subtest, according to how well the examinee performs. But this is a crude and inefficient form of adaptive administration. Its goal is to administer every item on which the examinee has a probability of passing that is greater than essentially 0 and less than essentially 1. Then, if the items are well ordered in difficulty, one can assume passes for all items below the basal and failures for all items above the ceiling. This gives an estimate of the raw score the person would have gotten if all items had been given.

This is an inefficient approach because it requires giving many items that are extremely easy or very hard for the examinee, in the process of establishing the basal and ceiling. More items are administered than are necessary to provide an accurate estimate of the person's ability.

Figure 3.3a illustrates how a basal-and-ceiling system works. It shows a person response curve, analogous to the item response curves presented earlier, which indicates the probability of a particular person passing an item as item difficulty increases. For very easy items the probability is nearly

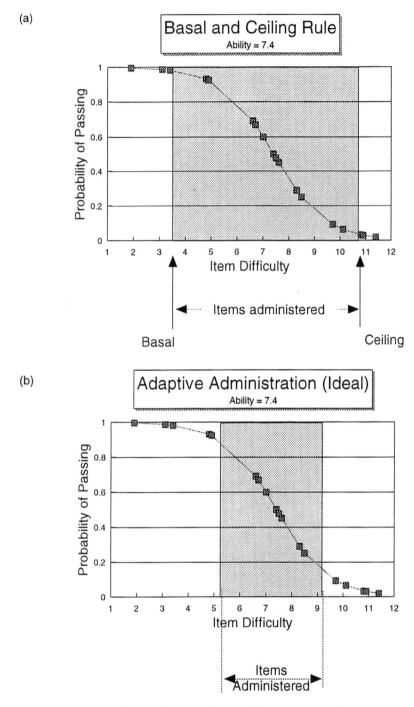

FIG. 3.3. Ranges of items administered under different adaptive-administration rules.

1 and as items become more difficult, the probability of passing declines to nearly 0.

With the basal-and-ceiling method of item administration, the examinee would be given all of the items in the shaded region of the difficulty scale. This range includes a number of items where the examinee's probability of passing is very close to 1 or 0. Those items give little extra information about the examinee's ability beyond what would be known from the examinee's performance on the items that have a moderate difficulty level. In contrast, an adaptive testing approach attempts to administer items in a narrower range of difficulty, such as the items in the shaded region of Fig. 3.3b. For items in this region, the examinee has a probability of passing that ranges between approximately .15 and .85. The information from the examinee's performance on just these items would be enough to produce an ability estimate that is almost as accurate as the one based on the wider set of items, in considerably less testing time and with less frustration for the examinee. Of course, no actual adaptive method is this perfect, but this is the ideal.

IRT opens up the possibility of designing individually administered tests that come closer to the ideal of efficient adaptive administration than the basal-and-ceiling method permits. However, it is not obvious how this can best be accomplished in practice. One of the first individually administered instruments to attempt IRT-based adaptive administration was the British Ability Scales (BAS; Elliott, Murray, & Pearson, 1979), a cognitive battery for children. On each BAS subtest, the items were divided into several overlapping subsets covering different levels of difficulty. The examiner would select a subset expected to be appropriate in difficulty based on the particular examinee's age, adjusted by any expectation that the child might score significantly above or below average for their age. Then, the child's score on a Rasch ability scale was estimated from their raw score on the particular item set they took.

The BAS administration method represented an advance in assessment efficiency because it did not require establishing a basal and ceiling. However, it had an administrative shortcoming. If the selected item set proved to be too easy or difficult for the child (as shown by a raw score near the maximum or minimum), the ability estimate would be relatively inaccurate, and a harder or easier item set would have to be administered. However, in this event, there was no way to use all of the child's item responses to compute an ability score. Instead, the examiner would have to choose from among the ability estimates produced by the two or more item sets that had been administered. This introduced subjectivity and failed to make use of all of the available information about the child's ability.

For the U.S. adaptation of the BAS, the Differential Ability Scales (DAS; Elliott, 1990a), a more sophisticated form of adaptive administration was developed. Like the BAS, the DAS groups items into overlapping subsets, but it provides the opportunity to augment the originally assigned item set with additional easier or harder items if the child obtains a near-zero or near-perfect score. For example, if the child passes all but one item in the initial set, the examiner gives more difficult items until reaching the upper end of the next-most-difficult item set. This can be continued if necessary until the child has failed at least three items altogether (the criterion for stopping used on the DAS). At that point, the child's ability can be estimated based on the complete set of items the child has taken.

As an illustration, consider the DAS Matrices subtest, which has 33 items. There are three item sets: Items 1 through 14 (for ages 5 to 7), Items 5 through 23 (ages 8 to 10), and Items 15 through 33 (ages 11 to 17). As long as the child has passed at least 3 items and failed at least 3 items by the time he or she reaches the designated stopping point, testing ends; the set of item responses is sufficient for an accurate ability estimate. If, however, the examinee has failed only 1 or 2 items, administration continues until reaching the next stopping point.

The subtest is scored using the raw-score-to-ability table reproduced in Fig. 3.4. There are five sets of items an examinee could reasonably take: the three standard item sets, plus the extended item sets that would be administered if the child did extremely well or extremely poorly on a standard set. The table converts the raw score on each item set to a Rasch ability score. (For convenience, the ability scores have been transformed to positive integers through multiplication by 10 and addition of a constant.) A raw score of 6 on the easiest item set yields a relatively low ability score of 56, whereas the same number correct on the hardest item set (Items 15 through 33) corresponds to an ability score of 101.

The method of adaptive administration used on the DAS, although far from optimally efficient, reduces the average number of items a child must take to arrive at an accurate score, and for many examinees does away with the need to fail a sequence of items before stopping. The item sets and stopping rules were designed through a procedure of computer simulation based on the known item difficulties and the distribution of abilities at each age (Elliott, 1990b). Under any particular system of item sets and stopping rules, it is possible to calculate the probability that an examinee with a given level of ability will take each of the several possible item sets or extended item sets. For each of these sets, the standard error of measurement for that examinee can also be calculated. This permits calculation of the expected standard error for each level of ability and an average expected standard error for all examinees in an age group. In these simulations, various combinations of item sets and stopping rules were evaluated according to the average accuracy of ability estimates and the average number of items administered. The final selections were those that yielded high accuracy with the fewest items.

Matrices
Raw Score to Ability Score

Raw Score	Item Set				
	1-14	1-23	5-23	5-33	15-33
0	10(15)	10(15)			
1	18(11)	18(11)	43(11)	42(11)	76(11)
2	28(9)	28(9)	52(9)	52(9)	84(8)
3	36(8)	36(8)	59(8)	59(8)	89(7)
4	43(8)	42(8)	65(7)	65(7)	94(6)
5	49(8)	49(8)	70(7)	70(7)	97(6)
6	56(8)	55(8)	74(6)	74(6)	101(6)
7	62(8)	60(7)	78(6)	77(6)	104(5)
8	68(8)	66(7)	82(6)	81(6)	107(5)
9	73(7)	70(7)	85(6)	84(6)	110(5)
10	78(7)	74(6)	88(6)	87(5)	112(5)
11	84(8)	78(6)	91(6)	90(5)	115(5)
12	90(8)	82(6)	95(6)	92(5)	118(6)
13	99(11)	85(6)	98(6)	95(5)	122(6)
14		88(6)	101(6)	98(5)	125(6)
15		91(6)	105(6)	100(5)	129(6)
16		95(6)	109(7)	103(5)	133(7)
17		98(6)	115(8)	105(5)	139(8)
18		101(6)	123(11)	108(5)	148(11)
19		105(6)		111(5)	156(17)
20		109(7)		113(5)	
21		115(8)		116(5)	
22		123(11)		119(5)	
23				122(6)	
24				125(6)	
25				129(6)	
26				134(7)	
27				139(8)	
28				148(11)	
29				156(17)	

FIG. 3.4. Raw-score-to-ability-score conversion table for the DAS Matrices subtest. Differential Ability Scales. Copyright © 1990 by The Psychological Corporation. Reproduced by permission. All rights reserved. "Differential Ability Scales" and "DAS" are registered trademarks of The Psychological Corporation.

The capacity of IRT to estimate an examinee's ability from an incomplete set of item data is valuable not only for the design of efficient administration procedures but also in the research phase of test development. Collecting representative norm samples for individually administered tests is difficult and costly. Particularly because research versions of new tests are unfamiliar to examiners, administrations sometimes are incomplete because of examiner error. Under a traditional raw-score-based model, such improperly administered cases usually would have to be discarded. With IRT, however, incomplete cases often can be used, as long as there is sufficient data to provide an accurate ability estimate.

Advantages of the Ability Scale Over the Raw-Score Scale. One might wonder whether it is desirable to require users of an IRT-based test to make use of an ability scale in the scoring process. After all, the DAS scoring tables could have been constructed to show conversions from the raw score on each item set to the predicted raw score on all items in the subtest, rather than to an ability score. Such predicted raw scores might be more easily understood by examinees. Also, because ability scores corresponding to near-zero or near-perfect raw scores can take on extreme values, the raw score scale may be preferable for some types of statistical analysis.

Yet there are several important benefits gained from using an ability scale. One benefit is educational: Such a scale communicates to test users that a new approach to test administration and scoring underlies the instrument. A second benefit is flexibility. For example, suppose a stimulus word on the DAS Word Definitions subtest changed in meaning over time or acquired a slang meaning that made it unusable, or suppose the item was found to be inappropriate for a particular population subgroup. Using the item difficulties published in the DAS Handbook (Elliott, 1990b), anyone familiar with the Rasch model could compute a new raw-score-to-ability table for item sets from which that item was deleted. This would permit practitioners to administer the subtest without the malfunctioning item and still use the published national norms that are based on ability scores.

A third benefit of expressing scores in the IRT ability scale is the ease and convenience of computing standard errors of measurement (*SEM*) of the ability estimates. (These *SEM*s are shown in parentheses in the raw-score-to-ability table reproduced in Fig. 3.4.) Yet another benefit derives from the fact that the IRT ability scale is not dependent, as the raw-score scale is, on the numbers of items at various levels of difficulty that are included in a particular test. This tends to make the ability score a superior basis for measuring growth or learning.

Finally, the ability scale has useful interpretive implications. Ability scores do not have normative meaning and thus they have no advantage over raw scores for purposes of normative interpretation. However, differences between ability scores on a subtest, or between an ability score and an item difficulty, can be interpreted in terms of (relative) probabilities of item success. In the Rasch model, by knowing a person's ability, one can calculate the probability that they will pass an item of known difficulty. Woodcock developed this idea in a number of interesting and valuable ways on several instruments including the Woodcock–Johnson Psycho-Educational Battery— Revised (WJ–R; Woodcock & Johnson, 1989). The WJ–R Relative Mastery Index tells how well an examinee is expected to do on tasks that members of the relevant norm group can do with 90% mastery. Other Woodcock concepts are the Instructional Range and the Developmental Level Band, each of which indicates the types of tasks that are in the person's range of ability.

Person Fit. Just as items vary in how well they differentiate examinees by ability, examinees vary in their sensitivity to differences in item difficulty. The person response curves of Fig. 3.3, analogous to the item response curves shown in Fig. 3.2, represent the probability (under the IRT model) that a person with a particular level of ability will pass items at various difficulty levels. A pattern of item passes and failures for a particular examinee that departs substantially from the expected curve suggests that the individual has been mismeasured, with the implication that an ability estimate based on the entire set of items may be invalid for that person.

There is a sizable literature on person misfit and appropriateness measurement and the implications of these indices for score interpretation (see, for example, Drasgow, Levine, & McLaughlin, 1987). Person fit is a useful tool for checking the accuracy of raw research data collected during test development, such as cases in a standardization sample. Serious misfit—that is, surprisingly poor performance on easy items or surprising success on hard items—could signal an error in administration or in the recording or keying of the data. Misfit could also occur because the test was inappropriate for the examinee. For example, language or cultural differences or a physical handicap could contribute to misfit. Although cases typically are not deleted from datasets solely because of poor fit, the person-fit index flags cases that deserve inspection.

LOCAL ACCURACY VERSUS OVERALL RELIABILITY

In addition to creating problems for item analysis, the prevalence of missing data seriously complicates the estimation of internal-consistency forms of reliability. To calculate a split-half or alpha coefficient from raw item scores, it is necessary to have a complete person-by-item data matrix. To obtain this for data collected using basal-and-ceiling rules, the missing values would have to be filled in with expected item scores (passes below the basal and failures above the ceiling). As in estimating item discrimination, the process of assigning scores to unadministered items presumes the very thing—high reliability—that is being investigated, and is for that reason an unsatisfactory procedure. When a test is administered in an adaptive fashion that is more efficient than the basal-and-ceiling method, any procedure that relies on filling in missing item responses is especially weak.

IRT makes possible several methods of computing internal consistency that do not require filling in missing data. One, commonly employed in the development of individually administered tests, is a split-half procedure in which an ability estimate is computed separately for each half of the test based on the set of items actually administered. The correlation between the two sets of abilities is then adjusted using the Spearman–Brown formula to estimate the correlation that would be found between parallel full-length tests. Other IRT-based methods estimate reliability from the relationship between the average of the local standard errors in a sample (representing the square root of overall error variance) and the variance of ability estimates in the sample (Elliott, 1990b; Lord, 1980).

Perhaps more importantly, however, IRT shows that it is possible, and often desirable, to use the local standard error instead of reliability for evaluating the accuracy of a test. Whereas reliability describes a test's accuracy for a group, the standard error describes its accuracy for an individual; and when individually administered tests are being employed, it is almost always the individual rather than the group that is the object of concern. IRT makes clear, in a way that reliability does not, that a test usually is more accurate for some members of a group than for others. Thus, reliability can be a misleading guide to the selection of an appropriate test for an individual. Furthermore, use of reliability as the sole index of a test's accuracy can inhibit the development of useful tests for special populations.

When selecting a test for a particular examinee, a clinician is concerned with how likely it is that the test will measure that individual accurately. This will depend partly on the expected position of the individual's ability level relative to others of the same age or grade. The examiner's objective is to select a test whose content is appropriately difficult for the examinee, because the accuracy of the resulting score will depend on how many such items are administered. Figure 3.5 illustrates this point by showing the relationship between the standard error of the ability estimate and true raw score for the DAS Word Definitions subtest. For examinees whose ability is so low or so high that the test offers almost no items of moderate difficulty

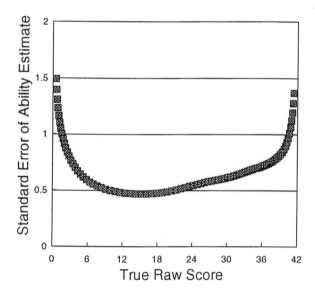

FIG. 3.5. Standard error of the ability estimate as a function of true raw score for the DAS Word Definitions subtest.

(i.e., whose true raw score is less than 3 or greater than 39), the standard error is high and the test is functioning poorly.

This same phenomenon can be seen in the standard errors printed in the raw-score-to-ability table of Fig. 3.4. There, the standard error of the ability estimate is fairly small except near the lowest and highest possible raw scores in each set of items. The table puts shading around those ability scores to remind the examiner that an examinee scoring at that level should be given additional harder (or easier) items.

Simply knowing the relationship between raw scores and the standard error of ability estimates is not enough, however, to make it easy for a practitioner to select a test that will be appropriate for a particular examinee. Even if the examiner has a good idea of the likely level of the examinee's normative score, he or she may not know (without referring to a norm table) what raw scores correspond to that level. A more convenient way of providing the information, then, is to show the standard error as a function of normative scores for the examinee's age or grade.

Figure 3.6 is an example of such a display, again using the DAS Word Definitions subtest (as in Fig. 3.5), with the horizontal axis now representing the *T*-score scale for the age group 6:3 (6 years 3 months) to 6:5. Six is the youngest age at which this subtest is routinely given. The horizontal axis covers a range of three standard deviations on either side of the mean—that is, *T*-scores from 20 to 80. The curve in Fig. 3.6 is a section of the one in

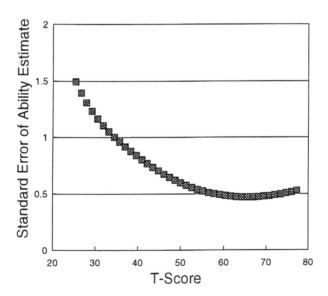

FIG. 3.6. Standard error of the ability estimate as a function of normative score, for an age at which the subtest is difficult (DAS Word Definitions subtest at ages 6:3–6:5).

Fig. 3.5; the shape is slightly different because the horizontal axis has been transformed nonlinearly from raw scores to ability scores and then to normalized *T*-scores.

This subtest has a reasonably high reliability coefficient (.81) for the general-population norm sample of 6-year-olds. Figure 3.6 shows that the subtest is quite accurate for young 6-year-olds who are no more than moderately below average in ability for their age—that is, those whose ability is at or above one standard deviation below the general-population mean. However, those at the low end of the ability range for this age are not being measured very accurately by this subtest, which contains relatively few items of appropriate difficulty for those children. When information on standard errors is presented in this format, it can easily be used by a clinician to select a test for an examinee.

Faced with the task of assessing a low-functioning child in the 6:3 to 6:5 age range, an examiner using the DAS would do well to consider choosing an alternative to Word Definitions (which is part of the standard battery at that age). The DAS includes another expressive-vocabulary subtest, Naming Vocabulary, which is in the standard battery for preschoolers but is also normed through age 8. Although this subtest is rather easy for most 6-year-olds (its reliability at that age is .78), for low-functioning children of that age it provides more items of appropriate difficulty than does Word Definitions. Figure 3.7 shows standard errors on Naming Vocabulary as a function

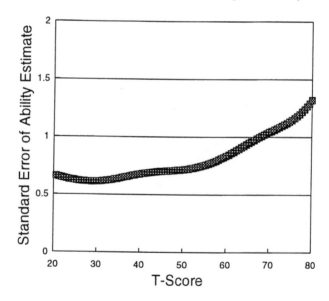

FIG. 3.7. Standard error of the ability estimate as a function of normative score, for an age at which the subtest is easy (DAS Naming Vocabulary subtest at ages 6:3–6:5).

of *T*-scores for ages 6:3 to 6:5, the same horizontal scale as in Fig. 3.6. Compared with Word Definitions, Naming Vocabulary has a larger standard error for children of average or high ability, but is considerably more accurate than Word Definitions for low-ability children, and would be a better choice for assessing such a child.

These examples demonstrate that the reliability coefficient is not a dependable guide to the accuracy with which a test measures different members of an age or grade group. The reliability coefficient reflects how accurate the test is on average for a group. A test with a particular reliability for a group might, perhaps, measure all members of that group with roughly equal accuracy, or it might measure some members much more accurately than others. The reliability coefficient, as an overall statistic for the group, cannot indicate which of these possibilities is the case. The standard error, in contrast, is a local statistic that gives information about accuracy at particular ability levels (i.e., for individuals rather than a group).

The example of Word Definitions given earlier showed how a moderately high reliability coefficient does not ensure accurate measurement for all individuals at that age or grade. The converse is also true: A test may have low reliability for a group, yet be quite accurate for certain members of that group. Consider a more extreme example, of the sort that might arise in assessing a child for developmental disabilities. According to traditional standards, the DAS Naming Vocabulary subtest ought not to be offered for use with 8-year-olds because its reliability coefficient for that age is only .64. Nevertheless, this subtest was given to the entire DAS norm sample at age 8, and Fig. 3.8 presents the relationship of its standard error to *T*-scores for ages 8:6 to 8:11. For 8-year-olds who are in the bottom third of the ability distribution, the subtest is quite accurate. Its extreme inaccuracy for above-average 8-year-olds causes its overall reliability to be poor, but this is of no consequence when considering use of the test with a low-functioning child.

Local Reliability

The local standard errors of ability estimates as a function of normative scores can be far more useful information than the overall reliability coefficient as a guide to selecting appropriate tests for individuals. Yet the reliability coefficient has a feature that makes it more interpretable than standard errors when evaluating tests: Reliability is expressed on a scale from 0 to 1 and has consistent meaning across tests, regardless of what the tests measure and the nature of their items. By contrast, the IRT ability scale in which standard errors are expressed is not test-free, in the sense that ability scores from completely independent instruments are not commensurable.

There would be benefit, then, in finding a way to express the information contained in local standard errors in a metric as generic and familiar as that of the reliability coefficient. A straightforward way to do this would be to

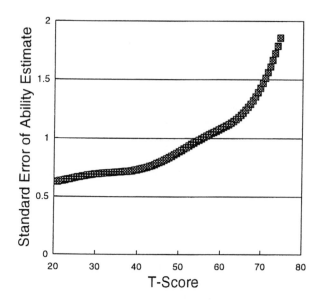

FIG. 3.8. Standard error of the ability estimate as a function of normative score, for a subtest administered out of level (DAS Naming Vocabulary subtest at ages 8:6–8:11).

insert the local standard error into the traditional formula that relates reliability to standard error

$$r_{xx} = 1 - SE^2/SD^2$$

where SD is the standard deviation of ability scores for the entire group. Using non-IRT procedures, the (overall) standard error of measurement computed from a reliability coefficient is, roughly, an average of the local standard errors for members of the group. When the local standard error is substituted for the average standard error in this formula, the resulting *local reliability* coefficient can be interpreted as the reliability of a test that, under the traditional model, would measure with that level of accuracy across the entire score range. In other words, a local reliability of 0.8 indicates that the test is functioning at that particular score level as if it had an overall reliability coefficient of 0.8.

Local reliability is only a quasi-reliability, designed as a aid to test selection. Unlike an actual reliability coefficient, it does not represent the proportion of observed variance that is true variance, nor does it indicate the correlation between parallel forms; each of those is a group-based statistic that is incompatible with the focus of local reliability on the individual score level.

Figure 3.9 shows how local reliabilities compare with overall reliability for a test administered at an age where it is appropriately difficult, the DAS

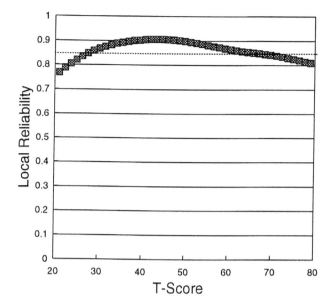

FIG. 3.9. Local reliability as a function of normative score for a subtest administered on level (DAS Word Definitions subtest at ages 10:0–10:5).

Word Definitions at ages 10:0 to 10:5. Local reliability is high across the full range of scores earned at that age. For example, for a 10-year-old with a T-score of 40, the standard error of the ability estimate is 0.47. The standard deviation of ability estimates for the entire age group is 1.52, so the local reliability for a T-score of 40 is computed as

$$1 - .47^2/1.52^2 = .90.$$

The curve of local reliabilities hovers around the overall reliability of .84, shown by the dashed line. Only for extremely low-ability 10-year-olds does the local reliability dip below .8.

Figure 3.10 shows local reliabilities for a subtest administered out-of-level: DAS Naming Vocabulary for 8-year-olds. This graph is another depiction of the information shown in Fig. 3.8. Again, local reliabilities are distributed above and below the overall reliability of .64, but their range is much greater than in Fig. 3.9. For most examinees of this age, the subtest functions poorly, but for low-ability 8-year-olds it functions like a test whose reliability is in the .80s.

The DAS provides norms for many subtests outside the range of ages for which the subtests have acceptable overall reliabilities, enabling practitioners to select those subtests in cases where their content better matches the examinee's ability level than would the content of the subtests typically

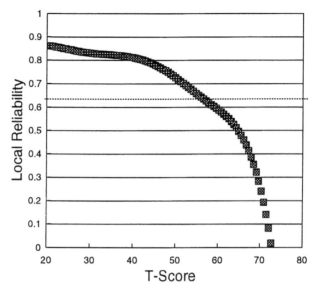

FIG. 3.10. Local reliability as a function of normative score for a subtest administered out of level (DAS Naming Vocabulary subtest at ages 8:6–8:11).

given at that age. To guide examiners in test selection, the DAS Handbook (Elliott, 1990b) provides a table of local reliabilities (or, more precisely, regional reliabilities), reproduced in Fig. 3.11. The values in this table are based on the average standard error in each of four T-score ranges. For example, in the case of the Early Number Concepts subtest given to children aged 2½, about the top 25% of children are measured as accurately as they would be by a test that had an overall reliability in the high .70s or above. For average and low-ability children of that age, the reliabilities are far too low to permit the test to be useful. The Early Number Concepts subtest may, therefore, be an appropriate tool in the assessment of a very bright 2-year-old, if there is a need to measure that domain of ability.

SCORING AND INTERPRETATION

Of the types of test-related information listed in Table 3.1, the only one that has not been affected by IRT is information about population score distributions. Because it is sample-free, IRT is primarily concerned with the scaling of item difficulties and person abilities and is little concerned with that branch of the classical test model that deals with normative interpretation of scores. However, for many kinds of tests, especially those such as cognitive-ability tests where item content is not an intrinsically meaningful guide

Out-of-Level Subtests: Reliability at Different Levels of Ability

Subtest	Age	T Score ≤40	41–50	51–59	≥60
Early Number Concepts	2:6–2:11	.24	.30	.74	.82
	3:0–3:5	.54	.83	.88	.89
	6:6–6:11	.90	.88	.83	.56
	7:0–7:11	.85	.76	.39	.16
Matching Letter-Like	4:0–4:5	.57	.82	.89	.84
Forms	6:0–6:11	.89	.87	.74	.08
	7:0–7:11	.87	.77	.46	.00
Naming Vocabulary	8:0–8:11	.79	.73	.61	.36
Pattern Construction	3:0–3:5	.47	.84	.90	.93
Pattern Construction	3:0–3:5	.06	.24	.54	.75
(Alternative)	13:0–13:11	.89	.87	.82	.52
	14:0–14:11	.85	.82	.72	.35
	15:0–15:11	.86	.83	.72	.41
	16:0–16:11	.84	.81	.45	—[a]
	17:0–17:11	.80	.70	.21	—[a]
Picture Similarities	6:0–6:11	.77	.70	.58	.15
	7:0–7:11	.66	.54	.35	.00
Recall of Digits	2:6–2:11	.69	.90	.91	.91
Recognition of Pictures	2:6–2:11	.38	.72	.78	.83
	8:0–8:11	.65	.65	.57	.18
	9:0–9:11	.73	.71	.61	.00
	10:0–10:11	.76	.71	.62	.01
	11:0–11:11	.74	.69	.56	.03
	12:0–12:11	.72	.65	.36	.00
	13:0–13:11	.73	.61	.27	.00
	14:0–14:11	.67	.53	.13	.00
	15:0–15:11	.71	.56	.20	.00
	16:0–16:11	.67	.53	.13	.00
	17:0–17:11	.61	.46	.00	.00
Seq. & Quant. Reasoning	5:0–5:11	.52	.79	.85	.85
Similarities	5:0–5:11	.63	.88	.89	.89
Verbal Comprehension	6:0–6:11	.90	.84	.70	.30
Word Definitions	5:0–5:11	.42	.73	.87	.90
Word Reading[b]	5:0–5:11	—	.60	.86	.95

Note. See text for explanation of how reliability is calculated for an ability level. Speed of Information Processing (for age 5) is omitted because its reliability is calculated by coefficient alpha rather than by the IRT-based method.
[a]For ages 16-17, the Pattern Construction (Alternative) norms do not extend above a T score of 59.
[b]The ranges for Word Reading standard scores are 86-100, 101-114, and ≥115. For age 5, the Word Reading norms do not extend below a standard score of 86.

FIG. 3.11. Regional reliabilities of DAS subtests administered out of level. Differential Ability Scales. Copyright © 1990 by The Psychological Corporation. Reproduced by permission. All rights reserved. "Differential Ability Scales" and "DAS" are registered trademarks of The Psychological Corporation.

to interpretation, norms are considered essential. Norms provide a unique type of information and are likely to continue to be valued even as sophisticated new systems for the interpretation of nonnormative scores are developed. The following discussion describes some new developments in the use and interpretation of normative scores.

The fundamental equation of the classical test model,

$$X = T + E$$

(i.e., the observed score is the sum of the true score and error), has not been repealed by IRT, and is applicable to tests scaled using IRT. For such tests, X represents the observed estimate of ability and T is the true ability (i.e., ability as measured with perfect accuracy). The observed ability score X is influenced by measurement error in a similar way as are raw scores. That is, the measurement errors that affect the person's performance on individual items are preserved in the translation from item scores to the IRT ability estimate. The ability estimate, like a traditional raw score, reflects the cumulative effect of these errors.

The equation $X = T + E$ underlies the familiar formula for estimating a person's true raw score from an observed raw score (see, for example, Feldt & Brennan, 1989). Given an estimate of the mean (M) of raw scores in a relevant reference sample (such as a norm group) and a reliability estimate (r_{xx}) for the sample, the estimated true raw score is:

$$\hat{X}_{\text{true}} = M + r_{xx}(X - M) \tag{3.1}$$

For the reasons just cited, this true-raw-score estimation formula can be applied equally well to an observed ability score from an IRT-calibrated test. In either case, the formula suggests that observed scores that are above the reference-group mean are more likely to have been increased than decreased by measurement error, and conversely for the lower scores. That is, relatively high raw scores (or ability scores) are likely to be overestimates of the true scores, and relatively low scores are likely to be underestimates. On retesting, the examinees who originally scored highest will tend to score somewhat lower.

This concept of measurement error inherent in estimated ability scores is distinct from the issue of whether the method of estimating ability from a set of item scores is free of systematic bias. Even if an ability-estimation procedure produces an unbiased estimate of the true ability that would generate the observed set of item scores, it does not take into account the type of bias in the item responses themselves that the true-score estimation procedure of the classical model addresses. The classical model views the individual examinee as a member of a group and uses information about the group to adjust the estimate of the individual's true score.

One common application of estimated true raw scores is to locate the center of true-score confidence intervals. Such an interval is interpreted as a range that has a specified probability of including the person's true raw score. Because the estimated true raw score is closer than the observed raw score to the reference-group mean, the confidence interval is not symmetrical about the observed raw score.

Although the methods for estimating true scores and true-score confidence intervals were developed on the basis of raw scores, they are frequently applied to normative scores such as standard scores. The measurement literature contains little analysis of whether these methods may be transferred legitimately from the domain of raw scores to that of normative scores. Indeed, the broader topic of the statistical properties of normative scores is relatively unexplored. The statistical basis for the estimation of true normative scores is worthy of analysis because of the practical utility of true-score estimation in test interpretation.

A true normative score may be defined as a score that describes the location of the person's true raw score in the norm group's distribution of true raw scores. In other words, it is the normative score that would be obtained if the examinee as well as all members of the norm group were measured without error.

In general, two pieces of information are required for estimating a true normative score: an estimate of the true raw score and an estimate of the distribution of true raw scores in the norm population. The first of these is given by Equation 3.1. The classical model also provides an estimate of the standard deviation of true raw scores in the norm sample, through a rearrangement of the definition of reliability as the ratio of true variance to observed variance:

$$\hat{SD}_{true} = r_{xx}^{1/2} SD \qquad (3.2)$$

where SD is the standard deviation of observed raw scores. Note that Equation 3.1 regresses the person's score toward the mean by the factor r_{xx}, whereas Equation 3.2 regresses the norm-group scores by a smaller amount, using the factor $r_{xx}^{1/2}$. Thus, the estimated standard deviation of true raw scores is larger than the standard deviation of estimated true raw scores.

The implication of these observations is that the distance of a true raw score from the mean in true-score standard deviation units is likely to be smaller than the distance of the observed raw score from the mean in observed-score standard deviation units. Thus, the best estimate of a person's true normative score will be closer to the mean than the observed normative score. For standard scores, the appropriate true-score estimation formula is

$$\hat{SS}_{true} = M_{ss} + r_{xx}^{1/2} (SS - M_{ss}) \qquad (3.3)$$

where M_{ss} is the nominal mean of the standard-score scale. The derivation of this formula is provided in the Appendix. The difference between it and Equation 3.1 is that the coefficient is $r_{xx}^{1/2}$ rather than r_{xx}.

As an illustration, consider a test whose reliability is .80 that reports standard scores on a scale where $M = 100$, $SD = 15$. Using Equation 3.3, for an observed standard score of 120 the best estimate of the examinee's true standard score is approximately 118. The magnitude of the regression toward the mean is only about half as great as would be obtained if Equation 3.1, the true-score estimation formula for raw scores, had been applied.

The estimated true standard score from Equation 3.3 should be used to center confidence intervals for true standard scores. The norm tables of both the KAIT and the DAS contain true-score confidence intervals calculated in this way.

There has been no reference in this discussion to the conceptualization of true score as the expected score, that is, as the average of the observed scores that would be obtained from a large number of independent administrations. In the case of raw scores, the concepts of expected score and error-free score converge on the same numerical value. However, the expected normative score is conceptually and numerically distinct from the normative score that would result from error-free measurement. This is a good example of how the statistical properties of normative scores and raw scores (including IRT ability scores) can differ. Because each observed normative score expresses the position of an observed raw score in the norm-sample distribution of observed raw scores, the average of an individual's set of observed normative scores will also be referenced to that distribution, rather than to the estimated distribution of true raw scores. However, the expected value of the person's raw score converges on the true raw score. Thus, the average, or expected, normative score is a score that describes the location of the true raw score in the norm-sample distribution of observed raw scores. Because this definition mixes true and observed scores, the expected normative score is uninterpretable as a normative score. In summary, when dealing with normative scores, the true score and the expected score are distinct concepts and the expected score does not converge on the true score. In the case of standard scores, the true score is estimated by Equation 3.3, and the expected score by Equation 3.1.

The foregoing analysis of true normative scores raises many interesting questions. For instance, could true normative scores be estimated using local standard errors rather than the overall reliability? What would be the practical implications of using estimated true normative scores in place of observed normative scores for interpretation? How would profile analysis be affected? Numerous aspects of the statistical properties of normative scores remain to be explored.

THE FUTURE OF INDIVIDUAL TESTING

Individual test administration is likely to continue to be viewed as desirable if not essential for the valid assessment of young children and individuals with special needs. Methods of using IRT to make these tests more efficient and accurate and their interpretation richer have only begun to be developed, and there is much room for improvement. It is possible that further improvements in the adaptiveness (and resulting efficiency) of individual administration will require computer assistance for the examiner. To be attractive, such computer-aided administration would need to avoid interfering with or slowing down the smooth flow of administration; otherwise, the reduction in the number of items administered might not reduce testing time sufficiently to justify the technology.

IRT now produces the information that can enable examiners to evaluate potential tests in terms of their appropriateness for particular examinees, taking into consideration the individual's level of ability. In order to encourage professionals to look at tests in this way, developers and publishers will need to find ways of communicating this information clearly and educating practitioners in the difference between local accuracy and overall reliability. At the same time, we should expect to see publication of an increasing number of tests that are accurate for specific subgroups even though they are unreliable for more general populations.

Finally, test interpretation will continue to be enhanced through further exploitation of the possibilities offered by IRT ability/difficulty scales and through better understanding of the meaning of normative scores. For many applications, nonnormative ability scales are likely to take over the functions now served by normative scales. IRT ability scores are less tied than raw scores to a specific measuring instrument. The fact that normative scores from different tests can be compared has always been one of their useful and distinctive features, but as different tests measuring the same construct are jointly calibrated using IRT, the ability scale may emerge as a superior basis for comparing and interpreting scores from varied instruments.

APPENDIX

DERIVATION OF EQUATION 3.3
(ESTIMATION OF THE TRUE STANDARD SCORE)

Let X represent the observed raw score, and M, SD, and r_{xx} the mean, standard deviation, and reliability of raw scores in the norm sample. The observed standard score SS is

$$SS = M_{ss} + SD_{ss}\left(\frac{X - M}{SD}\right) \tag{3.A1}$$

where M_{ss} and SD_{ss} are the mean and standard deviation of the standard-score scale (for example, 100 and 15 for the deviation IQ scale).

The true standard score SS_{true} is defined by the same formula (Equation 3.A1), except that the true raw score is substituted for the observed raw score, and the norm-sample mean and standard deviation of true raw scores are substituted for the mean and standard deviation of observed raw scores. Estimates of the true raw score (X_{true}) and the norm-sample standard deviation of true raw scores (SD_{true}) are given in Equations 3.1 and 3.2. Inserting these estimates into Equation 3.A1 gives:

$$\hat{SS}_{true} = M_{ss} + SD_{ss}\left(\frac{X_{true} - M_{true}}{SD_{true}}\right)$$

$$= M_{ss} + SD_{ss}\left[\frac{M + r_{xx}(X - M) - \hat{M}_{true}}{r_{xx}^{1/2}\,SD}\right]$$

Because $\hat{M}_{true} = M$,

$$\hat{SS}_{true} = M_{ss} + r_{xx}^{1/2}\,SD_{ss}\left(\frac{X - M}{SD}\right) \tag{3.A2}$$

Rearranging Equation 3.A1 gives

$$SD_{ss}\left(\frac{X - M}{SD}\right) = SS - M_{ss}$$

Substituting this into Equation 3.A2 yields

$$\hat{SS}_{true} = M_{ss} + r_{xx}^{1/2}\,(SS - M_{ss})$$

which is Equation 3.3, the formula for estimating a true standard score.

REFERENCES

Drasgow, F., Levine, M. V., & McLaughlin, M. E. (1987). Detecting inappropriate test scores with optimal and practical appropriateness indices. *Applied Psychological Measurement, 11,* 59–79.

Elliott, C. D. (1990a). *Differential Ability Scales.* San Antonio, TX: Psychological Corporation.

Elliott, C. D., Murray, D. J., & Pearson, L. S. (1979). *British Ability Scales.* Windsor, England: NFER-Nelson.

Embretson, S. E. (1996). The new rules of measurement. *Psychological Assessment, 8,* 341–349.

Feldt, L. S., & Brennan, R. L. (1989). Reliability. In R. L. Linn (Ed.), *Educational measurement* (3rd ed., pp. 105–146). New York: American Council on Education.

Lord, F. M. (1980). *Applications of item response theory to practical testing problems.* Hillsdale, NJ: Lawrence Erlbaum Associates.

Kaufman, A. S., & Kaufman, N. L. (1993). *Kaufman Adolescent and Adult Intelligence Test.* Circle Pines, MN: American Guidance Service.

Woodcock, R. W., & Johnson, M. B. (1989). *Woodcock–Johnson Psycho-Educational Battery— Revised.* Itasca, IL: Riverside.

CHAPTER FOUR

Fundamental Measurement for Psychology

Benjamin D. Wright
University of Chicago

A new measurement in psychology has emerged from a confluence of scientific and social forces that are producing a revolution in social science methodology. I begin by reviewing how the semiotics of Peirce (Buchler, 1955) revise and enrich our interpretation of Stevens' (1946) four kinds of measurement into a creative dynamic for the evolution of one kind of useful measurement. Then I recall two turning points in social history that remind me of the antiquity and moral force of the need for stable measures. Next I review the psychometric and mathematical histories of measurement, show how the obstacles to inference shape our measurement practice, and summarize Rasch's (1960) contributions. This brings me to some applications of the new measurement models produced by Rasch's work. Finally I review some mistakes that the history of measurement can teach us to stop making.

THE SEMIOTICS OF MEASUREMENT

Peirce Semiotics

Semiotics is the science of signs. It provides a developmental map of creative thought that shows how thinking progresses step-by-step from qualitative flashes of insight to the reproducible quantitative laws of process that are the tool and triumph of science. Table 4.1 outlines six levels of conscious signs through which science is reached (Buchler, 1940; Sheriff, 1994).

TABLE 4.1
Six Steps to Science

Peirce 1904 (see Lieb, 1953)	Stevens 1939	Kinston 1985	6 STEPS TO SCIENCE
5. possible ICON			FANCY qualitative
6. possible INDEX		Entity real idea	THOUGHT qualitative
7. factual INDEX	Nominal	Observable existent	OBJECT qualitative
8. possible SYMBOL	Ordinal	Comparable quantity	SCORE quantitative
9. factual SYMBOL	Interval Ratio	Measurable unit	MEASURE quantitative
10. arguable SYMBOL		Relatable process	RELATION quantitative

Peirce's complete set of signs mark out 10 steps in the evolution of knowing (Sheriff, 1994). The four earliest steps, however, precede the kind of awareness we ordinarily recognize as scientific so they are omitted here. Note how Peirce improved on Stevens in two ways: (a) Twice as many identifiable steps. (b) A clear sequence of connected thinking from the wildest qualitative hypothesis to the most objectively quantitatively measured process.

The first level of scientific consciousness is private fancy, a flash of thought, a wild hypothesis. The thought is ours alone. We may never rethink it. Peirce (Buchler, 1955) called this first level of awareness a possible icon. It is the seed of creativity.

Then some wild ideas acquire meaning. We think them again and encounter others who also think them. This is the step to Peirce's second level. A particular idea becomes more than a private fancy. It becomes something to return to, to talk about. It is still but a quality. We cannot point and say, "There it is." But we can think and talk it. Eddington (1946) and Kinston (1985) called this level an entity. Peirce called it a possible index.

The next step up is an invention of a way to see what we mean. We nominate an experience, a thing, to serve as an instance of our idea. This makes our idea observable and real. Now our idea is a thing of the world. We can do more than think it. We can seek it. We can count it. We have reached the third level at which Stevens' (1946) first kind of measurement, the nominal, finally emerges. Eddington and Kinston called this level an observable and Peirce called it a factual index.

Stevens Revised

Peirce's first two steps to science precede Stevens' (1946) nominal. This shows us that a nominal is not where science begins. A nominal is only reached as a consequence of an evolution of prior possible icons and indices. It is the successful development of these precursors that bequeath the nominal its potential merit as a qualitative thought with quantitative possibilities. We dream before we think. We think before we point. The scientific harvest that may follow depends on the fertility of our imagination and the cultivation of our thought.

Then, as we gather examples of our evolving entity, we discover preference. Some things please us. Others do not. The presence and absence of our entities acquire irresistible valence. We begin to count on more of their goodness, less of their badness. Our preferences propel us to a fourth level, a higher sign, a comparable, corresponding to Stevens' ordinal kind of measurement. We discover that entity nomination is not only a necessary step toward science, but that we are unable to nominate without preferring. Stevens called this ordinal measurement. Peirce called it a possible symbol. Our choices and pursuits of this latency are the crucible in which the tools of science are forged.

At this stage, the subtle and decisive invention of abstract quantification begins to emerge. Valuing more or less of particular things begins to imply valuing more or less of a common something these things imply, a latent variable. We begin to abstract from counting apples to ideas of appleness.

To count is to begin to measure. But counting concrete objects is ambiguous. Counts of real objects do not maintain the magnitude equivalence necessary to qualify as measures. When bricks do not approximate a single size, each piece requires individual attention; building is hard to plan, requires continuous readjustment, and suffers awkward irregularity. It takes uniform bricks to regularize construction, to draw plans. It is the same in trade. How could my grocer sell me a mix of apples and oranges without the currency they share?

This earthy necessity propels us upward to a fifth level. We invent an even more abstract sign, the Eddington and Kinston measurable, which reaches beyond a comparison of more or less to build an imaginary variable along which we can define and maintain an ideal of perfectly equal units that, although abstract in theory, are, nevertheless, approximable in practice. Stevens called this interval measurement. Peirce called it a factual symbol. It is the fundamental language of science. We will discover that its successful realization requires clear ideas as to the obstacles to inference and an understanding of their mathematical solutions.

Stevens distinguished ratios from intervals. But logarithms of ratios are intervals. And exponentiated intervals are ratios. If we have one, we have the other. The only basis for a distinction would be a belief in natural origins. But there are none. Look around. We put our origins wherever they work best: either end of a yardstick, where water (or alcohol) becomes solid, where molecular motion is extrapolated to cease or. . . . Our origins are convenient reference points for useful theories. When our theories change so do our origins (Wright & Masters, 1982).

Stevens' taxonomy stops here. Peirce and Kinston reached one step further to the level of Peirce's arguable symbol and Kinston's relatable. This is where theories of process begin. What good is one variable, if it does not lead to another? And now, at last, a job for linear statistics emerges. To see what our variables imply about process, we plot them against one another. We analyze their variance, estimate regressions, and model equations.

Implications for Practice

Peirce's semiotics specify six steps that we must climb through to reach our pride of science. A quick regression of raw data is always misleading. When we do not think and build our way through the five steps that precede statistical analysis with care and meaning, our research remains empty. We can always get some numbers. But they will not add up to reproducible meaning.

Mistaking Stevens' nominal/ordinal/interval/ratio taxonomy as four kinds of measurement, each with its own kind of statistics, has polarized social scientists into a qualitative/quantitative antipathy that cuts off communication, paralyzes progress, and overlooks the inevitability of a careful stepwise evolution beginning two steps before Stevens' nominal and going a step beyond his interval/ratio to reach, not two or four kinds of measurement but just one kind of science.

The moment we nominate a possible index as sufficiently interesting to observe, we experience a preference that elevates that nominal to an ordinal. Then as we replicate our observations, we cannot resist counting them and using these counts as though they were measures. The final step from concrete ordinals to abstract intervals is forced on us by the necessities of commerce. Just as we cannot trade without currency, we cannot reason quantitatively without linear measures.

Thus the discovery, invention, and construction of scientific knowledge begins with (a) a wild hypothesis that gets thought into (b) a reproducible idea, which becomes realized in (c) an observable instance, to be interpreted as (d) a concrete ordinal that is carefully built into (e) an abstract measurable suitable, finally, for analyses in relation to other measurables and so to the construction of (f) promising theories.

SOCIAL HISTORY

Long before science or mathematics emerged as professions, the commercial, architectural, political, and moral necessities for abstract, exchangeable units of unchanging value were recognized and pursued. A fair weight of seven was a tenet of faith among 7th century Muslims. Muslim leaders were censured for using less righteous standards (Sears, 1997).

Twelve centuries ago, Caliph 'Umar b. 'Abd al-'Aziz ruled that, "The people of al-Kufa have been struck with trial, hardship, oppressive governments and wicked practices. The righteous law is justice and good conduct. I order you to take in taxes only the weight of seven" (Damascus, 723 A.D.), (Sears, 1997).

Seven centuries ago, King John decreed that:

> There shall be one measure of wine throughout Our kingdom, and one of ale, and one measure of corn, to wit, the London quarter, and one breadth of cloth, to wit, two ells within the selvages. As with measures so shall it be with weights. (Magna Carta, Runnymede, 1215 A.D.)

Some say the crux of the French Revolution was outrage against unfair measures. The true origins of stable units for length, area, volume, and weight were the necessities of commerce and politics. The steam engine is responsible for our measures of temperature and pressure.

PSYCHOMETRIC HISTORY

Counting Events Does Not Produce Equal Units

The patriarch of educational measurement, Edward Thorndike (1904), observed:

> If one attempts to measure even so simple a thing as spelling, one is hampered by the fact that there exist no units in which to measure. One may arbitrarily make up a list of words and observe ability by the number spelled correctly. But if one examines such a list one is struck by the inequality of the units. All results based on the equality of any one word with any other are necessarily inaccurate. (p. 7)

Thorndike saw the irregularity in counting concrete events, however indicative they might seem (Engelhard, 1991, 1994). One might observe signs of spelling. But simply counting would not measure spelling. The problem of entity ambiguity is ubiquitous in science, commerce, and cooking. What is an apple? How many apples make a pie? How many little apples equal one big one? Why do three apples not always cost the same? With apples, we solve entity ambiguity by renouncing the concrete apple count and turning, instead, to abstract apple volume or weight (Wright, 1992, 1994).

Raw Scores Are Not Measures

Thorndike was not only aware of the inequality of the units counted but also of the nonlinearity of the raw scores counting produced. Raw scores are bound to begin at none right and end at all right. But the linear measures we intend raw scores to imply have no boundaries. Figure 4.1 is a typical raw score to measure ogive. It shows how the monotonically increasing ogival exchange of one more right answer for a measure increment is steepest in the middle where items are dense and flat at the extremes of 0% and 100%. One more right answer implies the least measure increment near 50%, but an infinite increment at each extreme. In Fig. 4.1, the measure distance along the horizontal axis that corresponds to a 10 percentile raw score increment from 88% to 98% up the vertical axis is 5 times greater than the measure distance corresponding to a 10 percentile raw score increment from 45% to 55%.

Table 4.2 shows the numerical magnitude of this raw score bias against extreme measures for tests of normally distributed and uniformly distributed item difficulties. The tabled values are ratios formed by dividing the measure increment corresponding to one more right answer at the next-to-largest extreme step by the measure increment corresponding to one more right answer at the smallest central step. Even when item difficulties spread out

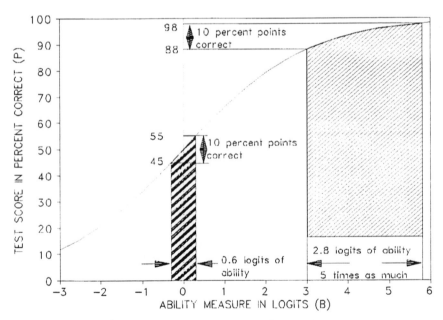

FIG. 4.1. Extreme Raw Scores are Biased Against Measures

TABLE 4.2
Raw Score Bias in Terms of Measure Increment Ratios for
One More Right Answer at the Largest and Smallest Score Steps

Number of Items	Normal Test	Uniform Test
10	2.0	3.5
25	4.6	4.5
50	8.9	6.0
100	17.6	8.0

These calculations are explained on pages 143–151 of *Best Test Design* (Wright & Stone, 1979). The ratio for a normal test of L items is:

$$\log\{2(L-1)/(L-2)\}/\log\{(L+2)/(L-2)\}$$

uniformly in equal increments, the raw score bias against measure increments at the extremes of a 25-item test is a factor of 4.5. When the item difficulties of a 50-item test distribute normally, the bias against extreme measures is a factor of 8.9!

Raw score bias is not confined to dichotomous responses. The bias is just as severe for partial credits, rating scales, and, of course, the infamous Likert Scale, the misuse of which pushed Thurstone's seminal 1920s work on how to construct linear measures from ordinal raw scores out of use (Thurstone, 1926, 1928).

This raw score bias in favor of central scores and against extreme scores means that any linear statistical method like analysis of variance, regression, generalizability, structural equation modeling, or factor analysis that misuses nonlinear raw scores or Likert scales as though they were linear measures will produce systematically distorted results. Like the nonlinear raw scores on which they are based, all results will be target biased and sample dependent and hence inferentially ambiguous (Wright & Linacre, 1989; Wright & Masters, 1982; Wright & Stone, 1979). Little wonder that so much social science remains a transient description of never-to-be-reencountered situations, easy to doubt with almost any replication.

An obvious first law of measurement is: Before applying linear statistical methods, use a measurement model to construct linear measures from your observed raw data.

There are many advantages to working with model-controlled linearization. Each measure is accompanied by a realistic estimate of its precision and a mean square residual-from-expectation evaluation of the extent to which the raw ordinal data from which the measure has been estimated fit the measurement model. When we now advance to graphing results and applying linear statistics to analyze relationships among variables, we not only have linear measures to work with, we also have estimates of their statistical precision and validity.

Thurstone's Measurement

Between 1925 and 1932, Thurstone published 24 articles and a book on how to construct good measures.

Unidimensionality. "The measurement of any object or entity describes only one attribute of the object measured. This is a universal characteristic of all measurement" (Thurstone, 1931, p. 257).

Linearity. "The very idea of measurement implies a linear continuum of some sort such as length, price, volume, weight, age. When the idea of measurement is applied to scholastic achievement, for example, it is necessary to force the qualitative variations into a scholastic linear scale of some kind" (Thurstone & Chave, 1929, p. 11).

Abstraction. "The linear continuum which is implied in all measurement is always an abstraction . . . There is a popular fallacy that a unit of measurement is a thing—such as a piece of yardstick. This is not so. A unit of measurement is always a process of some kind . . ." (Thurstone, 1931, p. 257).

Invariance. ". . . which can be repeated without modification in the different parts of the measurement continuum" (Thurstone, 1931, p. 257).

Sample-Free Item Calibration. "The scale must transcend the group measured. One crucial test must be applied to our method of measuring attitudes before it can be accepted as valid. A measuring instrument must not be seriously affected in its measuring function by the object of measurement. Within the range of objects intended, its function must be independent of the object of measurement" (Thurstone, 1928, p. 547).

Test-Free Person Measurement. "It should be possible to omit several test questions at different levels of the scale without affecting the individual score. It should not be required to submit every subject to the whole range of the scale. The starting point and the terminal point should not directly affect the individual score" (Thurstone, 1926, p. 446).

Guttman's Scale

In 1944, Guttman showed that the meaning of a raw score, including one produced by Likert scales, would be ambiguous unless the score defined a unique response pattern:

If a person endorses a more extreme statement, he should endorse *all* less extreme statements if the statements are to considered a scale . . . We shall call a set of items of *common content* a scale if [and only if] a person with a higher rank than another person is just as high or higher on *every* item than the other person. (Guttman, 1950, p. 62)

According to Guttman, only data that approximate this kind of conjoint transitivity can produce unambiguous measures. A deterministic application of Guttman's scale is impossible. But his ideal of conjoint transitivity is the kernel of Norman Campbell's (1920) fundamental measurement. Notice the affinity between Guttman's scalability and Ronald Fisher's (1922) sufficiency. Both call for a statistic that exhausts the information to which it refers.

MATHEMATICAL HISTORY

Although mathematics did not initiate the practice of measurement, it is the mathematics of measurement that provide the ultimate foundation for better practice and the final logic by which useful measurement evolves and thrives. As we review some of the ideas by which mathematicians and physicists built their theories, we discover that, although each worked on his own ideas in his own way, their conclusions converge to a single formulation for measurement practice.

Concatenation

In 1920, physicist Norman Campbell deduced that the fundamental measurement on which physics was built required the possibility of explicit concatenation, like joining the ends of sticks to concatenate length or piling bricks to concatenate weight. Because psychological concatenation seemed impossible, Campbell concluded that there could be no fundamental measures in psychology.

Sufficiency

In 1920, Ronald Fisher, while applying his likelihood version of inverse probability to invent maximum likelihood estimation, discovered a statistic so sufficient that it exhausted from the data in hand all information concerning its modeled parameter. Fisher's discovery is much appreciated for its informational efficiency. But it has a concomitant property that is far more important to the construction of measurement. A statistic that exhausts all modeled information enables conditional formulations by which a value for each parameter can be estimated independently of the values of all other parameters in the model.

This follows because the functional presence of any parameter can be replaced by its sufficient statistic (Andersen, 1977). Without this replacement each parameter estimation, each attempt to construct a generalizable measure, is forever foiled. The incidental distributions of the other parameters make every measure estimate situation-specific. Generality is destroyed.

This leads to a second law of measurement: When a model employs parameters for which there are no sufficient statistics, that model cannot construct useful measurement because it cannot estimate its parameters independently of one another.

Divisibility

Levy (Feller, 1957, p. 271) proved that the construction of a law for probability distributions that is stable with respect to arbitrary decisions as to what is countable required infinitely divisible parameters (Feller, 1957). Levy's divisibility is logarithmically equivalent to conjoint additivity (Luce & Tukey, 1964). Levy's conclusions were reenforced in 1932 when Kolmogorov (1950) proved that independent parameter estimation also requires divisibility.

In 1992, Bookstein reported his astonishment at the mathematical equivalence of every counting law he could find (1992, 1996). Provoked to decipher how this ubiquitous equivalence could have occurred, he discovered that the counting formulations were not only members of one simple mathematical family, but they were surprisingly robust with respect to ambiguities of *entity* (which elements to count), *aggregation* (at what hierarchical level to count) and *scope* (for how long and how far to count). As he sought to understand the source of this remarkable robustness, Bookstein discovered that the necessary and sufficient formulation was Levy's divisibility.

Additivity

American work on the mathematical foundations of measurement came to fruition with the proof by Luce and Tukey (1964) that Campbell's concatenation was a physical realization of the mathematical law which is necessary for fundamental measurement:

> The essential character of simultaneous conjoint measurement is described by an axiomatization for the comparison of effects of *pairs* formed from two specified kinds of "quantities" . . . Measurement on interval scales which have a common unit follows from these axioms.
>
> A close relation exists between conjoint measurement and the establishment of response measures in a two-way table . . . for which the "effects of columns" and the "effects of rows" are additive. Indeed the discovery of such measures

. . . may be viewed as the discovery, via conjoint measurement, of fundamental measures of the row and column variables. (Luce & Tukey, 1964, p. 1)

Their conclusion writes a third law of measurement: "When no natural concatenation operation exists, one should try to discover a way to measure factors and responses such that the 'effects' of different factors are additive" (Luce & Tukey, 1964, p. 4).

INFERENCE

The common measures by which we make life better are so familiar that we seldom think about why or how they work. A mathematical history of inference, however, takes us behind practice to the theoretical requirements that make measurement possible. Table 4.3 articulates an anatomy of inference into four obstacles that stand between raw data and the stable inference of measures they might imply.

Uncertainty is our motivation for inference. The future is uncertain by definition. We have only the past by which to foresee. Our solution is to capture this uncertainty in a matrix of inverse probabilities that regularize the irregularities that interrupt the continuity between what seems certain now but must be uncertain later.

Distortion interferes with the transition from observation to conceptualization. Our ability to figure things out comes from our faculty to visualize.

TABLE 4.3
An Anatomy of Inference

Obstacles	Solutions	Inventors
UNCERTAINTY	PROBABILITY	Bernoulli, 1713
have ⇒ want	binomial odds	Bayes, 1764
now ⇒ later	regular irregularity	Laplace, 1774
statistic ⇒ parameter	misfit detection	Poisson, 1837
DISTORTION	ADDITIVITY	Fechner, 1860
nonlinearity	linearity	Helmholtz, 1887
unequal intervals	concatenation	Campbell, 1920
incommensurability	conjoint additivity	Luce/Tukey, 1964
CONFUSION	SEPARABILITY	Rasch, 1958
interdependence	sufficiency	Fisher, 1920
interaction	invariance	Thurstone, 1926
confounding	conjoint order	Guttman, 1944
AMBIGUITY	DIVISIBILITY	Levy, 1937
of entity, interval,	independence	Kolmogorov, 1950
and aggregation	stability	Bookstein, 1992

For Bernoulli, Bayes, Laplace, Poisson, and Helmholtz, see Stigler (1986).

Our power of visualization evolves from the survival value of body navigation through the space in which we live. Our antidote to distortion is to represent our observations of experience in the bilinear form that makes them look like the mostly two dimensional space we see in front of us. To see what experience means, we map it.

Confusion is caused by interdependencies. As we look for tomorrow's probabilities in yesterday's lessons, confusing interactions intrude. Our resolution of confusion is to simplify the complexity we experience into a few shrewdly crafted dimensions. We define and measure our dimensions one at a time. Their authority is their utility. Truths may be unknowable. But when our inventions work, we have proven them useful. And when they continue to work, we come to believe in them and may even christen them real and true.

Ambiguity, a fourth obstacle to inference, occurs because there is no objective way to determine exactly which operational definitions of conceptual entities are the right ones. As a result, only models that are indifferent to levels of composition are robust enough to survive the vicissitudes of entity ambiguity. Bookstein (1992) showed that this requires functions that embody divisibility or additivity as in:

$$H(x/y) = H(x)/H(y) \quad \text{or} \quad G(x + y) = G(x) + G(y)$$

Fortunately the mathematical solutions to distortion, confusion, and ambiguity are identical. The parameters that govern the probability of the data must appear in either an entirely divisible or an entirely additive form. No mixtures of divisions and additions, however, are admissible.

The Probability Solution

The application of Jacob Bernoulli's 1713 binomial distribution as an inverse probability for interpreting the implications of observed events (Jacob Bernoulli, 1713; Thomas Bayes, 1764; Laplace, 1774, in Stigler, 1986) was a turning point in the mathematical history of measurement. Our interests reach beyond the data in hand to what these data might imply about future data, still unmet, but urgent to foresee.

The first problem of inference is how to predict values for these future data, which, by the meaning of inference, are necessarily missing. This meaning of missing, of course, must include not only the future data to be inferred but also all possible past data that were lost or never collected. Because the purpose of inference is to estimate what future data might be like before they occur, methods that require complete data (i.e., cannot analyze present data in which some values are missing) cannot be methods of inference. This realization engenders a fourth law of measurement: Any statistical method nominated to serve inference which requires complete data, by this requirement, disqualifies itself as an inferential method.

But if what we want to know is missing, how can we use the data in hand to make useful inferences about the missing data they might imply? Inverse probability reconceives our raw observations as a probable consequence of a relevant stochastic process with a useful formulation. The apparent determinism of formulae like F = MA depends on the prior construction of relatively precise measures of F and M (For a stochastic discussion of this formulation of the multiplicative law of accelerations in which M is realized by solid bodies and F is realized by instruments of force, see Rasch, 1960). The first step from raw observation to inference is to identify the stochastic process by which an inverse probability can be defined. Bernoulli's binomial distribution is the simplest process. The compound Poisson is the stochastic parent of all such measuring distributions (Rasch, 1960).

The Mathematical Solution

The second problem of inference is to discover which mathematical models can determine the stochastic process in a way that enables a stable, ambiguity-resilient estimation of the model's parameters from data in hand. At first glance, this step may look obscure. Table 4.3 suggests that its history followed many paths, traveled by many mathematicians and physicists. One might fear that there was no clear second step but only a variety of unconnected possibilities with seemingly different resolutions. Fortunately, reflection on the motivations for these paths and examination of their mathematics leads to a reassuring simplification. Although each path was motivated by a particular concern as to what inference must overcome to succeed, all solutions end up with the same simple, easy to understand, and easy to use formulation. The mathematical function that governs the inferential stochastic process must specify parameters that are either infinitely divisible or conjointly additive; that is, separable.

What does this summarize to?

1. Measures are inferences,
2. Obtained by stochastic approximations,
3. Of one dimensional quantities,
4. Counted in abstract units,
5. That are impervious to extraneous factors.

To meet these requirements, measurement must be an inference of values for infinitely divisible parameters that define the transition odds between observable increments of a theoretical variable.

RASCH'S MEASURING FUNCTIONS

The Fundamental Measurement Model

In 1953, Rasch (1960) found that the only way he could compare performances on different tests of oral reading was to apply the exponential additivity
of Poisson's 1837 distribution (Stigler, 1986) to data produced by a sample
of students responding simultaneously to both tests. Rasch used the Poisson
distribution as his model because it was the only distribution he could think
of that enabled the equation of two tests to be entirely independent of the
obviously arbitrary distribution of the reading abilities of the sample.

As Rasch worked out his solution to what became an unexpectedly successful test equating, he discovered that the mathematics of the probability
process, the measurement model, must be restricted to formulations that
produced sufficient statistics. Only when his parameters had sufficient statistics could these statistics replace and, hence, remove the unwanted person
parameters from his estimation equations and so obtain estimates of his test
parameters, which were independent of the incidental values of the person
parameters used in the model.

I never heard Rasch refer to Guttman's (1944) conjoint transitivity. Yet,
as Rasch described the necessities of his probability function, he defined a
stochastic solution to the impossible requirement that data conform to a
deterministic conjoint transitivity:

> A person having a greater ability than another should have the greater prob-
> ability of solving *any* item of the type in question, and similarly, one item
> being more difficult than another one means that for *any* person the prob-
> ability of solving the second item correctly is the greater one. (Rasch, 1960,
> p. 117)

Rasch completed his argument for a measurement model in his 1960
book (pp. 117–122). His measuring function specifies the divisible definition
of fundamental measurement for dichotomous observations as:

$$f(P) \equiv b/d \qquad \text{(p. 118)}$$

where P is the probability of a correct solution, f(P) is a function of P, still
to be determined, b is a ratio measure of person ability, and d is a ratio
calibration of item difficulty.

Rasch explained this measuring function as an inverse probability "of a
correct solution, which may be taken *as the imagined outcome* of an in-
definitely long series of trials" (p. 118). Because "*an additive system* . . . is
simpler than the original . . . *multiplicative system*" (p. 118), Rasch took
logarithms:

$$\log\{f(P)\} = \log b - \log d = B - D = G(P)$$

and transformed P into its logistic form:

$$L = \log\{P/(1 - P)\}$$

Then Rasch asked, *"Does there exist a function of the variable L which forms an additive system in parameters for person B and parameters for items D such that"*:

$$L = \log\{P/(1 - P)\} = B - D \qquad \text{(pp. 119–120)}$$

Finally, asking "whether the measuring function for a test, if it exists at all, is uniquely determined" (p. 120) Rasch proved that:

$$f(P) = C\{f_0(P)\}^A$$

"is a measuring function for any positive values of C and A, if $f_0(P)$ is," which "contains all the possible measuring functions which can be constructed from $f_0(P)$." So that "By suitable choice of dimensions and units, i.e. of A and C for f(P), it is possible to make the b's and d's vary within any positive interval which may . . . be . . . convenient" (p. 121).

Because of "the validity of a *separability theorem (due to sufficiency)*":

> It is possible to arrange the observational situation in such a way that from the responses of a number of persons to the set of items in question we may derive two sets of quantities, the distributions of which depend only on the item parameters, and only on the personal parameters, respectively. Furthermore the conditional distribution of the whole set of data for given values of the two sets of quantities does not depend on any of the parameters.

With respect to separability the choice of this model has been lucky. Had we for instance assumed the "Normal-Ogive Model" [as did Thurstone in the 1920s] with all $s_i = 1$—which numerically may be hard to distinguish from the logistic—then the separability theorem would have broken down. And the same would, in fact, happen for any other conformity model which is not equivalent—in the sense of $f(P) = C\{f_0(P)\}^A$ to $f(P) = b/d$ . . . as regards separability.

The possible distributions are . . . limited to rather simple types, but . . . lead to rather far reaching generalizations of the Poisson . . . process. (p. 122)

The Compound Poisson

Rasch (1960, 1961, 1963, 1968, 1969, 1977) showed that formulations in the compound Poisson family, such as Bernoulli's binomial, are not only sufficient for the construction of stable measurement, but that the multiplicative

Poisson (Feller, 1957) is the only mathematical solution to the formulation of an objective, sample and test-free measuring function. Andrich (1995, 1996) confirmed that Rasch separability required the Poisson distribution for estimating measures from discrete observations. Bookstein (1996) showed that the stochastic application of the divisibility necessary for ambiguity resilience requires the compound Poisson.

Conjoint Additivity and Rasch

Although conjoint additivity is acknowledged to be a decisive theoretical requirement for measurement, few psychologists realize that Rasch models are its practical realization. Rasch models construct conjoint additivity by applying inverse probability to empirical data and then testing these data for their goodness-of-fit to this construction (Fischer, 1968; Keats, 1967; Perline, Wright, & Wainer, 1979):

> The Rasch model is a special case of additive conjoint measurement . . . a fit of the Rasch model implies that the cancellation axiom (i.e. conjoint transitivity) will be satisfied . . . It then follows that items and persons are measured on an interval scale with a common unit. (Brogden, 1977, p. 633)

Rasch models are the only laws of quantification that define objective measurement, determine what is measurable, decide which data are useful, and expose which data are not.

A MEASUREMENT MODEL

Our data can be obtained as responses to nominal categories like:

yes/no,
right/wrong,
present/absent,
always/usually/sometimes/never,
strongly agree/agree/disagree/strongly disagree.

Nominal labels like these invite ordinal interpretation from more to less: more yes, more right, more presence, more occurrence, more agreement. Almost without further thought, we take the asserted hierarchy for granted and imagine that our declared categories will inevitably implement a clear and stable ordinal scale. But whether our respondents actually use our categories in the ordered steps we intend cannot be left to imagination. We must find out by analyzing real responses how respondents actually use our categories. When this is carefully done, it frequently emerges that an intended rating scale of five or six seemingly ordinal categories has actually functioned as a simple dichotomy.

Binomial transition odds like P_{nix}/P_{nix-1} can implement the inferential possibilities of data collected in nominal categories interpreted as ordered steps. When we label our categories: $x = 0,1,2,3,4, \ldots$ in their intended order, then each numerical label can count one more step up our ordered scale. Our response categories may be labeled and scored as:

Wrong	Right
$x = 0$	$x = 1$

or

Strongly Disagree	Disagree	Agree	Strongly Agree
$x = 0$	$x = 1$	$x = 2$	$x = 3$

We can connect each x to the situation for which we are trying to construct measures by subscribing x as x_{ni} so that it can stand for a rating recorded by (or for) a person n on an item i and then specify P_{nix} as the inverse probability that person n obtains x as their rating on item i.

The transition odds that the rating is x rather than $x - 1$ become P_{nix}/P_{nix-1}.

	P_{nix-1}	P_{nix}	
$x - 2$	$x - 1$	x	$x + 1$

Then we can introduce a mathematical model that explains P_{nix} as the consequence of a conjointly additive function that specifies exactly how we want our parameters to govern P_{nix}.

Our parameters can be B_n, the location measure of person n on the continuum of reference; D_i, the location calibration of item i, the instrumental operationalization of this continuum and F_x, the gradient up the continuum of the transition from response category $(x - 1)$ to category (x).

The necessary and sufficient measurement models are:

$$P_{nix}/P_{nix-1} \equiv b_n/d_i f_x$$

or

$$\log(P_{nix}/P_{nix-1}) \equiv B_n - D_i - F_x$$

in which the symbol $\equiv$ means *by definition* rather than merely *equals*.

The first model satisfies the Levy/Kolmogorov/Bookstein divisibility requirement. The second model satisfies the Campbell/Luce/Tukey conjoint additivity requirement. On the left of either formula a concrete datum x_{ni} is replaced by its abstract Bernoulli/Bayes/Laplace stochastic proxy P_{nix}. In practice we apply the second formulation because its additivity produces parameter estimates in the linear form to which our eyes and feet are accustomed. Our penchant for linearity is more than visual. Fechner (1860) showed that when we experience a ratio impact of light, sound, or pain, our nervous system takes a logarithm so that we can see how the impact feels on a linear scale. Nor was Fechner the first to notice this neurology. Pythagorean tuning puts musical instruments out of tune at each key change. Tuning to notes that increase in frequency by equal ratios, however, produces an equally tempered scale of notes that sound equally spaced in any key. Pythagorean tuning is key-dependent. Equally tempered tuning is key-free. Bach's motive for writing "The Well-Tempered Clavier" was to demonstrate the validity of this 17th century discovery.

APPLICATIONS OF RASCH MEASUREMENT

Measuring Applied Self-Care

Here is an example of a Rasch analysis of 3,128 administrations of the eight-program PECS© Applied Self-Care LifeScale™.
This scale asks about the success of eight self-care programs:

1. BOWEL
2. URINARY
3. SKIN CARE
4. Health COGNIZANCE
5. Health ACTIVITY
6. Health EDUCATION
7. SAFETY Awareness
8. MEDICATION Knowledge

Nurses rate patients on their competence in each of these self-care programs according to a seven category scale (labeled 1–7 in this case). This scale rises from Ineffective at label $x = 1$ through three levels of dependence at $x = 2,3,4$ and two levels of independence at $x = 5,6$ to normal at label $x = 7$.
The data matrix we analyze has 3,128 rows and 8 columns, a row for each patient n and a column for each program i with cell entries for patient n on program i of x_{ni} recorded as an ordinal rating from 1 to 7. This matrix of 25,024 data points is analyzed to estimate the best possible:

1. 8 self-care program calibrations to define a self-care construct,
2. 48 rating step gradients to define each program's rating scale structure,
3. 3,128 patient reports, with self-care measures when data permit.

All estimates are expressed in linear measures on the one common scale that marks out a single dimension of self-care.

Here are excerpts from a BIGSTEPS (Wright & Linacre, 1997) analysis of these data. As you scan this example, do not worry about every detail. Relax and enjoy how this kind of analysis can reduce potentially complicated data into a few well-organized tables and pictures.

Summarizing Results

Table 4.4 summarizes the results of a 91% reduction of the raw data (from $3,128 \times 8 = 25,024$ ordinal observations to $2,145 + 8 + 56 = 2,209$ linear measures) and documents the success of its reconstruction into one unidimensional measurement framework. The linear logits for this analysis were rescaled to center the eight test programs at 50 and mark out 10 units per logit. The resulting measures reach from -10 to 110 with 98% of the action between 0 and 90.

1. Of the 3,128 patient records reported in Table 4.4:

   2,145 nonextreme records are measured on the self-care construct,

   5 are rated at the high extreme of normal on all programs,

   94 are rated at the low extreme of ineffective on all programs,

   884 lack all but one or two ratings and are set aside.
2. The data for the 2,145 measured patients are 94.3% complete.

TABLE 4.4
Measure Summary
PECS[©] LifeScales: Applied Self-Care

ENTERED: 3,128 PATIENTS   ANALYZED: 2145 PATIENTS   8 PROGRAMS   56 CATEGORIES

Summary of 2,145 Measured (Nonextreme) Patients

	RAW SCORE	COUNT	MEASURE	MODEL ERROR	INFIT MNSQ	OUTFIT MNSQ
MEAN	26.2	7.5	41.56	4.94	.88	.89
S.D.	11.0	.9	22.09	1.35	1.06	1.10
REAL RMSE	5.80	ADJ.SD	21.32	SEPARATION 3.68	RELIABILITY	.93
S.E. OF PATIENT MEAN		.48				

MAXIMUM EXTREME SCORE: 5 PATIENTS   MINIMUM EXTREME SCORE: 94 PATIENTS
LACKING RESPONSES: 884 PATIENTS   VALID RESPONSES: 94.3%
Output from BIGSTEPS (Wright & Linacre, 1997)

3. The mean patient measure for the 2,145 measured patients = 41.56.
4. The observed patient S.D. = 22.09 measure units.
5. Root Mean Square Measurement Error [RMSE] = 5.80 Measure Units.
6. Correction for measurement error and misfit adjusts the observed S.D. = 22.09 to the more realistic value of ADJ.S.D. = 21.32.
7. The separation ratio for distinguishing among these 2,145 self-care measures is (ADJ.S.D.)/RMSE = 21.32/5.80 = 3.68.
8. The corresponding test reliability = $(3.68)^2/[1 + (3.68)^2]$ = .93.

Program Calibrations

Table 4.5 lists the eight-program calibrations by which the operational definition of this self-care construct will be mapped. This table shows the programs in their order of difficulty to accomplish. (Note that Health Cognizance matches Skin Care and Health Education matches Knows Medications in difficulty.)

Listed for each self-care program is a program calibration MEASURE, calibration standard ERROR, and two mean square ratio [MNSQ] fit statistics by which the validity of that calibration can be judged. The MNSQ fit statistics are ratios of observed residual variance to expected residual variance. When observed variance is no more than expected, these fit statistics are near 1.00. Their values in Table 4.5 show that the only program afflicted with tangible calibration uncertainty is the Skin Care program, with mean square residual ratios of observed to expected at 1.22 and 1.29.

This slight misfit suggests that Skin Care may interact with other variables like patient age, sex, or impairment for some patients. Other pages of BIGSTEPS output identify exactly which patients manifest such interactions and bring out the rating pattern diagnostics most useful for understanding the ratings of these particular patients.

The analysis of the extent to which any particular set of data cooperates with a measurement model to define an intended variable and so to estimate useful measures along that variable is decisive in the construction of good measures. I cannot do justice to this important topic here. But an excellent place to find articulate explanations and applications is in the work of Smith (1985, 1986, 1988, 1991, 1994, 1996).

Rating Scale Analysis

Figure 4.2, derived from a larger sample of patients rated on the same instrument, shows how BIGSTEPS analyzes the way each set of rating categories works to obtain patient ratings on each program. The program shown is the Bowel program.

TABLE 4.5
Program Calibrations
PECS© LifeScales: Applied Self-Care

PROGRAMS STATISTICS: MEASURE ORDER

ENTRY NUM	RAW SCORE	COUNT	MEASURE	ERROR	INFIT MNSQ	OUTFIT MNSQ	PTBIS	HARDEST PROGRAM
8	5,964	1,866	57.4	.3	.96	.97	.82	KNOWS MEDICATIONS
6	5,828	1,832	57.1	.3	.66	.68	.89	HEALTH EDUCATION
5	6,294	1,800	52.1	.3	.72	.74	.87	HEALTH ACTIVITY
7	7,458	2,137	48.9	.3	.71	.78	.86	SAFETY AWARENESS
4	7,413	2,135	48.2	.3	.47	.49	.91	HEALTH COGNIZANCE
3	7,290	2,139	48.1	.3	1.22	1.29	.77	SKIN CARE PROGRAM*
1	7,858	2,141	44.6	.3	.82	.92	.83	BOWEL PROGRAM
2	8,168	2,135	43.7	.3	1.09	1.16	.80	URINARY PROGRAM
MEAN	7,034.	2,023.	50.0	.3	.83	.88		EASIEST PROGRAM
S.D.	829.	148.	4.8	.0	.23	.24		

*The SKIN CARE PROGRAM shows slight misfit with INFIT & OUTFIT = 1.22 & 1.29

INPUT: 3,128 PATIENTS, 8 PROGRAMS
ANALYZED: 2,145 PATIENTS, 8 PROGRAMS   56 CATEGORIES

Output from BIGSTEPS (Wright & Linacre, 1997)

85

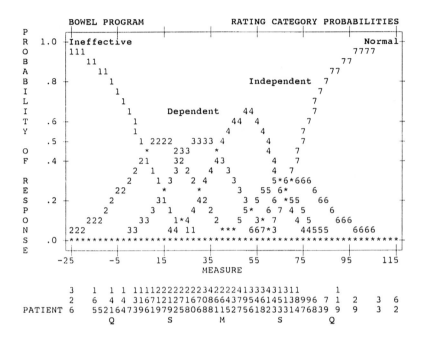

```
          BOWEL PROGRAM              RATING CATEGORY PROBABILITIES
P  ┌─────────────┼───────────┼──────────┼─────────────┼──────────┐
R  1.0 ┤Ineffective                                        Normal├
O      111                                            7777
B         11                                          77
A         11                                     77
B  .8 ┤     1                    Independent    7                ├
I          1                                 7
L          1                               7
I          1         Dependent    44      7
T  .6 ┤     1                   44  4      7                     ├
Y          1                  4      4    7
   .5 ┤     1 2222    3333 4        4    7
O          *      233      *       4   7
F  .4 ┤     21      32      43      4  7                         ├
        2   1   3  2    4  3      4  7
R        2     1 3    2 4      3      5*6*666
E          22       *      *     3   55 6*     6
S  .2 ┤    2      31      42     3  5   6 *55    66              ├
P      2       3  1    4  2    5*   6  7 4  5     6
O      222      33    1*4    2    5  3* 7   4 5      666
N  222         33     44 11     ***  667*3    44555    6666
S  .0 ┤*********************************************************├
E  └─────┼───────────┼──────────┼─────────────┼──────────┘
    -25      -5      15     35     55     75     95     115
                                MEASURE
```

```
        3    1   1  1  111122222222342222413334313 1 1       1
        2    6   4  4  316712127167086643795461451389 96  7 1  2   3   6
PATIENT 6    5521647396197925806881152756182333147 6839 9  9   3   2
                       Q            S          M      S    Q
```

BOWEL PROGRAM   **RATING STEP CALIBRATIONS**

CATEGORY STEP LABEL	STEP VALUE	OBSERVED COUNT	STEP MEASURE	STEP ERROR	EXPECTED SCORE MEASURES STEP-.5	AT STEP	STEP+.5
Ineffective	1	618	NONE		(-6)		13
2	2	1049	7	.6	13	13	22
Dependent	3	1794	21	.4	22	30	40
4	4	2503	38	.3	40	50	58
Independent	5	860	66	.4	58	63	67
6	6	727	66	.4	67	72	78
Normal	7	1010	70	.5	78	(84)	
			──mode──		──mean──		

Output from BIGSTEPS (Wright, & Linacre, 1997)

FIG. 4.2. Rating Category Step Structure PECS© LifeScales: Applied Self-Care Construct

The plot in the top half of Fig. 4.2 shows how the probabilities of category use, 1 to 7, move to the right across the variable from low measures below −20 to high measures above +110. Each rating category in turn, from left to right, shows a distinct region of greatest probability, except categories 5 and 6, which were underused in these data. This discovery raises a question about the utility of trying to distinguish between categories 5 and 6 when rating the Bowel program. If raters do not use categories 5 and 6 to distinguish successive levels of Bowel program success in a reliable way, it could be more efficient to combine 5 and 6 into one category of independence for rating success on this program. This rescoring might be mistaken as throwing away data. But experience with this kind of analysis has shown that rescoring to combine indistinct adjacent categories increases the reliability of measurement.

The table at the bottom of Fig. 4.2 gives a statistical summary of how these ratings performed. Successive columns show Observed Counts, Step Measures and Expected Score Measures at each rating level from 1 to 7. In the Observed Count column, we see that the use of categories 5 and 6, at counts of 860 and 727, fall below the use of category 4, at a count of 2,503. This is why the probability curves for those two categories do not surface in the plot. Rescoring these categories together produces a combined count of 1,587, which fits right into a unimodal distribution of observed counts from 618 through 1,048, 1,794, 2,503, 860 + 727 = 1,587 to 1,010.

Making a MAP

To expedite interpretation of this self-care construct, the distribution of patient measures and the program calibrations from Table 4.5 are plotted on the construct MAP in Fig. 4.3. The left column benchmarks the linear units of the measurement framework from 0 to 90 units.

The second column plots the frequency distribution of the 2,096 patients measuring between 0 and 90. M marks the mean patient measure. The two Ss mark plus and minus one standard deviation. The two Qs mark plus and minus two standard deviations.

Finally the right column of the MAP shows the calibration locations of the six most distinct self-care programs. The relative positions of these programs provide define this self-care construct. The programs are shown at four of their rating seven levels:

1 marking "Ineffective,"

3 and 4 marking two levels of "Dependence," and

6 marking "Independence."

This MAP shows how this definition of self-care moves up from ratings of ineffectiveness in the 0 to 10 measure region, through successive levels of dependence in the 25 to 60 measure region, to ratings of independence in the 75 to 90 measure region.

The program difficulty hierarchy in each level begins with the Urinary and Bowel programs that are the easiest programs to succeed on and moves up through Skin Care, Safety and Activity to reach Medications, which is the hardest to succeed on.

The clinical implications of this hierarchy are that self-care education has the best chance of success when it begins at the easy end with Urinary and Bowel programs and does not attempt the more challenging Activity and

```
MEASURE    PATIENTS        RATING.APPLIED SELF-CARE

  90           . +          6.KNOWS MEDICATIONS
               . |
             .# Q|          6.HEALTH ACTIVITY
               . |          6.SAFETY AWARENESS
  80         .## +          6.SKIN CARE PROGRAM
            .### |          6.BOWEL PROGRAM
             .## |          6.URINARY PROGRAM
           .#### |
  70        .### +
           .#### |
        ######## |
        ######## S|
  60    .####### +          4.KNOWS MEDICATIONS
      .######### |
           .#### |          4.HEALTH ACTIVITY
      .######### |          4.SAFETY AWARENESS
  50       .#### +          4.SKIN CARE PROGRAM
        .###### |           4.BOWEL PROGRAM
          #### |            4.URINARY PROGRAM
       ####### M|
  40 .########## +          3.KNOWS MEDICATIONS
    .########## |
      .######## |           3.HEALTH ACTIVITY
       .##### |             3.SAFETY AWARENESS
  30   .##### +             3.SKIN CARE PROGRAM
      .###### |             3.BOWEL PROGRAM
      .###### |             3.URINARY PROGRAM
       .##### |
  20    .#### S+
      .##### |
       .#### |
       .#### | 1.KNOWS MEDICATIONS
  10   .#### +
         .# | 1.HEALTH ACTIVITY
          . | 1.SAFETY AWARENESS
        .## | 1.SKIN CARE PROGRAM
   0     .# + 1.BOWEL PROGRAM
       .### Q| 1.URINARY PROGRAM
```

Output from **BIGSTEPS** (Wright, & Linacre 1997)

FIG. 4.3. A MAP of PECS[©] Lifescales: Applied Self-Care

Medications programs until the mastery of the easier programs is well underway.

Diagnostic KEYs

MAPs and numerical summaries of program and category performance are essential to the analysis of the measurement quality of a test. Our ultimate concern, however, is the measurement and diagnosis of each patient. This brings us to the two diagnostic KEYs illustrated in Fig. 4.4.

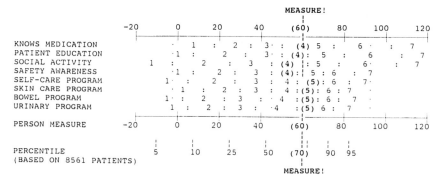

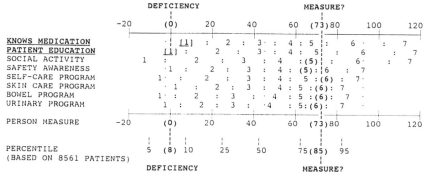

Output from BIGSTEPS (Wright, & Linacre, 1997)

FIG. 4.4. KEY Forms for A Typical and An Atypical Patient

After the construct MAP of Fig. 4.3, KEYs like those in Fig. 4.4 are the second-most useful outcome of a BIGSTEPS analysis. Figure 4.4 shows two patients who received the same rating totals of 36 raw score points, but who differ decisively in the best estimates of their overall self-care measures and in the diagnostic implications of their different self-care rating patterns.

The typical (i.e., fitting) patient at the top of Fig. 4.4 measures at 60 self-care units, which puts them at the 70th percentile among a normative group of 8,561 patients. This patient is verging on self-care independence but can still benefit from additional help with the hardest programs, Medication and Education.

The atypical (i.e., misfitting) patient at the bottom of Fig. 4.4 has the same raw score. But, as soon as we draw a vertical line through their ratings of 5s and 6s on the easiest six programs, the implications of their pattern of ratings are quite different. Now we see that when their totally ineffective ratings of 1s on Medication and Education are set aside, they measure at 73 units and the 85th percentile.

This patient is well into independence on everything except Education and Medication. But, for these two programs, their training must go back to the beginning and start over again at the earliest levels. The KEY record makes it obvious that their self-care curriculum can ease up on everything except Education and Medication.

Notice how easily we become aware of the idiosyncratic aspects of a patient's status when a well-defined frame of reference has been constructed. The KEYs make it clear that the two patients in Fig. 4.4 should not be treated the same just because they happen to have the same raw score of 36. On the contrary, when we have a frame of reference, we learn more about each patient than just the overall measure their score may imply. We learn how they got their score. And, when their pattern of ratings contains values that, because of the structure of our measurement frame of reference are unexpected, we can identify and respond to these explicit expressions of the needs of those particular patients.

Methodological Summary

1. Raw scores are not measures. Raw scores are biased against off-target performance, test and sample dependent, and nonlinear.

2. Inverse probability explained by conjointly additive parameters enables the construction of clear measures from raw ratings.

3. Measures enable MAPs to define a variable in a one-page, easy-to-grasp graphical report of the construct our analysis has realized as a measurable variable.

4. Measures enable KEYs, which apply the variable individually to each person, to bring out their personal particulars in an easy-to-work-from one-page report.

WHAT HISTORY TELLS US NOT TO DO

The history of social science measurement not only teaches us what to do in order to succeed as scientists. It also shows us what not to do.

Do Not Use Raw Scores as Though They Were Measures

Some social scientists still believe that misusing raw scores as measures does no harm. They are unaware of the consequences for their work of the raw score bias against extreme scores. Some believe they can construct measures by decomposing raw score matrices with some kind of factor analysis. There is an incomplete relation between measurement construction and factor analysis, but factor analysis does not construct measures (Smith, 1996; Wright, 1996, especially Table 5). All supposedly useful results from raw score analyses are spoiled by their nonlinearity, extreme score bias and sample dependency (Embretson, 1996).

Do Not Use Models That Fail to Converge

Among those who have seen their way beyond raw scores to Item Response Theory, there is a self-destructive misunderstanding concerning the measurement necessity for conjoint additivity. These adventurers cannot resist the blandishments of Birnbaum's (1968) 2P and 3P IRT models:

$$\log(P_{ni1}/P_{ni0}) = A_i(B_n - D_i)$$

and

$$\log\{(P_{ni1} - C_i)/P_{ni0}\} = A_i(B_n - D_i)$$

These nonadditive models are mistaken as improvements over what they refer to as a 1P Rasch model because they bring in an item scaling parameter A_i to estimate a discrimination and a lower asymptote parameter C_i to estimate a guessing level for each item.

Here is what happens when these models are applied:

- Item discriminations "increase without limit." Person abilities "increase or decrease without limit" (Lord, 1968, pp. 1015–1016).
- Even for data generated to fit the 3PL model exactly, "only item difficulty [the Rasch parameter] is satisfactorily recovered by [the 3P computer program] LOGIST" (Lord, 1975, p. 13). "If restraints are not imposed, the estimated value of discrimination is likely to increase without limit" (Lord, 1975, p. 14). "Left to itself, maximum likelihood estimation pro-

cedures would produce unacceptable values of guessing" (Lord, 1975, p. 16).

- During "estimation in the two and three parameter models . . . the item parameter estimates drift out of bounds" (Swaminathan, 1983, p. 34).

- "Bias [in person measures] is significant when ability estimates are obtained from estimated item parameters . . . And, in spite of the fact that the calibration and cross-validation samples are the same for each setting, the bias differs by test." (Stocking, 1989, p. 18)

- "Running LOGIST to complete convergence allows too much movement away from the good starting values" (Stocking, 1989, p. 25).

The reason why 2P and 3P IRT models do not converge is clear in Birnbaum's (1968, pp. 421–422) estimation equations:

$$\sum_i a_i x_{\theta i} = \sum_i a_i P_{\theta i} \rightarrow \theta$$

$$\sum_\theta \theta x_{\theta i} = \sum_\theta \theta P_{\theta i} \rightarrow a_i$$

These equations are intended to iterate reciprocally to convergence. When the first equation is applied to a person with a correct response $x_{\theta i} = 1$ on an item with discrimination $a_i > 1$, their ability estimate Θ is increased by the factor a_i. When the second equation is applied, the same person response $x_{\theta i} = 1$ is multiplied by their increased ability estimate Θ, which further increases discrimination estimate a_i. The presence of response $x_{\theta i} = 1$ in both equations produces a feedback that escalates the estimates for item discrimination a_i and person measure Θ to infinity.

Do Not Use Models That Fail to Minimize Residuals

The *sine qua non* of a statistical model is its success at predicting its data. The simplest evaluation of success is the mean square residual between each piece of data x and its modeled expectation E_x, as in the mean of (x $- E_x)^2$ over all observed values of x. Ordinarily, the more parameters a model uses, the smaller the mean square residual must become. Otherwise why add more parameters? Should we encounter a parameter the addition of which increases our mean square residuals, we have exposed a parameter that does not belong in our model.

Hambleton and Martois (1983) used LOGIST (Stocking, 1989) to analyze 18 sets of data twice, first with a 1-item parameter Rasch model and second with a 3-item parameter Birnbaum model. In 12 of their 18 experiments, much to their surprise, two less item parameters, that is, the Rasch model, produced smaller mean square residuals than the 3-item parameter model. In the six data sets where this did not happen, the tests were unusually difficult for the students. As a result, attempting to estimate guessing parameters reduced residuals slightly more than the Rasch model without a guessing constant.

Had a single *a priori* guessing constant been set at a reasonable value like C = .25 for all items and the data reanalyzed with a 1P Rasch model so modified, Hambleton and Martois would have discovered that one well-chosen *a priori* guessing constant did a better job than attempting to estimate a full set of item-specific guessing parameters. When we encounter a situation in which the addition of a parameter makes things worse, we have proven to ourselves that the parameter in question does not belong in our model.

Do Not Destroy Additivity

The additivity of the parameters of a model can be tested by attempting to separate parameters for independent estimation by subtraction.

Letting $G_{ni} = \log[P_{ni}/(1 - P_{ni})]$ stand for the log odds side of the measurement model for a dichotomy, consider the Rasch equations:

when $G_{ni} = B_n - D_i$ $G_{mi} = B_m - D_i$ $G_{nj} = B_n - D_j$

then $G_{ni} - G_{mi} = B_n - B_m$ and D_i drops out of consideration.

and $G_{ni} - G_{nj} = D_j - D_i$ and B_n drops out of consideration.

Now consider the corresponding 2P equations:

when $G_{ni} = A_i(B_n - D_i)$ $G_{mi} = A_i(B_m - D_i)$ $G_{nj} = A_j(B_n - D_j)$

then $G_{ni} - G_{mi} = A_i(B_m - B_n)$ and we are stuck with A_i

and $G_{ni} - G_{nj} = B_n(A_i - A_j) + A_jD_j - A_iD_i$ and we are stuck with B_n

When we add an item discrimination parameter, we cannot separate A and B in order to estimate them independently.

But Parameter Additivity Is Not Enough

Additive parameters can be asserted to govern a monotonic probability function over an infinite range, yet fail to construct fundamental measurement. The stochastic formulation of G_{ni} is also decisive.

Consider Goldstein (1980):

$$\log[-\log(P_{ni})] = B_n - D_i$$

and Samejima (1997):

$$\{\log[P_{ni}/(1 - P_{ni})]\}^{-A} = B_n - D_i$$

two stochastic models for G_{ni} that appear to specify conjoint additivity but do not construct fundamental measurement.

Not only does neither model provides sufficient statistics for B and D, but both models fail to construct unique measures. To see this, reverse the direction of the latent variable and focus on person deficiency $(-B_n)$, item easiness $(-D_i)$ and task failure $(1 - P_{ni})$.

Rasch: $\log[P_{ni}/(1 - P_{ni})] = B_n - D_i$

becomes $\log[(1 - P_{ni})/P_{ni}] = -(B_n - D_i) = -\log[P_{ni}/(1 - P_{ni})]$

in which nothing changes but direction. However,

Goldstein: $\log[-\log(P_{ni})] = B_n - D_i$

becomes $\log[-\log(1 - P_{ni})] = -(B_n - D_i)$

that does NOT equal $-\log[-\log(P_{ni})]$ unless $[\log P_{ni}][\log(1 - P_{ni})] = 1$

and

Samejima: $\{\log[P_{ni}/(1 - P_{ni})]\}^{-A} = B_n - D_i$

becomes $\{\log[(1 - P_{ni})/P_{ni}]\}^{-A} = -(B_n - D_i)$

that does not equal $-\{\{\log[P_{ni}/(1 - P_{ni})]\}^{-A}\}$ unless $A = 1$

making Samejima's model a Rasch model.

For Goldstein and Samejima, merely measuring from the other end of the ruler produces a second set of measures that are incommensurable with the first. The mere assertion of additivity on one side of a model is not enough. To produce fundamental measurement, the whole model must reproduce itself.

Do Not Destroy Construct Stability

Finally there is a substantive illogic in attempting to define a construct with item characteristic curves (ICC) that cross because their slopes differ due to differing discriminations or their asymptotes differ due to differing guessing parameters. Crossing curves cause the hierarchy of relative item difficulty to change at every ability level. This destroys the variable's criterion definition. Table 4.6 shows a word recognition ruler built by Woodcock (1974). The left column marks the Mastery Scale inches, which measure equal intervals of word recognition mastery. The center column gives norms from 1st to 12th Grade. The right column lists some of the words that define this construct. Red, a short easy word, is recognized at 1st Grade. When we finally reach heterogeneous, we see that it takes a 12th Grader to recognize it. Woodcock's ruler implements a continuous construct that can be used to make detailed word-by-word interpretations of children's word-recognition measures.

Figure 4.5 shows the relative locations of Rasch item calibrations for five words from Woodcock's ruler. It does not matter whether you are a 1st, 2nd, or 3rd Grader, red, away, drink, octopus, and equestrian remain in the same order of experienced difficulty, at the same relative spacing. This ruler works the same way and defines the same variable for every child whatever their grade. It obeys the Magna Carta.

TABLE 4.6
A Useful Measuring Instrument

WOODCOCK
READING MASTERY TESTS

	DIFFICULTY		SAMPLE TASK	
	Mastery Scale	Grade Scale 50% Mastery		
	25	1.1	is	
	41	1.3	*red*	A
	58	1.4	down	
	70	1.5	black	
	86	1.7	*away*	B
	101	1.8	cold	
	114	2.0	*drink*	C
	124	2.2	shallow	
	143	2.8	through	
	159	3.3	*octopus*	D
	174	4.1	allowable	
	192	5.7	hinderance	
	211	9.3	*equestrian*	E
	240	12.9	heterogeneous	

WORD RECOGNITION RULER — *MEASURE* — *NORM* — *CRITERIA*

FIXED ITEM POSITIONS
DEFINE VARIABLE

To obtain the construct stability manifest in Fig. 4.5, we need the kind of item response curves that follow from the standard definition of fundamental measurement. Figure 4.6 shows that these Rasch curves do not cross. In fact, when we transform the vertical axis of these curves into log-odds instead of probabilities, the curves become parallel straight lines, thus demonstrating their conjoint additivity.

Figure 4.7, in contrast, shows five 3P Birnbaum curves for the same data. These five curves have different slopes and different asymptotes. There is no sign of conjoint additivity.

Figure 4.8 shows the construct destruction produced by the crossing curves of Fig. 4.7. For a 1st Grader, red is said to be easier than away, which is easier than drink, which is easier than octopus. But for a 3rd Grader, the order of item difficulty is different. Now it is away rather than red that is easier. Red has become even harder than drink! And octopus is now almost as easy to recognize as red, instead of being up near equestrian. What is the criterion definition of this variable? What construct is defined? The definition is different at every ability level. There is no construct! No ruler! No Magna Carta!

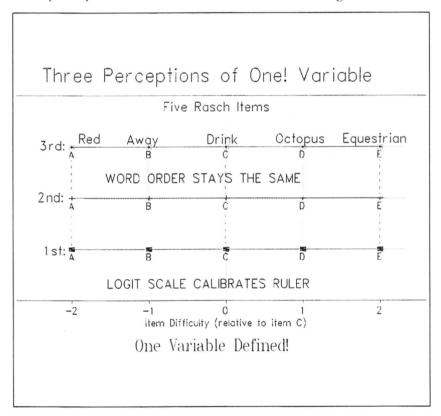

FIG. 4.5. Five Sample-Free RASCH Items

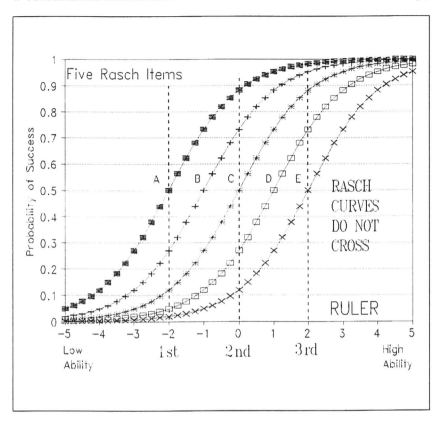

FIG. 4.6. Five Sample-Free RASCH Curves

Much as we might be intrigued by the complexity of the Birnbaum 3P curves in Fig. 4.7, we cannot use them to construct measures. To construct measures we require orderly, cooperating, noncrossing curves like the Rasch curves in Fig. 4.6. This means that we must take the trouble to collect and refine data so that they serve this clearly defined purpose, so that they approximate a stochastic Guttman scale.

When we go to market, we eschew rotten fruit. When we make a salad, we demand fresh lettuce. We have a recipe for what we want. We select our ingredients to follow. It is the same with making measures. We must think when we select and prepare our data for analysis. It is foolish to swallow whatever comes. Our data must be directed to building a structure like the one in Figs. 4.5 and 4.6—one ruler for everyone, everywhere, every time—so we can achieve a useful, stable construct definition like Woodcock's word-recognition ruler.

The lamentable history of the Birnbaum model is a cautionary tale of myopic promiscuity. Guessing is celebrated as an item asset. Discrimination

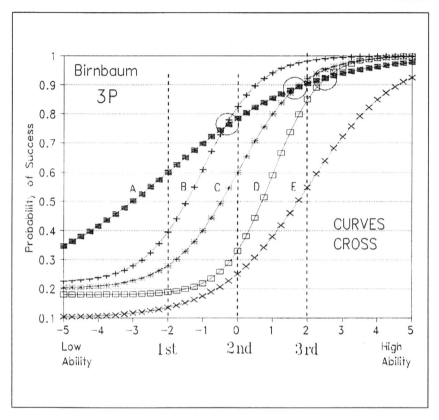

FIG. 4.7. Five Sample-Dependent Birnbaum Curves

is saluted as a useful scoring weight. Crossed item characteristic curves are swallowed without hesitation.

Models that build fundamental measurement are more choosy. They recognize guessing, not as an item asset but as an unreliable person liability. They identify variation in discrimination as a symptom of item bias and multidimensionality (Masters, 1988). Instead of parameterizing discrimination and guessing and then forgetting them, models for fundamental measurement analyze the data for statistical symptoms of misfit including variations in discrimination and guessing, identify their item and person sources, and weigh their impact on measurement quality.

In practice, guessing is easy to minimize. All one has to do is to test on target. Should a few lucky guesses crop up, it will not be items that produce them. The place to look for lucky guessing is among lucky guessers. The most efficient and fairest way to deal with lucky guessing, when it does occur, is to detect it, to measure the advantage it affords the lucky guesser, in case that matters, and, finally, to decide what is the most reasonable thing to do with the improbably successful responses that lucky guessing chanced on.

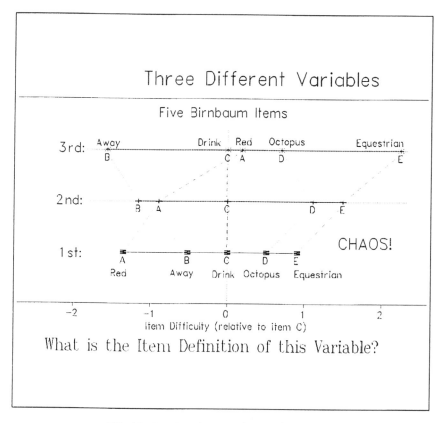

FIG. 4.8. Five Sample-Dependent Birnbaum Items

In the history of science there are vast differences between gerrymandering models to give best local descriptions of transient data and searching, instead, for better data that brings inferentially stable meaning to parameter estimates. It is the search for better data that begets discovery. The only way discovery can emerge is as an unexpected discrepancy from an otherwise stable frame of reference. When we study data misfit, we discover new things about what we are measuring and how people tell us about it. These discoveries strengthen and evolve our constructs as well as our ability to measure them.

CONCLUSIONS

The social history of stable units for fair trade makes clear that when units are unequal, when they vary from time to time and place to place, it is not only unfair, it is immoral. So, too, with the misuse of necessarily unequal and so unfair raw score units.

The purpose of measurement is inference. No measurement model that fails to meet the requirements for inference of probability, additivity, separability, and divisibility can survive actual practice. Physics and Biology do not use and would never consider using models with intersecting trace lines. We measure to inform our plans for what to do next. If our measures are unreliable, if our units vary in unknown ways, our plans will go wrong and, eventually, our work will perish.

This simple point is sometimes belittled. It is not negotiable. It is vital and decisive! We will never build a useful, let alone moral, social science until we stop deluding ourselves by analyzing local concrete ordinal raw scores as though they were general abstract linear measures.

Thurstone's New Measures

Thurstone (1928, 1931) outlined his necessities for a new measurement in the 1920s:

1. Measures must be linear, so that arithmetic can be done with them.
2. Item calibrations must not depend on whose responses they were estimated from—must be sample-free.
3. Person measures must not depend on which items they were estimated from—must be test-free.
4. Missing data must not matter.
5. The method must be easy to apply.

The mathematics needed to satisfy Thurstone's necessities and to make them practical were latent in Campbell's 1920 concatenation, Fisher's 1920 sufficiency, and the divisibility of Levy (1937) and Kolmogorov (1950) and realized by Rasch's (1960) Poisson measurement model.

Rasch's New Models

The implications of Rasch's discovery have taken many years to reach practice (Masters & Wright, 1984; Wright, 1968, 1977, 1984). Even today there are social scientists who do not understand or benefit from what Campbell, Levy, Kolmogorov, Fisher, and Rasch have proven (Wright, 1992). Yet, despite this hesitation to use fundamental measurement models to transform raw scores into linear measures so that subsequent statistical analysis can become fruitful, there have been many successful applications (Engelhard & Wilson, 1996; Fisher & Wright, 1994; Wilson, 1992, 1994; Wilson, Engelhard, & Draney, 1997).

Infinitely divisible (conjointly additive) models for the inverse probabilities of observed data enable:

1. The conjoint additivity that Campbell (1920) and Luce and Tukey (1964) required for fundamental measurement (Brogden, 1977; Perline, Wright, & Wainer, 1979; Wright, 1985, 1988).
2. The exponential linearity that Fisher (1922) required for estimation sufficiency (Andersen, 1977; Wright, 1989).
3. The parameter separability that Thurstone (1926) and Rasch (1960) required for objectivity (Wright & Linacre, 1989).

Measurement is an inference of values for infinitely divisible parameters that define the transition odds between observable increments of a theoretical variable.

No other formulation can construct results that a rational scientist, engineer, businessperson, tailor, or cook would be willing to use as measures. Only data that can be understood and organized to fit this model can be useful for constructing measures. When data cannot be made to fit this model, the inevitable conclusion is that those data are inadequate and must be reconsidered (Wright, 1977).

Rasch's models are applicable to every imaginable raw observation: dichotomies, rating scales, partial credits, binomial, and Poisson counts (Andrich, 1978; Masters & Wright, 1984) in every reasonable observational situation including ratings faceted to: persons, items, judges, and tasks (Linacre, 1989).

Computer programs that apply Rasch models have been in circulation for 30 years (Wright & Panchapakesan, 1969). Today, convenient, easy-to-use software for applying Rasch's measuring functions is readily available (Linacre & Wright, 1997; Wright & Linacre, 1997). Today it is easy for any social scientist to use computer programs like these to take the decisive step from unavoidably ambiguous, concrete raw observations to well-defined, abstract linear measures with realistic estimates of precision and explicit quality control. Today there is no methodological reason why social science cannot become as stable, as reproducible, and as useful as physics.

REFERENCES

Andersen, E. B. (1977). Sufficient statistics and latent trait models. *Psychometrika, 42,* 69–81.

Andrich, D. (1978). A rating formulation for ordered response categories. *Psychometrika, 43,* 561–573.

Andrich, D. (1995). Models for measurement: Precision and the non-dichotomization of graded responses. *Psychometrika, 60,* 7–26.

Andrich, D. (1996). Measurement criteria for choosing among models for graded responses. In A. von Eye & C. C. Clogg (Eds.), *Analysis of categorical variables in developmental research* (pp. 3–35). Orlando, FL: Academic Press.

Birnbaum A. (1968). Some latent trait models and their use in inferring an examinee's ability. In F. M. Lord & M. R. Novick (Eds.), *Statistical theories of mental test scores* (pp. 397–479). Reading, MA: Addison-Wesley.

Bookstein, A. (1992). Informetric distributions, Parts I and II. *Journal of the American Society for Information Science, 41*(5), 368–388.

Bookstein, A. (1996). Informetric distributions. III. Ambiguity and randomness. *Journal of the American Society for Information Science, 48*(1), 2–10.

Brogden, H. E. (1977). The Rasch model, the law of comparative judgement and additive conjoint measurement. *Psychometrika, 42*, 631–634.

Buchler, J. (1940). *Philosophical writings of Peirce.* New York: Dover.

Campbell, N. R. (1920). *Physics: The elements.* London: Cambridge University Press.

Eddington, A. S. (1946). *Fundamental theory.* London: Cambridge University Press.

Embretson, S. E. (1996). Item response theory models and spurious interaction effects in multiple group comparisons. *Applied Psychological Measurement, 20*, 201–212.

Engelhard, G. (1991). Thorndike, Thurstone and Rasch: A comparison of their approaches to item-invariant measurement. *Journal of Research and Development in Education, 24*(2), 45–60.

Engelhard, G. (1994). Historical views of the concept of invariance in measurement theory. In M. Wilson (Ed.), *Objective measurement: Theory into practice* (Vol. 2, pp. 73–99). Norwood, NJ: Ablex.

Engelhard, G., & Wilson, M. (Eds.). (1996). *Objective measurement: Theory into practice* (Vol. 3). Norwood, NJ: Ablex.

Fechner, G. T. (1860). *Elemente der psychophysik.* Leipzig: Breitkopf & Hartel. [Translation: Adler, H. E. (1966). *Elements of psychophysics.* New York: Holt, Rinehart & Winston.].

Feller, W. (1957). *An introduction to probability theory and its applications.* New York: Wiley.

Fischer, G. (1968). *Psychologische testtheorie.* Bern, Switzerland: Huber.

Fisher, R. A. (1920). A mathematical examination of the methods of determining the accuracy of an observation by the mean error and by the mean square error. *Monthly Notices of the Royal Astronomical Society, 53*, 758–770.

Fisher, R. A. (1922). On the mathematical foundations of theoretical statistics. *Philosophical Transactions of the Royal Society of London, 222*, 309–368.

Fisher, W. P., & Wright, B. D. (1994). Applications of probabilistic conjoint measurement. Special Issue. *International Journal Educational Research, 21*, 557–664.

Goldstein, H. (1980). Dimensionality, bias, independence and measurement scale problems in latent trait test score models. *British Journal of Mathematical and Statistical Psychology, 33*, 234–246.

Guttman, L. (1944). A basis for scaling quantitative data. *American Sociological Review, 9*, 139–150.

Guttman, L. (1950). The basis for scalogram analysis. In Stouffer et al. (Eds.), *Measurement and Prediction* (Vol. 4, pp. 60–90). Princeton NJ: Princeton University Press.

Hambleton, R., & Martois, J. (1983). Evaluation of a test score prediction system. In R. Hambleton (Ed.), *Applications of item response theory* (pp. 196–211). Vancouver, BC: Educational Research Institute of British Columbia.

Keats, J. A. (1967). Test theory. *Annual Review of Psychology, 18*, 217–238.

Kinston, W. (1985). Measurement and the structure of scientific analysis. *Systems Research, 2*(2), 95–104.

Kolmogorov, A. N. (1950). *Foundations of the theory of probability.* New York: Chelsea Publishing.

Levy, P. (1937). *Theorie de l'addition des variables aleatoires.* Paris.

Lieb, I. C. (Ed.). (1953). *Charles S. Peirce's Letters to Lady Welby.* New Haven, CT: Whitlochs.

Linacre, J. M. (1989). *Many-faceted Rasch measurement.* Chicago: MESA Press.

Linacre, J. M., & Wright, B. D. (1997). *FACETS: many-faceted Rasch analysis.* Chicago: MESA Press.

Lord, F. M. (1968). An analysis of the Verbal Scholastic Aptitude Test Using Birnbaum's Three-Parameter Model. *Educational and Psychological Measurement, 28,* 989–1020.

Lord, F. M. (1975). *Evaluation with artificial data of a procedure for estimating ability and item characteristic curve parameters.* (Research Report RB-75-33). Princeton: ETS.

Luce, R. D., & Tukey, J. W. (1964). Simultaneous conjoint measurement. *Journal of Mathematical Psychology, 1,* 1–27.

Masters, G. N. (1988). Item discrimination: When more is worse. *Journal of Educational Measurement, 24,* 15–29.

Masters, G. N., & Wright, B. D. (1984). The essential process in a family of measurement models. *Psychometrika, 49,* 529–544.

Perline, R., Wright, B. D., & Wainer, H. (1979). The Rasch model as additive conjoint measurement. *Applied Psychological Measurement, 3,* 237–255.

Rasch, G. (1960). *Probabilistic models for some intelligence and attainment tests.* Chicago: MESA Press.

Rasch, G. (1961). On general laws and meaning of measurement in psychology. *Proceedings of the Fourth Berkeley Symposium on Mathematical Statistics and Probability, 4,* 321–333. Berkeley: University of California Press.

Rasch, G. (1963). The Poisson process as a model for a diversity of behavioral phenomena. *International Congress of Psychology.* Washington, DC.

Rasch, G. (1968). A mathematical theory of objectivity and its consequences for model construction. In *Report from European Meeting on Statistics, Econometrics and Management Sciences.* Amsterdam.

Rasch, G. (1969). Models for description of the time-space distribution of traffic accidents. *Symposium on the Use of Statistical Methods in the Analysis of Road Accidents. Organization for Economic Cooperation and Development Report 9.*

Rasch, G. (1977). On specific objectivity: An attempt at formalizing the request for generality and validity of scientific statements. *Danish Yearbook of Philosophy, 14,* 58–94.

Samejima, F. (1997). Ability estimates that order individuals with consistent philosophies. *Annual Meeting of the American Educational Research Association.* Chicago: AERA.

Sears, S. D. (1997). *A monetary history of Iraq and Iran.* Unpublished doctoral dissertation. Chicago: University of Chicago.

Sheriff, J. K. (1994). *Charles Peirce's guess at the riddle.* Bloomington: Indiana University Press.

Smith, R. M. (1985). Validation of individual test response patterns. *International Encyclopedia of Education,* Oxford: Pergamon Press, 5410–5413.

Smith, R. M. (1986). Person fit in the Rasch Model. *Educational and Psychological Measurement, 46,* 359–372.

Smith, R. M. (1988). The distributional properties of Rasch standardized residuals. *Educational and Psychological Measurement, 48,* 657–667.

Smith, R. M. (1991). The distributional properties of Rasch item fit statistics. *Educational and Psychological Measurement, 51,* 541–565.

Smith, R. M. (1994). A comparison of the power of Rasch total and between item fit statistics to detect measurement disturbances. *Educational and Psychological Measurement, 54,* 42–55.

Smith, R. M. (1996). A comparison of methods for determining dimensionality. *Structural Equation Modeling, 3*(1), 25–40.

Stevens, S. S. (1939). On the problem of scales for the measurement of psychological magnitudes. *Journal for the Unification of Science, 9,* 94–99.

Stevens, S. S. (1946). On the theory of scales and measurement. *Science, 103,* 667–680.

Stigler, S. M. (1986). *The history of statistics.* Cambridge, MA: Harvard University Press.

Stocking, M. L. (1989). *Empirical estimation errors in item response theory as a function of test properties.* Research Report RR-89-5. Princeton, NJ: ETS.

Swaminathan, H. (1983). Parameter estimation in item response models. In R. Hambleton (Ed.), *Applications of item response theory* (pp. 24–44). Vancouver, BC: Educational Research Institute of British Columbia.

Thorndike, E. L. (1904). *An introduction to the theory of mental and social measurements.* New York: Teacher's College.

Thurstone, L. L. (1926). The scoring of individual performance. *Journal of Educational Psychology, 17,* 446–457.

Thurstone, L. L. (1928). Attitudes can be measured. *American Journal of Sociology, 23,* 529–554.

Thurstone, L. L. (1931). Measurement of social attitudes. *Journal of Abnormal and Social Psychology, 26,* 249–269.

Thurstone, L. L., & Chave, E. J. (1929). *The measurement of attitude.* Chicago: University of Chicago Press.

Wilson, M. (Ed.). (1992). *Objective measurement: Theory into practice* (Vol. 1). Norwood, NJ: Ablex.

Wilson, M. (Ed.). (1994). *Objective measurement: Theory into practice* (Vol. 2). Norwood, NJ: Ablex.

Wilson, M., Engelhard, G., & Draney, K. (Eds.). (1997). *Objective measurement: Theory into practice* (Vol. 4). Norwood, NJ: Ablex.

Woodcock, R. W. (1974). *Woodcock reading mastery tests.* Circle Pines, MN: American Guidance Service.

Wright, B. D. (1968). Sample-free test calibration and person measurement. *Proceedings 1967 Invitational Conference on Testing* Princeton: Educational Testing Service, 85–101.

Wright, B. D. (1977). Solving measurement problems with the Rasch model. *Journal of Educational Measurement, 14,* 97–116.

Wright, B. D. (1984). Despair and hope for educational measurement. *Contemporary Education Review, 1,* 281–288.

Wright, B. D. (1985). Additivity in psychological measurement. In E. Roskam (Ed.), *Measurement and personality assessment* (pp. 101–112). Amsterdam: North-Holland.

Wright, B. D. (1988). Rasch model from Campbell concatenation for mental testing. In J. M. Linacre (Ed.), *Rasch Measurement Transactions* (Part 1, p. 16). Chicago: MESA Press.

Wright, B. D. (1989). Rasch model from counting right answers. In J. M. Linacre (Ed.), *Rasch Measurement Transactions* (Part 1, p. 62). Chicago: MESA Press.

Wright, B. D. (1992). IRT in the 1990's: Which models work best? In J. M. Linacre (Ed.), *Rasch Measurement Transactions* (Part 2, pp. 196–200). Chicago: MESA Press.

Wright, B. D. (1994). Measuring and counting. In J. M. Linacre (Ed.), *Rasch Measurement Transactions* (Part 2, p. 371). Chicago: MESA Press.

Wright, B. D. (1996). Comparing Rasch measurement and factor analysis. *Structural Equation Modeling, 3*(1), 3–24.

Wright, B. D., & Linacre, J. M. (1989). Observations are always ordinal: Measures, however, must be interval. *Archives of Physical Medicine and Rehabilitation, 70,* 857–860.

Wright, B. D., & Linacre, J. M. (1997). *BIGSTEPS: Rasch computer program for all two facet problems.* Chicago: MESA Press.

Wright, B. D., & Masters, G. N. (1982). *Rating scale analysis: Rasch measurement.* Chicago: MESA Press.

Wright, B. D., & Panchapakesan, N. (1969). A procedure for sample-free item analysis. *Educational and Psychological Measurement, 29,* 23–48.

Wright, B. D., & Stone, M. H. (1979). *Best test design: Rasch measurement.* Chicago: MESA Press.

CHAPTER FIVE

What Can Rasch-Based Scores Convey About a Person's Test Performance?[1]

Richard W. Woodcock
University of Virginia

[1]

It has been 26 years since publication of the first Rasch-based test in the United States—the *KeyMath Diagnostic Arithmetic Test* (Connolly, Nachtman, & Pritchett, 1971). Many tests published since have utilized the item calibration and test linking features that emanate from the Rasch model. Only a few tests have capitalized on the powerful interpretation features that become accessible when person abilities and item difficulties have been calibrated on a common Rasch scale. The basis for these interpretation features is summarized by Embretson (1996):

- In CTT [Classical Test Theory], score meaning is determined by a norm-referenced standard. . . . An objection that is often raised to norm-referenced meaning is that scores have no meaning for what the person actually can do.

- . . . in IRT [Item Response Theory] models, the meaning of a score can be referenced directly to the items . . . The probability that a person passes a particular item is derived from the match of item difficulty to trait level.

- If these items are further structured by content, substantive trait level meaning can be derived.

- In some tests . . . IRT trait levels are also linked to norms. . . . Thus, IRT trait levels also can have norm-referenced meaning. (pp. 345–346)

[1]Appreciation is expressed to Benjamin Wright, as the work described in this chapter could not have been accomplished without his frequent advice and support.

This chapter presents a broad look at the interpretation of test performance emphasizing the role of Rasch-based scores in that framework. It then describes the four steps used to apply Rasch-based test score interpretation to tests for which I have had responsibility either as an editor or as an author. A primary purpose of this chapter is to urge more test developers to apply these procedures to their instruments. The chapter concludes with an example test report that highlights the application of Rasch-based interpretation statements to describe the test performance of a bilingual child.

HIERARCHY OF TEST INFORMATION

Table 5.1 displays four levels of information that contribute to the evaluation of test performance (Woodcock, 1991). This formulation demonstrates the variety of information that can be reported about an individual's test performance and also provides the organization to which several Rasch-derived interpretation procedures will be related.

At Level 1, qualitative information is obtained by observing behavior during testing and by analyzing response errors to individual items. The *KeyMath Diagnostic Profile* (described later and in Fig. 5.1) is an example of an interpretation device that facilitates the analysis of responses by identifying the location of each item along a Rasch scale, indicating whether the item was passed or failed, and providing a mnemonic to the item's content.

The second level of information consists of scores that report level of development in the trait measured. The raw score is the fundamental score associated with this level, but raw scores may be transformed into Rasch ability scores (e.g., logits or *W* scores) and, thus, acquire the advantages of an equal interval scale for statistical computations and for charting growth. For most tests, raw scores or Rasch ability scores are transformed into age equivalents (AE) or grade equivalents (GE) which are the traditional derived scores used to report level of development.

For many test applications, Level 3 (level of proficiency) may provide the most useful information about an individual's test performance. Unfortunately, this level of information is absent from the interpretation plan for many tests. Level 3 includes criterion-referenced scores that describe proficiency or quality of performance. Two such measures are the Relative Proficiency Index (RPI) and the Developmental Zone. Level 3 scores are common in some other areas of measurement. For example, visual acuity is described by the familiar Snellen Index. An individual with 20/20 vision is predicted to see an object at a distance of 20 feet as well as a person with normal vision. If the person's vision is 20/200, however, that person needs to be within 20 feet of an object to see it as well as a person with normal vision can see the object from 200 feet. The Snellen Index is a criterion-referenced statement about the quality of an individual's visual acuity. The dB

TABLE 5.1
Hierarchy of Information Potentially Available From Any Test

Level	Type of Information	Basis	Information and Scores	Uses
1	Qualitative (Criterion-Referenced)	Observations during testing and analysis of responses	Description of subject's reaction to the test situation Performance on finely defined skills at the item content level (e.g., *KeyMath Diagnostic Profile*)	• Appreciation of the subject's behavior underlying obtained test score • Prediction of the subject's behavior and reactions in instructional situations • Specific skill instructional recommendations
2	Level of Development (Norm-Referenced)	Sum of item scores Age or grade level in the norming sample at which the average is the same as the subject's score.	Raw score *Rasch ability score (e.g., logit, *W*) Age Equivalent (AE) Grade Equivalent (GE)	• Reporting a subject's level of development • Basis for describing the implications of developmental strengths and weaknesses • Basis for initial recommendations regarding instructional level and materials • Placement decisions based on a criterion of significantly advanced or delayed development • Measuring growth and change

(Continued)

TABLE 5.1
(Continued)

Level	Type of Information	Basis	Information and Scores	Uses
3	Level of Proficiency (Criterion-Referenced)	Subject's distance on a Rasch scale from an age or grade reference point	*Rasch Difference Score Quality of performance on reference tasks: Relative Proficiency Index (RPI) Instructional or Developmental Zone	• Proficiency on tasks of criterion difficulty for peers • Developmental level at which typical tasks will be perceived as very easy by the subject • Developmental level at which typical tasks will be perceived as very difficult by the subject • Placement decisions based on a criterion of significantly good or poor proficiency
4	Relative Standing in a Group (Norm-Referenced)	Relative position (A linear or area transformation of a difference score)	Rank Order *Standard Score (including z, T, NCE) Percentile Rank (PR)	• Communication of a subject's competitive position among peers • Placement decisions based on a criterion of significantly high or low standing among peers

Note. From *Woodcock Language Proficiency Battery—Revised: Examiner's Manual* (p. 56) by R. W. Woodcock, 1991, Itasca, IL: Riverside Publishing. Copyright 1991 by The Riverside Publishing Company. Adapted with permission. The * indicates equal unit scales; preferred for statistical calculations.

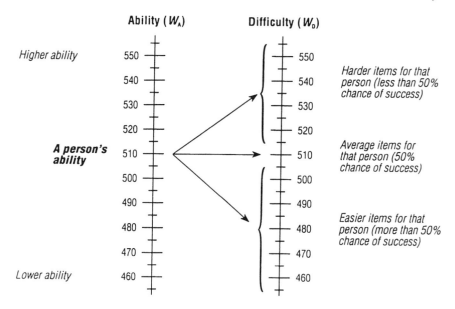

FIG. 5.1. Relationship of person ability to item difficulty on the *W* scale. From *Development and Standardization of the Woodcock–Johnson Psycho-Educational Battery* (p. 78) by R. W. Woodcock, 1978, Itasca, IL: Riverside. Copyright 1978 by The Riverside Publishing Company. Adapted with permission.

scale, when used as an index of hearing acuity, is another example. Normal hearing is referenced at zero on the dB scale. If an individual has a hearing loss of −40 dB, this indicates the additional amplitude necessary for that individual to hear a standard signal that a normal hearing person would hear at zero dB.

Persons with visual or hearing problems are usually classified as handicapped or in need of special services because they have significant deficits in the quality of their visual or aural performance, not because they fall below some point on a norm-referenced scale. On the other hand, mental retardation has been based primarily on a norm-referenced criterion such as having an IQ that falls in the lower 3% of the general population (below 70). A learning disability diagnosis is often based on a similar criterion applied to the difference between scores on an aptitude measure and an achievement measure. Thus, mental retardation and learning disabilities are often determined by statistical fiat rather than demonstrating some criterion degree of performance deficit.

The fourth level in the hierarchy encompasses norm-referenced scores that report relative standing in a group. This type of score includes the percentile rank and several varieties of standard score.

Each of the four levels in Table 5.1 provides unique information about a person's test performance that is not provided by the information from any of the other three levels. On the other hand, scores in each level report the same type of information. For example, percentile ranks and standard scores in Level 4 both report standing in a group. Information from all four levels is required to provide a complete description of an individual's test performance.

Certain scores within Levels 2, 3, and 4 have the quality of being equal interval scales. These scores are the preferred metric at that level for statistical calculations and are identified by an asterisk (*) in Table 5.1.

The next section describes the outcome of four steps undertaken to exploit the potential interpretation advantages of Rasch-scaled tests.

EVOLUTION OF STEPS TOWARD INTERPRETING RASCH-SCALED TESTS

The practice of test interpretation has been significantly impacted by IRT over the past 25 years. Several million children and adults each year are now administered tests that incorporate Rasch-derived statements in the interpretation of their test performance. The interpretation plans of many other tests could be enriched by incorporating similar features.

The present status of several Rasch-based interpretation procedures has evolved through four steps:

1. derivation of the *W* scale;
2. publication of the *KeyMath Diagnostic Arithmetic Test*;
3. development of the Relative Proficiency Index and Developmental Zone concepts; and
4. development of descriptive/predictive labels for designated regions along a Rasch difference scale.

The *W* Scale

The earliest Rasch scaling program (Wright & Panchapakesan, 1969) used in the United States produced an item difficulty scale called EASY and two ability scales called RAW ABILITY and LOG ABILITY. It was undetermined at that time which of the two ability scales would be the most useful, or if a rescaling of one or the other could provide a more convenient scale for interpreting test performance. Over the course of a year, Dahl and Woodcock at American Guidance Service, in consultation with Wright, experimented with many transformations of the two ability scales and evaluated plots of the resulting growth curves for a wide age-range set of test data. The transformation eventually selected is called the *W* scale, and its derivation and characteristics are described by Woodcock and Dahl (1971). The chosen scale is a base$_{(9)}$ log transformation of the RAW ABILITY scale. Alternatively, the equation may be expressed as a direct transformation of the logits scale.

$$W = 9.1024 \text{ logits} + 500. \tag{5.1}$$

If the BIGSTEPS program (Wright & Linacre, 1991–1997) is used to conduct a Rasch calibration, the W scale is produced by setting the UMEAN control code to 500 and the USCALE control code to 9.1024.

Woodcock and Dahl's W scale provides four practical advantages over the scales produced by the original Wright and Panchapakesan program:

1. Negative values are eliminated by setting the centering constant at 500. (This centering constant may be further adjusted to some meaningful point such as 500 set equal to beginning grade 5 W ability.)
2. The need for decimal values in many applications is eliminated by the multiplicative scaling constant of 9.1024.
3. The signs of the item difficulty and person ability scales are set so that low values imply either low item difficulty or low person ability. High values imply either high item difficulty or high person ability.
4. Distances along the W scale have probability implications that are more convenient to remember and to use than distances along the logits scale.

In our applications of the W scale, we customarily set 500 as the W ability associated with beginning grade 5 ability on any measured trait (e.g., short-term memory, handwriting legibility, or reading vocabulary). Because the typical ability spread on tests that we have developed is from preschool to superior adult, the relative difficulty of items in a test must range from extremely easy to extremely difficult. A typical spread of item difficulties may run from a low of 430 to a high of 550 (about 13 logits). The lowest W difficulty I have observed is 185 for an item in which a 24-month-old child is asked to draw a line with a pencil. The highest W difficulties are about 600 (e.g., simple matrix algebra transformations or reading a word such as *chaotic* or *assiduous* and then orally providing an antonym or synonym).

An important characteristic of the W scale is that person ability and item difficulty are calibrated on a common scale. Figure 5.1 illustrates the implications of person ability relative to item difficulty. When item difficulty is at the same level as a person's ability, the person has a 50% chance of success on that item. If item difficulties are higher than person ability, then the chance of success is less than 50%. If item difficulties are lower than person ability, then the person has a greater than 50% chance of success.

Table 5.2 extends the information illustrated in Fig. 5.1 by indicating the probability of success for individuals whose W ability is displaced from an item's W difficulty (e.g., a W difference of +20 indicates that the person's

TABLE 5.2
Probability of Success on Items Displaced From Person Ability

W *Ability Minus* W *Difficulty*	*Probability of Success*	W *Ability Minus* W *Difficulty*	*Probability of Success*
+50	.995	−5	.366
+45	.993	−10	.250
+40	.988	−15	.161
+35	.979	−20	.100
+30	.954	−25	.060
+25	.940	−30	.036
+20	.900	−35	.021
+15	.839	−40	.012
+10	.750	−45	.007
+ 5	.634	−50	.004
0	.500		

Note. From *Development and Standardization of the Woodcock–Johnson Psycho-Educational Battery* (p. 79) by R. W. Woodcock, 1978, Itasca, IL: Riverside Publishing. Copyright 1978 by The Riverside Publishing Company. Adapted with permission.

W ability is 20 W units higher than the item's W difficulty; therefore, the probability of a correct response is .900). Note that the information in Table 5.2 is centered on a W difference of zero (with a probability of .500) and that the probabilities change symmetrically (e.g., if a W difference is −20, the probability of a correct response is .100). Note also that the probability intervals are not linearly related to W differences. Furthermore, it is convenient, and a consequence of the chosen log base$_{(9)}$ transformation, that the probabilities associated with +20, +10, 0, −10, and −20 W differences are exact values (.90, .75, .50, .25, and .10). All other probabilities are rounded decimal fractions. The probabilities in Table 5.2 are the foundation for the Relative Proficiency Index, which is described later.

An important characteristic of any Rasch scale is that a given difference along the scale has the same implication for performance at any level and in any area measured. If a person has grown 10 W units (e.g., if W ability on that trait has increased from 510 to 520), this person can now perform with 75% success the tasks they were able to perform before with only 50% success. This relationship is true for any 10-point difference on the W scale, whether the test performance is a kindergartner's ability to blend speech sounds or a college student's ability to solve calculus problems.

This constancy of interpretation across Rasch scales is an important feature for application to developmental studies and other types of research. For example, Fig. 5.2 compares the cross-sectional growth curves for seven cognitive abilities. These seven abilities are measured reliably from age 5

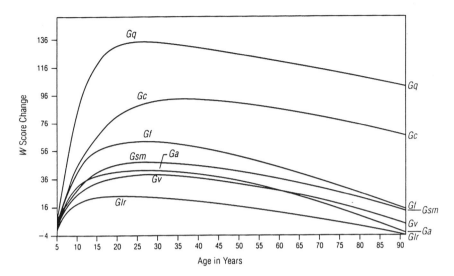

FIG. 5.2. Seven WJ-R cognitive factor growth curves plotted on the *W* scale. From *WJ-R Technical Manual* (p. 80) by K. S. McGrew, J. K. Werder, and R. W. Woodcock, 1991, Itasca, IL: Riverside. Copyright 1991 by The Riverside Publishing Company. Reprinted with permission. *Note. Gq* is quantitative ability, *Gc* is comprehension-knowledge, *Gf* is fluid reasoning, *Gsm* is short-term memory, *Ga* is auditory processing, *Gv* is visual processing, and *Glr* is long-term retrieval.

and above, using two tests for each ability drawn from the *Woodcock–Johnson Psycho-Educational Battery—Revised* (Woodcock & Johnson, 1989). The curves are based on the mean *W* score by age, with the mean *W* score at age 5 subtracted from all other age means for a given cognitive ability. Thus, the vertical scale represents change on the *W* scale from the arbitrary baseline at age 5. The seven different means at each age level are based on the same subset of subjects from the norming sample. Note how the seven growth curves can be compared directly when they have been plotted on a Rasch scale. For example, *Glr* (long-term retrieval) shows a relatively small change over the life span, whereas *Gq* (quantitative ability) shows considerable change. In fact, statements can be made such as "*Gq* changes about five times as much from age 5 to age 20 as does *Glr*," or "At age 90 in this cross-sectional study, *Gq* has declined to the former age 11 level, but *Glr* has declined below the former age 5 level."

A more complete description of the *W* scale and its applications may be found in Woodcock (1973, 1978, 1982) and in McGrew, Werder, and Woodcock (1991). These works may prompt other test developers and researchers to consider using the convenient *W* transformation of the Rasch scale. Other applications of the *W* scale are presented in later sections of this chapter.

The KeyMath Diagnostic Arithmetic Test

The *KeyMath Diagnostic Arithmetic Test* was published in 1971. The instrument's 14 subtests are designed to measure arithmetic skills from kindergarten through grade six. The test's Diagnostic Profile (shown in part in Fig. 5.3) displays the 209 items on a common Rasch scale. As the examiner administers the KeyMath, he/she scores each item, resulting in a map of the examinee's known and unknown arithmetic skills (Table 5.1, Level 1 information). Raw scores for each subtest and for the total test are plotted beneath each line (Table 5.1, Level 2 information). As a result, person ability for each subtest and for the total test are plotted on the same Rasch scale as are the item difficulties. The grade equivalent score for the Total Test (more Table 5.1, Level 2 information) is also represented on the Total Test line. Although the *W* scale was used for scaling the *KeyMath*, no other interpretive features of the *W* scale were applied to that test as the scale and its applications were still in an early stage of conceptualization.

The most recent application of this graphical concept is by Roid and Miller (1997), who developed a similar Rasch-scaled item map as part of their interpretation plan for the *Leiter International Performance Scale—Revised.*

The Relative Proficiency Index and the Developmental Zone

The RPI and the Developmental Zone were introduced in 1973 as features of the *Woodcock Reading Mastery Tests* (Woodcock, 1973), where they were called the Relative Mastery Score and Instructional Range, respectively. The following two enhancements of the *W* scale concept were necessary to provide these new interpretations of test performance:

1. norming the *W* scale, which provided grade and age reference points along the scale;
2. reporting the individual's level of proficiency on tasks performed by others at the same age or grade level with 90% proficiency rather than 50% (this 90% proficiency level was chosen because it is a frequently used criterion of mastery).

By definition, relative proficiency is an individual's predicted level of success on those tasks performed with 90% success by average individuals at a given age or grade level. Such tasks are 20 *W* units easier than the tasks falling at the exact age or grade level. (Tasks with a difficulty level falling at the exact age or grade level are performed with 50% success.) Table 5.3 presents a list of RPIs, referenced to a 90% level of success, associated with

FIG. 5.3. Portion of the 1971 *KeyMath Diagnostic Profile*. From A. J. Connolly, W. Nachtman, and E. M. Pritchett, 1971, Circle Pines, MN: American Guidance Service. Copyright 1971 by American Guidance Service. Reprinted with permission.

115

TABLE 5.3
Relative Performance Indexes (RPIs) Associated
With Differences Along the W Scale

W Difference	RPI	W Difference	RPI	W Difference	RPI
29 and	100[1]/90	−1	89/90	−36	15/90
above		−2	88/90	−37	13/90
28	99/90	−3	87/90	−38	12/90
27	99/90	−4	85/90	−39	11/90
26	99/90	−5	84/90	−40	10/90
25	99/90	−6	82/90	−41	9/90
24	99/90	−7	81/90	−42	8/90
23	99/90	−8	79/90	−43	7/90
22	99/90	−9	77/90	−44	7/90
21	99/90	−10	75/90	−45	6/90
20	99/90	−11	73/90	−46	5/90
19	98/90	−12	71/90	−47	5/90
18	98/90	−13	68/90	−48	4/90
17	98/90	−14	66/90	−49	4/90
16	98/90	−15	63/90	−50	4/90
15	98/90	−16	61/90	−51	3/90
14	98/90	−17	58/90	−52	3/90
13	97/90	−18	55/90	−53	3/90
12	97/90	−19	53/90	−54	2/90
11	97/90	−20	50/90	−55	2/90
10	96/90	−21	47/90	−56	2/90
9	96/90	−22	45/90	−57	2/90
8	96/90	−23	42/90	−58	2/90
7	95/90	−24	39/90	−59	1/90
6	95/90	−25	37/90	−60	1/90
5	94/90	−26	34/90	−61	1/90
4	93/90	−27	32/90	−62	1/90
3	93/90	−28	29/90	−63	1/90
2	92/90	−29	27/90	−64	1/90
1	91/90	−30	25/90	−65	1/90
0	90/90	−31	23/90	−66	1/90
		−32	21/90	−67	1/90
		−33	19/90	−68	1/90
		−34	18/90	−69 and	0[2]/90
		−35	16/90	below	

[1]Approximate value (>99.5).
[2]Approximate value (<0.5).

differences between person W ability and the median W for an age or grade level.

An RPI of 90/90 indicates that the subject is predicted to demonstrate 90% success with tasks that average individuals in the comparison group (same age or grade) would perform with 90% success. If applied to a test of arithmetic calculation, for example, the RPI predicts the percentage of success for a person given arithmetic calculation problems that the reference group would perform with 90% success. (The reference group success rate is the denominator of the index.) An RPI of 32/90 means that the subject is predicted to perform with 32% success those tasks that others at the subject's age or grade level would perform with 90% success. On the other hand, an RPI of 99/90 means that the subject is predicted to perform with 99% success those tasks that average subjects at the same age or grade level would perform with 90% success.

RPIs are valuable for two reasons. First, they describe relative quality of performance, not relative standing in a group. Second, if the population becomes better or worse in performing the trait over the years, relative performance scores still have the same meaning (just as the Snellen Index does). Scores such as percentile ranks, on the other hand, are statements describing standing in a group. Standing at the fifth percentile will be associated with a different absolute level of performance if the distribution of that ability in the population changes from one norming to the next.

The Developmental Zone (called the Instructional Range or Developmental Band in some tests) is an extension of the RPI concept. It is a band along an age or grade scale that extends from a point 10 W units lower than the subject's measured ability (RPI = 96/90) to a point that is 10 W units higher than the subject's measured ability (RPI = 75/90). The subject will find tasks below the lower end of the zone quite easy but will find tasks above the higher end of the zone quite difficult. Thus, the Developmental Zone defines the segment along a developmental scale that encompasses the subject's range of functioning from an easy level to a difficult level. Test scores derived through CTT can only indicate a point in the middle of this range and provide no useful information about offset points of easiness or difficulty.

The concept of the Developmental Zone directly parallels the difference between the easy reading level and the frustration reading level obtained by the Informal Reading Inventory (IRI) procedure described by Betts (1946, 1957). Although this technique is traditionally used by reading teachers, the concept was extended by Woodcock and Johnson (1977) to include other areas of achievement and intellectual functioning.

Profiles often provide the most meaningful interpretation of test performance, particularly when planning instructional or service needs with parents, teachers, or the subject. All of our tests since 1973 have included a Rasch-scaled "Age/Grade Profile." Figure 5.4 presents a completed Age/Grade Profile from

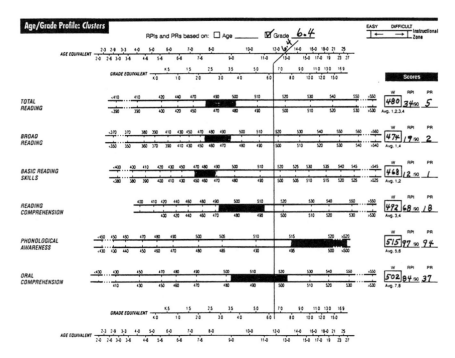

FIG. 5.4. Completed Age/Grade Profile from the *Woodcock Diagnostic Reading Battery* (Woodcock, 1997) for a sixth-grade girl.

the *Woodcock Diagnostic Reading Battery* (Woodcock, 1997). Each bar in the profile has a set of numbers representing *W* scores running across the top, and the same set of numbers, displaced to the right, running across the bottom of the bar. To draw the Developmental Zone, called the Instructional Zone in this test, the examiner shades in the region between the subject's *W* score in the top and bottom line of numbers. The subject's actual AE or GE is at the center of the Developmental Zone. A vertical line representing the subject's actual age or grade placement may be drawn on the profile for reference purposes. Space is provided at the right end of the profile to record the RPI and percentile rank for each measure. Note that after the Age/Grade Profile is completed, score information from Table 5.1, Levels 2, 3, and 4 are all provided in a single display to simplify test interpretation.

An examination of Fig. 5.4 indicates that this sixth-grade girl is achieving below grade placement in several of the areas measured. For example, Basic Reading Skills, which measures the ability to identify familiar and unfamiliar words, falls at a low second-grade level. The Developmental Zone indicates that basic reading tasks at the high first-grade level will be perceived as easy by this girl but such tasks by the middle second-grade level will be perceived as difficult and frustrating. Her RPI of 12/90 indicates that if she were asked to perform basic reading tasks that average students at the 6.4 grade level would perform with 90% success, she would perform them with only 12% success. Her percentile rank of 1 indicates that she is in the lowest 1% of students at her grade level in these skills.

Her performance on the Phonological Awareness tests, which measure the ability to analyze and synthesize the sounds of speech, is above average for her sixth-grade placement. She will perceive eighth-grade level phonological awareness tasks as easy. Her RPI of 97/90 indicates that she will perform with 97% success those phonological tasks that her average classmates in grade 6 would perform with 90% success. Her percentile rank is 94 in Phonological Awareness.

In a single display, the completed Age/Grade Profile presents a variety of test performance information that helps in identifying this student's strengths and weaknesses and planning a remedial program for her. Without the contribution of the Rasch model, it would not have been possible to identify this subject's easy and difficult levels in each area measured or to predict her level of success if she were assigned grade-level tasks. The only information available using traditional procedures would have been the GE point score and the percentile rank or standard score.

This example also illustrates that the width of the Developmental Zone may vary from one trait to another and from one point in age to another for the same trait. Depending on the inclination of the underlying growth curve, the width of these zones may differ even if the point value of the AE or GE scores is identical. The relative width of the Developmental Zone is inversely related to the steepness of the growth curve for that trait at that age. For example, the growth curve in Fig. 5.2 for *Gq* is steep in the 5- to 20-year age range. Therefore, the Developmental Zone is narrow on the Age/Grade Profile. In comparison, Developmental Zones for traits such as *Glr* will be wide, reflecting a slow rate of developmental change.

Descriptive/Predictive Labels for Regions Along a Scale of Rasch Difference Scores

A recent effort has been made to standardize a system of labels for designated regions along the *W* difference scale. This system both identifies the region and states the predicted instructional or performance implications for an individual falling in that region. Except for the lowest and highest regions, which are open-ended, each region is 20 *W* units wide with one region centered at zero on the difference scale. This system was first applied to the *Woodcock–Muñoz Language Survey*, a series of language proficiency tests (Woodcock & Muñoz-Sandoval, 1993a, 1993b). The purpose of the system was to describe a subject's language proficiency and instructional

CALP Level	Language Demands of Monolingual Instruction at Age or Grade Level	W Difference	RPI
5 Advanced English Advanced Spanish	Very Easy	+30 & above +20 +10	100/90 99/90 96/90
4 Fluent English Fluent Spanish	Manageable	0 −10	90/90 75/90
3 Limited English Limited Spanish	Difficult	−20 −30	50/90 25/90
2 Very Limited English Very Limited Spanish	Extremely Difficult	−40 −50	10/90 4/90
1 Negligible English Negligible Spanish	Impossible	−60 −70 & below	1/90 0/90

FIG. 5.5. Levels of language proficiency with predicted instructional implications. From *Woodcock–Muñoz Language Survey: Examiner's Manual* (p. 38) by R. W. Woodcock and A. F. Muñoz-Sandoval, 1993, Itasca, IL: Riverside. Copyright 1993 by The Riverside Publishing Company. Reprinted with permission.

implications relative to others at that person's age or grade. Figure 5.5 presents the classification system for the five levels of language proficiency. Level 4 in Fig. 5.5 is the 20-point band centered on the average score at any particular age or grade. In this application, the level of language proficiency is labeled as fluent. The instructional implication is that someone who falls at this level will find the language demands of monolingual instruction in the measured language manageable. If a subject falls at Level 2 (Very Limited), the predicted outcome for handling monolingual language demands is Extremely Difficult. Table 5.4 presents another example of the

TABLE 5.4
Neuropsychological Functional Level/Deficits and Predicted Performance

RPI	W Difference Score	Functional Level	Patient will find the demands of related age-level tasks:
97/90 to 100/90	+11 and above	Advanced	Very Easy
75/90 to 96/90	−10 to +10	Within Normal Limits	Manageable
25/90 to 74/90	−30 to −11	Mildly Impaired	Very Difficult
4/90 to 24/90	−50 to −31	Moderately Impaired	Extremely Difficult
0/90 to 3/90	−51 and below	Severely Impaired	Impossible

Note. From *The WJ-R and Batería-R in Neuropsychological Assessment: Research Report Number 1* (p. 19), by R. W. Woodcock, 1998, Itasca, IL: Riverside Publishing. Copyright 1998 by The Riverside Publishing Company. Adapted by permission.

TABLE 5.5
Generic Table of Labels for Levels and Implications

Proficiency Level	W Difference	RPI	Subject will find demands of related tasks at age or grade level:
Very Advanced	**+34 and above**	**100/90**	**Extremely Easy**
Advanced to Very Advanced	+27 to +33	99/90 to 100/90	Very Easy to Extremely Easy
Advanced	**+14 to +26**	**98/90 to 99/90**	**Very Easy**
Average to Advanced	+7 to +13	96/90 to 97/90	Easy
Average	**−6 to +6**	**82/90 to 95/90**	**Manageable**
Limited to Average	−13 to −7	68/90 to 81/90	Difficult
Limited	**−26 to −14**	**34/90 to 67/90**	**Very Difficult**
Limited to Very Limited	−33 to −27	19/90 to 33/90	Very Difficult to Extremely Difficult
Very Limited	**−46 to −34**	**5/90 to 18/90**	**Extremely Difficult**
Very Limited to Negligible	−53 to −47	3/90 to 4/90	Extremely Difficult to Impossible
Negligible	**−54 and below**	**0/90 to 2/90**	**Impossible**

system modified for neuropsychological applications (Woodcock, 1998). Table 5.5 is a generic table, with intermediate levels added, used by us to generate similar tables for other applications. Perhaps other test developers will find this classification system useful with their Rasch-scaled tests.

EXAMPLE TEST REPORT UTILIZING RASCH-BASED INTERPRETATION STATEMENTS

Figure 5.6 is an example of the report generated by the *Woodcock–Muñoz Language Survey* software. Carlos is bilingual, speaking both Spanish and English, and is in the fourth grade. He was administered the Spanish- and English-language versions of this language proficiency test. The first page of the report describes Carlos' proficiency in oral and written English. The second page describes his proficiency in oral and written Spanish and concludes with comparative information about both languages. The report illustrates most of the interpretation procedures described in this chapter, including RPIs, Developmental Zones, and descriptive proficiency labels with associated implications. The Comparative Language Index (CLI) on page 2 of the report is a special application of the RPI. The numerators from the Spanish and English RPIs are combined into a single index with the numerator of the Spanish RPI being the CLI numerator, and the numerator of the English RPI being the CLI denominator.

REPORT OF LANGUAGE PROFICIENCY TESTING
English and Spanish

NAME: Flores, Carlos   SCHOOL: Kennedy Middle
DATE OF TESTING: 02/03/1997   GRADE: 4.5
DATE OF BIRTH: 11/10/1986   TEACHER/ID: Miss Strickland
AGE: 10 years 3 months   EXAMINER: R. B. Berg

TABLE OF SCORES: Woodcock-Munoz Language Survey, English Form

CLUSTER/Test	GE	EASY	DIFF	PR -1	SEM +1	RPI LEVEL	
BROAD ENGLISH ABILITY	1.8	1.3	2.4	1	1 - 2	27/90	2-3
ORAL LANGUAGE ABILITY	2.4	1.2	4.0	16	10 - 23	68/90	3-4
Picture Vocabulary	2.0	K.9	3.2	10	5 - 19	58/90	
Verbal Analogies	3.0	1.6	4.6	30	19 - 42	77/90	
READING-WRITING ABILITY	1.6	1.3	1.9	<1	<1 - <1	5/90	2
Letter-Word Identification	2.1	1.8	2.6	4	2 - 6	15/90	
Dictation	1.1	K.7	1.4	<1	<1 - <1	2/90	

Broad English Ability is an overall measure of cognitive-academic language
proficiency (CALP) in English. This scale of language ability is a
combined measure of Carlos's oral language, reading, and writing abilities
in English. **On this measure, Carlos demonstrated Very Limited to Limited
English proficiency (Level 2-3).** His performance on this measure is
comparable to that of the average English-speaking student in grade 1.8.
**CALP tasks requiring English below the grade 1.3 level will be quite easy
for Carlos; those above the grade 2.4 level will be quite difficult for
him.**

122

Oral Language Ability includes CALP measures of vocabulary and verbal reasoning in English. **Carlos demonstrated Limited to Fluent English oral language proficiency (Level 3-4).** His performance on this measure is comparable to that of the average English-speaking student in grade 2.4. **English oral language tasks below the grade 1.2 level will be quite easy for Carlos; those above the grade 4.0 level will be quite difficult for him.**

Reading-Writing Ability includes CALP measures of reading and writing skills in English. **Carlos demonstrated Very Limited English reading-writing proficiency (Level 2).** His performance on this measure is comparable to that of the average English-speaking student in grade 1.6. **English reading-writing tasks below the grade 1.3 level will be quite easy for Carlos; those above the grade 1.9 level will be quite difficult for him.** However, inspection of his test scores shows significant variability in reading-writing performance. Performance on the writing test was significantly lower than performance on the reading test.

In summary, when compared to others at his grade level, Carlos's Broad English Ability, an overall measure of CALP, is at Level 2-3 (Very Limited to Limited English). Carlos's English Oral Language proficiency is at Level 3-4 (Limited to Fluent English). Carlos's English Reading-Writing proficiency is at Level 2 (Very Limited English).

Carlos will find the English oral language demands of grade-level tasks difficult. He will find the English written language demands extremely difficult.

FIG. 5.6. *(Continued)*

TABLE OF SCORES: Woodcock-Munoz Language Survey, Spanish Form

CLUSTER/Test	GE	EASY	DIFF	PR	-1 SEM +1		RPI	LEVEL
BROAD SPANISH ABILITY	6.8	5.0	9.2	93	90 -	95	98/90	5
ORAL LANGUAGE ABILITY	5.6	3.6	8.0	70	61 -	79	94/90	4
Picture Vocabulary	5.2	3.4	7.4	63	47 -	77	93/90	
Verbal Analogies	6.0	4.1	9.3	77	66 -	86	96/90	
READING-WRITING ABILITY	7.7	6.0	10.0	96	95 -	98	99/90	5
Letter-Word Identification	8.0	6.5	10.0	96	93 -	98	99/90	
Dictation	7.1	5.6	9.6	94	88 -	97	98/90	

Broad Spanish Ability is an overall measure of cognitive-academic language proficiency (CALP) in Spanish. This scale of language ability is a combined measure of Carlos's oral language, reading, and writing abilities in Spanish. **On this measure, Carlos demonstrated Advanced Spanish proficiency (Level 5).** His performance on this measure is comparable to that of the average Spanish-speaking student in grade 6.8. **CALP tasks requiring Spanish below the grade 5.0 level will be quite easy for Carlos; those above the grade 9.2 level will be quite difficult for him.**

Oral Language Ability includes CALP measures of vocabulary and verbal reasoning in Spanish. **Carlos demonstrated Fluent Spanish oral language proficiency (Level 4).** His performance on this measure is comparable to that of the average Spanish-speaking student in grade 5.6. **Spanish oral language tasks below the grade 3.6 level will be quite easy for Carlos; those above the grade 8.0 level will be quite difficult for him.**

Reading-Writing Ability includes CALP measures of reading and writing skills in Spanish. **Carlos demonstrated Advanced Spanish reading-writing proficiency (Level 5).** His performance on this measure is comparable to that of the average Spanish-speaking student in grade 7.7. **Spanish reading-writing tasks below the grade 6.0 level will be quite easy for Carlos; those above the grade 10.0 level will be quite difficult for him.**

In summary, when compared to others at his grade level, Carlos's Broad Spanish Ability, an overall measure of CALP, is at **Level 5 (Advanced Spanish).** Carlos's Spanish Oral Language proficiency is at **Level 4 (Fluent Spanish).** Carlos's Spanish Reading-Writing proficiency is at **Level 5 Advanced Spanish).**

Carlos will find the Spanish oral language demands of grade-level tasks manageable. He will find the Spanish written language demands very easy.

COMPARATIVE LANGUAGE INDEXES (Spanish compared to English)

BROAD ABILITY 98/27   ORAL LANGUAGE 94/68   READING-WRITING 99/5

For his grade level, Carlos performs overall CALP tasks with 98% success in Spanish and with 27% success in English. On parallel oral language tasks, Carlos performs with 94% success in Spanish and with 68% success in English. On parallel reading-writing tasks, Carlos performs with 99% success in Spanish and with 5% success in English.

FIG. 5.6. Language proficiency report for Carlos, a bilingual student in the fourth grade. Scores and text highlighted by bold type identify the information derived from Rasch-based scales.

The scores and text highlighted by bold type in Fig. 5.6 identify the information derived from Rasch-based scales that could not have been provided by traditional CTT procedures. In this report, half of the information, and arguably the most important information, about Carlos' language proficiency is derived from the Rasch-based scales. Further, all of the statements in the report are empirically generated and do not depend on the examiner's subjective judgment.

CONCLUSION

The potential for expanding the interpretation of test scores based on the Rasch model is analogous to walking out the end of a tunnel. Inside the tunnel it is possible to see only one point on the horizon. However, on emerging from the tunnel, the whole horizon is visible. CTT-derived scores predict performance only at the point represented by the obtained test score. Rasch-based interpretation predicts performance on any task given its scaled distance from the individual's measured ability. This capability allows test developers to enrich the interpretation schemes of their tests by providing additional important information about a subject's test performance.

REFERENCES

Betts, E. A. (1946, 1957). *Foundations of reading instruction.* New York: American Book.

Connolly, A. J., Nachtman, W., & Pritchett, E. M. (1971). *KeyMath Diagnostic Arithmetic Test.* Circle Pines, MN: American Guidance Service.

Embretson, S. E. (1996). The new rules of measurement. *Psychological Assessment, 8,* 341–349.

McGrew, K. S., Werder, J. K., & Woodcock, R. W. (1991). *WJ-R technical manual: A reference on theory and current research.* Itasca, IL: Riverside.

Roid, G. H., & Miller, L. J. (1997). *Leiter International Performance Scale—Revised.* Chicago: Stoelting.

Woodcock, R. W. (1973). *Woodcock Reading Mastery Tests.* Circle Pines, MN: American Guidance Service.

Woodcock, R. W. (1978). *Development and standardization of the Woodcock–Johnson Psycho-Educational Battery.* Itasca, IL: Riverside.

Woodcock, R. W. (1982, March). *Interpretation of the Rasch ability and difficulty scales for educational purposes.* Paper presented at the meeting of the National Council on Measurement in Education, New York, NY. (Available from Measurement/Learning/Consultants, LLC, PO Box 161, Tolovana Park, OR 97145)

Woodcock, R. W. (1991). *Woodcock Language Proficiency Battery—Revised: Examiner's manual.* Itasca, IL: Riverside.

Woodcock, R. W. (1997). *Woodcock Diagnostic Reading Battery.* Itasca, IL: Riverside.

Woodcock, R. W. (1998). *The WJ-R and Batería-R in neuropsychological assessment: Research report number 1.* Itasca, IL: Riverside.

Woodcock, R. W., & Dahl, M. N. (1971). *A common scale for the measurement of person ability and test item difficulty* (AGS Paper No. 10). Circle Pines, MN: American Guidance Service.

Woodcock, R. W., & Johnson, M. B. (1977). *Woodcock–Johnson Psycho-Educational Battery.* Itasca, IL: Riverside.

Woodcock, R. W., & Johnson, M. B. (1989). *Woodcock–Johnson Psycho-Educational Battery— Revised.* Itasca, IL: Riverside.

Woodcock, R. W., & Muñoz-Sandoval, A. F. (1993a). *Woodcock–Muñoz Language Survey— English Form.* Itasca, IL: Riverside.

Woodcock, R. W., & Muñoz-Sandoval, A. F. (1993b). *Woodcock–Muñoz Language Survey— Spanish Form.* Itasca, IL: Riverside.

Wright, B. D., & Linacre, J. M. (1991–1997). *A user's guide to BIGSTEPS: Rasch-model computer program.* Chicago: MESA Press.

Wright, B. D., & Panchapakesan, N. A. (1969). A procedure for sample-free item analysis. *Educational and Psychological Measurement, 29,* 23–48.

CHAPTER SIX

Generalizability Theory: Picking Up Where the Rasch IRT Model Leaves Off?

George A. Marcoulides
California State University at Fullerton

Measurement pervades almost every aspect of modern society. Measurement is generally considered the assigning of numbers to individuals in a systematic way as a means of representing properties of the individuals. For example, a great variety of things about individuals (e.g., achievement, aptitude, intelligence, height, weight) are measured by various people (e.g., teachers, doctors) on a regular basis. At a first glance, to obtain some of these measurements seems quite simple. Unfortunately, a major problem with many kinds of measurements is that there is often no basis to assume that the numerical value provided truthfully and accurately represents the underlying quantity of interest. Because the results of these measurements can have a profound influence on an individual's life, it is important to understand how these scores are derived and the accuracy of the information they contain.

There are two major psychometric theories for the study of measurement procedures: random sampling theory and item response theory (Bejar, 1983; Suen, 1990). Wright (chap. 4, this volume) and Reise (chap. 10, this volume) offer a complete discussion of item response theory models. In random sampling theory there are two approaches, the classical theory approach and the generalizability theory approach. To date, most of the standard strategies for creating and evaluating measurement procedures are based on a set of assumptions that follow the commonly called classical true-score theory approach. Although classical theory is a simple model that describes how errors of measurement can influence observed scores, the assumptions that follow the model are often unreasonable. In an attempt to be liberalized from the restrictive classical theory assumptions, Cronbach and his associates (Cronbach, Gleser, Nanda, & Rajaratnam, 1972; Cronbach, Rajaratnam, & Gleser, 1963; Gleser, Cronbach, & Rajaratnam, 1965) developed generalizability theory.

Since the major publication by Cronbach et al. (1972), generalizability theory has gained increasing attention, as evidenced by the growing number of studies in the literature that apply it (Shavelson, Webb, & Burstein, 1986). The diversity of measurement problems that generalizability theory can solve has developed concurrently with the frequency of its application (Marcoulides, 1989a). Some researchers have gone so far as to consider generalizability theory "the most broadly defined psychometric model currently in existence" (Brennan, 1983, p. xiii). Clearly, the greatest contribution of generalizability theory lies in its ability to model a remarkably wide array of measurement conditions through which a wealth of psychometric information can be obtained (Marcoulides, 1989b; Shavelson & Webb, 1981).

The purpose of this chapter is to provide an overview of generalizability theory and illustrate its use as a comprehensive method for studying measurement procedures. To gain a perspective from which to view the application of this measurement approach and to provide a frame of reference, generalizability theory is compared with the more traditionally used classical theory. The chapter also introduces some new developments that have emerged since the publication of Cronbach et al.'s (1972) monograph. In particular, the chapter focuses on recent developments that extend generalizability theory to a special type of item response theory (IRT) model capable of estimating latent traits such as ability estimates, item difficulties, and rater severity. To gain a perspective from which to view these recent developments, generalizability theory is also compared with the extended version of the Rasch IRT model (Linacre, 1989; Lunz & Linacre, 1998; Wright, chap. 4, this volume).

WHY THE NEED FOR G THEORY?

Although classical theory is the earliest theory of measurement, it continues to have a strong influence among measurement practitioners today (Cardinet, Tourneur, & Allal, 1976; Suen, 1990). In fact, many tests currently in existence provide psychometric information based only on the classical theory approach. Classical theory assumes that when a test is administered to an individual, the observed score (X) is comprised of two components, the true underlying ability of the examinee (T) and some combination of unsystematic error in the measurement (E), such that $X = T + E$. The individual's true score (T) is fixed, but the observed score (X) and error score (E) are random variables. Additionally, it is assumed that corresponding true scores and error scores are uncorrelated and that error scores from different measurements are also uncorrelated. The error scores have an expected value of zero for the population of individuals being measured. The better a test is at providing an accurate indication of an examinee's ability, the more accurate the T component will be and the smaller the E component.

Classical theory also provides a reliability coefficient that permits the estimation of the degree to which the T component is present in a measurement. The reliability coefficient is typically expressed as a ratio of the variance of true scores to the variance of observed scores and as the error variance decreases, the reliability coefficient increases. Mathematically this relationship is expressed as:

$$r^2{}_{xt} = \frac{\sigma^2{}_T}{\sigma^2{}_X}$$

Evaluation of the reliability of a measurement procedure is basically a question of determining how much of the variation in a set of observed scores is a result of the systematic differences among individuals and how much is the result of other sources of variation. Test–retest reliability estimates provide an indication of how consistently a test ranks examinees over time. This type of reliability requires administering a test on two different occasions and examining the correlation between the two test occasions to determine stability over time. Internal consistency is another method for estimating reliability and measures the degree to which individual items in a given test provide similar and consistent results about an examinee. Another method of estimating reliability involves administering two parallel forms of the same test at different times and examining the correlation between the forms.

These methods for estimating reliabilities of measurements illustrate that it is unclear which interpretation of error is the most appropriate. Obviously, the error variance estimates will vary according to the measurement design used (i.e., test–retest, internal consistency, parallel forms), as will the estimates of reliability. For example, if one computes a test–retest reliability coefficient, then the day-to-day variation in the observed score is counted as error, but the variation due to the sampling of items is not. On the other hand, if one computes an internal consistency reliability coefficient, the variation due to the sampling of different items is counted as error, but the day-to-day variation is not. However, because classical theory provides only one definition of error, it is unclear how one should choose between these reliability estimates. Thus, in classical theory one often faces the uncomfortable fact that data obtained from the administration of the same test to the same individuals may yield different reliability coefficients (Webb, Rowley, & Shavelson, 1988).

In contrast, generalizability theory explicitly recognizes that multiple sources of error may exist simultaneously (e.g., errors due to the use of different occasions, raters, or items) in a measurement and can estimate each source of error and the interaction among sources of error (Brennan, 1983; Cronbach et al., 1972; Shavelson & Webb, 1981). Therefore, generalizability theory extends beyond the classical theory approach and permits the estimation of multiple sources of error in a measurement.

OVERVIEW OF GENERALIZABILITY (G) THEORY

Generalizability (G) theory is a theory of the multifaceted errors of measurement. In G theory, any measurement is considered a sample from a universe of admissible observations described by one or more facets. These facets, for example, could be one of many possible tests administered to an examinee on one of many possible testing occasions. According to Cronbach et al. (1972), the conceptual framework underlying G theory is that "an investigator asks about the precision or reliability of a measure because he wishes to generalize from the observation in hand to some class of observations to which it belongs" (p. 15). Thus, the classical theory concept of reliability is replaced by the broader notion of generalizability (Shavelson, Webb, & Rowley, 1989). Instead of asking "how accurately observed scores reflect corresponding true scores," G theory asks "how accurately observed scores permit us to generalize about persons' behavior in a defined universe" (Shavelson et al., 1989).

This G theory question demonstrates how essential it is that the universe an investigator wishes to generalize about be defined by specifying which facets can change without making the observation unacceptable or unreliable. For example, if test scores might be expected to fluctuate from one occasion to another, then multiple testing occasions must be included in the measurement procedure. As such, the whole process of implementing the G theory approach begins with the first conceptualization of the measurement problem. Obviously, one would like to know an examinee's score (the universe score) over all combinations of facets and conditions (e.g., all possible occasions or all possible test items). However, because the universe score can only be estimated, the choice of a particular occasion or test item will inevitably introduce error in the measurement. Thus, the basic approach underlying G theory is to separate the variability in measurement that is due to error. This is accomplished by decomposing an observed score into a variance component for the universe score and variance components for any other sources of variability associated with the measurement study.

To illustrate this decomposition, consider a simple one-facet crossed measurement design. A common example of this one-facet design is a paper-and-pencil, multiple-choice test with n_i items administered to some sample of examinees. Table 6.1 presents data for a hypothetical study in which a group of five examinees are administered a test with four items (although

TABLE 6.1
Data From Hypothetical One-Facet Study

Examinee	Item 1	Item 2	Item 3	Item 4
1	8	5	5	7
2	6	4	5	5
3	9	7	6	7
4	6	4	5	3
5	8	4	5	2

in real applications one would usually administer a longer test to more examinees, the example is kept simple for illustrative purposes).

If X_{pi} is used to denote the observed score for any person (p) on any item (i), the universe score (a person's average score over the entire item universe) is defined as the expected value of a person's observed score across items or simply $\mu_p \equiv E_i X_{pi}$. In a similar manner, the population mean for item i is defined as the expected value over persons or $\mu_i \equiv E_p X_{pi}$, and the mean over both the population and the universe is $\mu \equiv E_p E_i X_{pi}$ (Brennan, 1983). An observed score for one person on one item can be expressed in terms of the following linear model:

$$X_{pi} = \mu \qquad \textit{(grand mean)}$$
$$+ \mu_p - \mu \qquad \textit{(person effect)}$$
$$+ \mu_i - \mu \qquad \textit{(item effect)}$$
$$+ X_{pi} - \mu_p - \mu_i + \mu \qquad \textit{(residual)}$$

In this model, for each score effect there is an associated variance component of the score effect. For example, the variance component for persons is:

$$\sigma_p^2 = E_p (\mu_p - \mu)^2$$

Similarly, the variance component for items is:

$$\sigma_i^2 = E_i (\mu_i - \mu)^2$$

and for the interaction of persons and items is:

$$\sigma_{pi,e}^2 = E_p E_i (X_{pi} - \mu_p - \mu_i + \mu)^2$$

The total variance of the observed scores is equal to the sum of each variance component:

$$\sigma^2 X_{pi} = \underset{p}{E}\, \underset{i}{E}\, (X_{pi} - \mu)^2 = \sigma_p^2 + \sigma_i^2 + \sigma_{pi,e}^2$$

The focus of G theory is on these variance components because their magnitude provides information about the sources of error variance influencing a measurement. Variance components are determined by means of a G study and can be estimated from an analysis of variance (ANOVA) of sample data. Because estimated variance components are the basis for indexing the relative contribution of each source of error and determining the dependability of a measurement, the estimation of variance components is often referred to as the Achilles heel of G theory (Shavelson & Webb, 1981).

It is important to note that there is no restriction on the mechanism that one can use to estimate variance components. In fact, numerous other methods of estimation can be used to provide the same information as ANOVA (for further discussion, see Marcoulides, 1987, 1989c, 1990, 1996). For example, Bayesian methods, minimum variance methods, restricted maximum likelihood methods, and covariance structure methods can all be used to estimate variance components (Marcoulides, 1987, 1996; Marcoulides & Schumacker, 1996; Shavelson & Webb, 1981). In some cases (e.g., small sample sizes, dichotomous data, unbalanced designs, or data with missing observations) the just-mentioned procedures have been found to provide more accurate estimates of variance components than ANOVA (Marcoulides, 1987; Muthén, 1983). However, because ANOVA is much easier to implement, it continues to be the most commonly used method in G theory.

Table 6.2 provides the ANOVA results for the hypothetical one-facet study. Estimation of the variance components is achieved by equating the observed mean squares from an analysis of variance to their expected values and solving the set of linear equations; the resulting solution for the components

TABLE 6.2
ANOVA Estimates of Variance Components for One-Facet Design

Source of Variation	df	SS	MS	Expected Mean Square
Persons (p)	4	23.3	5.82	$\sigma^2_{pi,e} + n_i\sigma^2_p$
Items (i)	3	22.8	7.60	$\sigma^2_{pi,e} + n_p\sigma^2_i$
Residual (pi,e)	12	12.7	1.06	$\sigma^2_{pi,e}$

The estimates for each variance component are obtained from the ANOVA as follows:

$$\hat{\sigma}_p^2 = \frac{MS_p - MS_{pi,e}}{n_i} = \frac{5.82 - 1.06}{4} = 1.19$$

$$\hat{\sigma}_i^2 = \frac{MS_i - MS_{pi,e}}{n_p} = \frac{7.60 - 1.06}{5} = 1.31$$

$$\hat{\sigma}_{pi,e}^2 = MS_{pi,e} = 1.06$$

comprises the estimates. The estimation of variance components for this one-facet design is also illustrated in Table 6.2.

G theory also considers two types of error variance corresponding to two different types of decisions: relative and absolute decisions. Relative decisions focus on individual differences between persons and absolute decisions focus on the level of performance. As such, relative error is of primary concern when one is interested in a decision that involves the rank ordering of individuals (e.g., the ranking of ice skaters in the Winter Olympics). With this type of error definition, all the sources of variation that include persons are considered measurement error. Accordingly, relative error is defined as σ_δ^2 and includes the variance components due to the interaction of persons with items averaged over the number of items used in the measurement. Using the estimates obtained from the example study (with number of items = 4), this value is found to be:

$$\sigma_\delta^2 = \frac{\sigma_{pi,e}^2}{n_i} = \frac{1.06}{4} = .26$$

The square root of this index is considered the δ-type (relative) standard error of measurement (SEM). This SEM is analogous (at least in the one-facet design) to the SEM in classical theory. Using the δ-type SEM, a confidence interval that contains the universe score (with some degree of certainty) can easily be determined.

Absolute error allows one to concentrate on a decision to determine whether an examinee can perform at a prespecified level (rather than knowing only whether the individual has performed better than others—e.g., a driver's license test). The absolute error variance, therefore, not only reflects the disagreements about the rank ordering of persons, but also reflects any differences in average scores. Absolute error is defined as σ_Δ^2 and includes all error variances in the design. Using the estimates from the example study, this value is found to be:

$$\sigma_\Delta^2 = \frac{\sigma_i^2}{n_i} + \frac{\sigma_{pi,e}^2}{n_i} = \frac{1.31}{4} + \frac{1.06}{4} = .58$$

The square root of this index is considered the Δ-type (absolute) SEM. It is important to note that $\sigma_\delta^2 \leq \sigma_\Delta^2$ because σ_δ^2 does not contain all sources of error variance.

Besides the relative and absolute error variances in G theory, another error variance that is sometimes considered involves the sampling error associated with using a sample mean as an estimate of the population mean in a measurement procedure (Marcoulides, 1993, 1995a, 1995b). The amount of sampling error is generally represented by the standard error of the mean or the square of it, the mean error variance (a term used more often in G theory). In the example one-facet design, the mean error variance is the error variance involved when using the mean (i.e., $\bar{X} = 5.55$) over the sample of both persons and items as an estimate of the mean over both the population of persons and the universe of items (Brennan, 1983). The mean error variance in the one-facet design was shown by Brennan to be equal to:

$$\sigma_{\bar{X}}^2 = \frac{\sigma_p^2}{n_p} + \frac{\sigma_i^2}{n_i} + \frac{\sigma_{pi,e}^2}{n_p n_i} = \frac{1.19}{5} + \frac{1.31}{4} + \frac{1.06}{20} = .62$$

Although G theory stresses the importance of variance components, it also provides a generalizability coefficient analogous to the classical theory reliability coefficient. The generalizability coefficient also ranges from 0 to 1.0 and is influenced by the amount of error variation observed in an individual's score and by the number of observations made. As the number of observations increase, error variance decreases and the generalizability coefficient increases. The generalizability coefficient can be intepreted as the ratio of universe score variance to expected observed score variance ($E\rho^2 = \sigma_p^2/E\sigma^2 X_{pi}$), and is somewhat analogous to the traditional reliability coefficient. However, unlike classical theory, G theory recognizes that error variance is not a monolithic entity but that multiple sources can contribute error to a measurement design (Shavelson & Webb, 1991). Thus, a generalizability coefficient can be determined for each type of decision, relative or absolute:[1]

$$E\rho_\delta^2 = \frac{\sigma_p^2}{\sigma_p^2 + \sigma_\delta^2} = \frac{1.19}{1.19 + .26} = .82$$

and

$$\rho_\Delta^2 = \Phi = \frac{\sigma_p^2}{\sigma_p^2 + \sigma_\Delta^2} = \frac{1.19}{1.19 + .58} = .67$$

Of course, sample estimates of the parameters in the generalizability coefficients are once again used to estimate the appropriate level of generalizability.

In the event that the emphasis is placed on a particular domain-referenced interpretation of examinee scores (i.e., a criterion referenced interpretation), a generalizability index can also be determined (Brennan & Kane, 1977a, 1977b). The index is denoted by $\Phi(\lambda)$ and represents domain-referenced

---

[1]The notation presented for the absolute coefficient is often used interchangeably. It is also referred to as the *index of dependability.*

interpretations involving a single fixed cut-off score (e.g., a proportion of items correct). The value of $\Phi(\lambda)$ is determined by using the following equation:

$$\Phi(\lambda) = \frac{\sigma_p^2 + (\mu - \lambda)^2}{\sigma_p^2 + (\mu - \lambda)^2 + \sigma_\Delta^2}$$

It is important to note that an unbiased estimator of the value $(\mu - \lambda)^2$ is determined by using $(\bar{X} - \lambda)^2 - \sigma_{\bar{x}}^2$. For example, if the cut-off score in the hypothetical study were $\lambda = 9$, the value of $\Phi(\lambda)$ is:

$$\Phi(\lambda) = \frac{\sigma_p^2 + (\mu - \lambda)^2 - \sigma_{\bar{X}}^2}{\sigma_p^2 + (\mu - \lambda)^2 + \sigma_\Delta^2} = \frac{1.19 + (5.55 - 9)^2 - .62}{1.19 + (5.55 - 9)^2 - .62 + .58} = .96$$

Thus, G theory permits the development of decisions about measurements designs based on information provided from the G study. Once the sources of measurement error have been pinpointed through estimating the variance components, one can determine how many conditions of each facet are needed to obtain an optimal level of generalizability (Goldstein & Marcoulides, 1991; Marcoulides, 1993, 1995a; Marcoulides & Goldstein, 1990, 1991, 1992a, 1992b). For example, if the number of test items were increased to 10 (i.e., $n_i = 10$), the generalizability coefficient for a relative decision is increased to 0.92.

The previous example illustrates the important distinction that exists between a G study and a decision (D) study. In general terms, G studies are associated with the development of a measurement procedure, whereas D studies apply the procedure in practical terms (Shavelson & Webb, 1981). If the results of a G study show that some sources of error are very small, then one may elect to reduce the number of levels of that facet (e.g., number of items) or may even ignore that facet in a D study (something that can be especially important in multifaceted designs—see next section). Alternatively, if the results of a G study show that some sources of error in the design are very large, then one may need to increase the levels of that facet in order to obtain an acceptable level of generalizability. Therefore, resources might be better spent by increasing the sample of conditions that contribute large amounts of error in order to increase generalizability.

There is a lot of confusion among practitioners, however, concerning the differences between what constitutes a G study and a D study. In general, the D study should be conceptualized as the point at which one looks back at the G study and examines the measurement procedure in order to make recommendations for change. In its simplest form, one can conceptualize the D study as an implementation of the Spearman–Brown Prophecy Formula developed in classical theory (for determining the appropriate test length).

In other words, what should be done differently if one were going to rely on this measurement procedure. In the case where no changes can or should be made, the G study will act as the D study. A major contribution of G theory, therefore, is that it permits one to pinpoint the sources of measurement error and increase the appropriate number of observations accordingly in order to obtain a certain level of generalizability (Shavelson et al., 1986).

GENERALIZABILITY THEORY EXTENDED TO MULTIFACETED DESIGNS

G theory provides a framework for examining the dependability of measurements in almost any type of design. This is because G theory explicitly recognizes that multiple sources of error may be simultaneously operating in a measurement design. As such, G theory can be used in multifaceted designs to estimate each source of error and the interactions among the sources of error. For example, when studying the dependability of measures of job performance, Marcoulides and Mills (1988) considered supervisor ratings and the items in the rating forms as important factors that could lead to the undependability of the measurement procedure. Such a study would be considered a person by item by supervisor ($p \times i \times s$) two-faceted crossed design.[2]

The following two-faceted study of the dependability of performance ratings of ice skaters during the 1988 Winter Olympics will be used to illustrate G theory's treatment of error in multifaceted designs (Marcoulides, 1988). In this study, ratings of the performance of 11 ice skaters were obtained on two occasions. Nine judges independently rate the ice skaters in terms of their performance on the two occasions.[3] This design is a person (skater) by judges by occasion ($p \times j \times o$) two-faceted crossed design.

For this study there are several sources of variability that can contribute to error in determining the dependability of the measures of performance. Because skaters are the object of measurement, their variability does not constitute error variation. In fact, we expect that skaters will perform differently. However, judges and occasions are potential sources of error because they can contribute to the undependability of the measurement of ice skaters' performance.

Using the ANOVA approach, seven variance components must be estimated. These correspond to the three main effects in the design (persons, judges, occasions), the three two-way interactions between effects, and the

---

[2]It is important to note that in a crossed design, every condition of the one facet occurs in combination with the every condition of the other facet. This is in contrast to a nested design where certain conditions of one facet may occur with only one condition of the other facet.

[3]In the 1988 Winter Olympic competition, the two occasions were referred to as artistic impression and technical merit occasions.

three-way interaction confounded with random error (due to the one observation per cell design). Thus, the total variance of the observed score would be equal to the sum of each of these variance components:

$$\sigma^2 X_{pjo} = \sigma_p^2 + \sigma_j^2 + \sigma_o^2 + \sigma_{pj}^2 + \sigma_{po}^2 + \sigma_{jo}^2 + \sigma_{pjo,e}^2$$

As discussed in the previous section, estimation of these variance components is achieved by equating the observed mean squares from an analysis of variance to their expected values and solving the sets of linear equations; the resulting solution for the components comprises the estimates (for more details, see Shavelson & Webb, 1991, or Marcoulides, 1998). Table 6.3 provides the ANOVA source table and the estimated variance components for this example. As can be seen in Table 6.3, the variability due to judges is a small source of error variation (3.44%). It appears that the judges are rating skaters using basically the same criteria. In addition, the judges are rank ordering the skaters somewhat similarly as evidenced by the small variance component for the person by judge interaction (6.90%). The variance due to the occasion of rating is also quite small (0.57%), indicating that there is no difference in the ratings of the performance of skaters across the two occasions. This is also reflected in the small variance components due to the person by occasion interaction (5.17%), and the judges by occasion interaction (0.57%).

As indicated in the previous section, G theory permits one to consider different types of error variance associated with measurement procedures. For example, if one decided that relative decisions were essential in determining the performance of ice skaters (i.e., decisions concerning the rank ordering of ice skaters for awarding the gold, silver, and bronze medals), the relative error variance would be determined as:

$$\sigma_\delta^2 = \frac{\sigma_{pj}^2}{n_j} + \frac{\sigma_{po}^2}{n_o} + \frac{\sigma_{pjo,e}^2}{n_j n_o}$$

TABLE 6.3
ANOVA Estimates of Variance Components for
1988 Winter Olympics Ice Skating Data

Source of Variation	df	SS	MS	V.C.	% Var.
Persons (p)	10	25.58	2.56	0.136	78.16
Judges (j)	8	1.38	0.17	0.006	3.44
Occasions (o)	1	0.16	0.16	0.001	0.57
p × j	80	2.69	0.03	0.012	6.90
p × o	10	0.88	0.09	0.009	5.17
j × o	8	0.18	0.02	0.001	0.57
pjo,e	80	0.74	0.01	0.009	5.17
Total	197	31.61			100

or simply:

$$\sigma_\delta^2 = \frac{.012}{9} + \frac{.009}{2} + \frac{.009}{18} = .006$$

The generalizability coefficient for such a relative decision would be determined to be:

$$E\rho_\delta^2 = \frac{\sigma_p^2}{\sigma_p^2 + \sigma_\delta^2} = \frac{.136}{.136 + .006} = 0.96$$

Similarly, using only one judge and one occasion will produce an estimated relative generalizability coefficient of 0.82, compared to 0.92 when using one occasion and nine judges. Table 6.4 provides the estimated variance components and generalizability coefficients for a variety of D studies using different combinations of number of judges and occasions.

There is no doubt that occasions are contributing very little error variability and can be reduced in subsequent measurements of performance. In addition, the number of judges may be reduced with little loss of generalizability. As indicated by Marcoulides and Goldstein (1990), one should always consider potential resource constraints imposed on measurement procedures before making final decisions. Although Cronbach et al. (1972) indicated that generalizability will generally improve as the number of conditions in a facet are increased, this increment can ultimately enter the realm of fantasy. More important is the question of the exchange rate or trade-off between conditions of a facet in some cost considerations (Cronbach et al., 1972). Typically, in multifaceted studies there can be several D study designs that yield the same level of generalizability. For example, if one desires to develop a measurement procedure with a generalizability coefficient of 0.90, there might be two distinct D study designs from which to choose. In such cases one must consider resource constraints in order to choose the appropriate D study design. The question then becomes how to maximize generalizability in a prespecified set of limited resources. As shown in the previous one-facet design, the question of satisfying resource constraints while maximizing generalizability is simple. One chooses the greatest number of items needed to give maximum gener-

TABLE 6.4
Variance Components and Generalizability
Coefficients for a Variety of D Studies

n_J	1	3	3	9
n_O	1	1	2	2
$E\rho_\delta^2$	0.82	0.90	0.93	0.96
ρ_Δ^2	0.78	0.88	0.92	0.95

alizability without violating the budget (Cleary & Linn, 1969). When other facets are added to the design, obtaining a solution can be quite complicated. Extending on this idea, Goldstein and Marcoulides (1991), Marcoulides and Goldstein (1990, 1991), and Marcoulides (1993, 1995a, 1995b, 1997b) developed procedures that can be used in any measurement design to determine the optimal number of conditions that maximize generalizability under limited budget and other constraints. For example, if the total available budget (B) for the above measurement procedure is $100 and if the cost (c) per judge per occasion is $5.00, then the optimal number of judges and occasions can be determined using the following equations (for a complete discussion, see Marcoulides, 1993, 1995a, 1995b, 1997b):[4]

$$n_j = \sqrt{\frac{\sigma_{pj}^2}{\sigma_{po}^2}\left(\frac{B}{c}\right)} = \sqrt{\frac{.012}{.009}\left(\frac{100}{5}\right)} = 5$$

and

$$n_o = \sqrt{\frac{\sigma_{po}^2}{\sigma_{pj}^2}\left(\frac{B}{c}\right)} = \sqrt{\frac{.009}{.012}\left(\frac{100}{5}\right)} = 4$$

Additional constraints, for example on the upper bounds of the number of judges, could easily be imposed on the problem before optimizing the solution. Such additional constraints might become important when, besides the budgetary constraints, one is aware of other design restrictions (such as the actual number of available judges). Thus, D studies are very important when attempting to improve the dependability of measurement procedures because they provide values for both realistic and optimum number of conditions.

GENERALIZABILITY THEORY
AS A LATENT TRAIT MODEL

Latent trait theory, also known as IRT, is a measurement theory that is used to describe, explain, and predict the encounter of an individual with a measurement device (for further discussion see Reise, chap. 10, this volume). IRT assumes that an individual's performance on the measurement device

---

[4]When the values of n_j and n_s are nonintegers, they must be rounded to the nearest feasible integer values—see Marcoulides & Goldstein (1990) for discussion of optimality when rounding integers. Marcoulides (1993, 1997b) also illustrates optimization procedures for more complex designs.

(e.g., a test item)[5] can be accounted for by defining characteristics called traits—hypothetical or unobserved characteristics or traits. Thus, in a testing situation, an IRT model permits one to assume that the most important aspects of test performance can be described by an examinee's standing on some latent traits. IRT models also describe how the latent trait influences performance on each measurement device. Typically, the relationship between the unobserved trait and the observed measure (or test score) is described in terms of some mathematical model (Schmidt-McCollam, 1998).

To date, there is no generally accepted model for describing the relationship between a given trait and performance on a measure of the trait. In fact, many latent trait models have been proposed in the literature for a variety of applications and with many different mathematical functions employed. One popular class of models that have found widespread application in the psychometric literature has been labeled the Rasch family (Masters & Wright, 1984; Rasch, 1960/1980; Wright, chap. 4, this volume). This family of models includes the logistic model (Wright & Panchapakesan, 1969), the rating scale and partial credit models (Andrich, 1978), the partial order model (Wislon, 1989), and the FACETS model (Linacre, 1988, 1989; Wright, chap. 4, this volume), to name a few.

Recently, Stahl and Lunz (1993), Bachman et al. (1993), Marcoulides (1997a), and Stahl (1994) provided a comparison of generalizability theory and the multifaceted (FACETS) Rasch IRT model and illustrated how both methods can be used to provide information concerning future test construction. Although both methods were found to provide similar information with respect to measurement designs that involve judged ratings, G theory was criticized for its focus on group behavior and the interaction of groups:

> G theory focuses on the performance of groups: 1) the variation of the examinees as a group, 2) the variance of the judges as a group, and 3) the variance of the tasks as a group. This group oriented focus minimizes the diagnostic information that is available at the individual level but may be useful information for developing judging schedules. (Stahl & Lunz, 1993, p. 4)

In response to the above criticism, Marcoulides and Drezner (1995, 1997a, 1997b) introduced an extension to G theory that can be used to provide specific information on the reliability of individual ability estimates and diagnostic information at the individual and group levels. As illustrated by Marcoulides & Drezner (1997a), their extension to G theory can be used to analyze performance assessments to provide three important pieces of information:[6] (a) a diagnostic scatter diagram—that can be examined for un-

---

[5]Although in traditional IRT models the measurement device is usually a test item, there can be a variety of measurement devices employed.

[6]Although Marcoulides and Drezner (1997a) illustrated their method using performance assessment designs, the model can be used with any type of design and with any number of conditions of facets and observations.

TABLE 6.5
Hypothetical Data Set of Teacher Performance
(Shavelson & Webb, 1991, p. 69)

	Subject Area					
	Mathematics			*Reading*		
Judges	*1*	*2*	*3*	*1*	*2*	*3*
Teacher						
1	4	4	4	5	5	6
2	6	7	6	7	9	5
3	8	7	7	4	3	2
4	6	8	7	9	11	7
5	2	1	1	5	5	3
6	5	4	4	7	6	5
7	4	5	6	6	8	9
8	7	7	6	5	9	9

usual patterns for each examinee and each judge in the measurement design, (b) an Index for Examinees—that can be used to examine the ability levels of examinees, and (c) an Index for Judges—that can be used to examine judge severity. Recently, Marcoulides (1997a) emphasized that this extension to G theory can be considered a special type of IRT model capable of estimating latent traits such as examinee ability estimates, rater severity, and item difficulties.

To illustrate the Marcoulides and Drezner (1997a, 1997b) latent trait extension to G theory, an example study is analyzed later in this chapter and the results are compared to those obtained from the extended version of the Rasch IRT model (i.e., the FACETS model—see Stahl & Lunz, 1993).[7] In this example study, eight teachers were observed by three judges on their presentation of two subject areas (mathematics and reading)—the data in this example study are based on an hypothetical example compiled by Shavelson and Webb (1991). The design is completely crossed because each judge rated each teacher on both subjects. The grades given by each judge to each teacher in the two subject areas range from 1 to 11—with each score representing a rating scale on which the overall quality of the teachers performance was rated. Following the Stahl and Lunz (1993) study, the subject area is considered a random facet selected from a universe of possible subjects. Table 6.5 presents the data from the example compiled by Shavelson and Webb (1991).

The results of a traditional G study analysis are presented in Table 6.6. As expected, the variance component for teachers (i.e., the object of meas-

---

[7]The same example study is presented by Stahl and Lunz (1993) in their comparison of a traditional G theory analysis and the FACETS model.

TABLE 6.6
G Study Results for Teacher Performance Data

Source of Variation	df	SS	MS	V.C.	% Var.
Teachers (p)	7	111.65	15.95	1.173	22.950
Judges (j)	2	4.88	2.44	0.015	0.293
Subject (s)	1	12.00	12.00	0.158	3.091
p × j	14	26.46	1.89	0.506	9.900
p × s	7	55.30	7.90	2.342	45.823
j × s	2	2.38	1.19	0.039	0.763
pjs,e	14	12.32	0.88	0.878	17.179
Total	47			5.111	100.000

urement) indicates that there are differences among the teachers' perform-ances. The teacher by judge interaction (9.9%) suggests that judges graded each teacher's performance somewhat differently. In addition, the teacher by subject interaction (45.82%) indicates that the relative ranking of each teacher differs substantially across the two subjects areas. An examination of the data in Table 6.5 reveals that the greatest difference in the ranking occurs for teacher #3, who was ranked first in mathematics and eighth in reading. Of course, in a larger data set it would be extremely difficult to discern which teacher (or teachers) are exhibiting unusual performances or discern the most able teacher from the least able. In addition, with a more complex judging plan it would be very difficult to identify unusual judges or identify problem subject areas.

The Marcoulides and Drezner (1997a) latent trait extension to G theory model is based on the assumption that n points (i.e., examinees, judges, items, or any other set of observations that define a facet of interest) are located in an n-dimensional space and that weights (w_{ij}) between two points need to be determined for $i,j = 1, \ldots \ldots n$. The weights express the importance of the proximity between points in space (e.g., the similarity in examinee ability level estimates, judge severity estimates, or item difficulty). The model is then formulated as the minimization of the objective function:

$$f(X) = \frac{\displaystyle\sum_{i,j=1}^{n} w_{ij}d_{ij}^2}{\displaystyle\sum_{i,j=1}^{n} d_{ij}^2}$$

where X is a vector of values for the points (defined according to the latent trait of interest—either examinee ability, judge severity, or item difficulty) that ensures that points with an associated large weight are close to each other,

d_{ij}^2 is the squared Euclidean distance between points i and j, and the weights (with $w_{ii} = 0$ for $i = 1, \ldots, n$ and $w_{ij} = w_{ji}$) are determined by using:

$$w_{ij} = \frac{1}{D_{ij}^p}$$

where D is the n-dimensional distance between points i and j, and the power p is a parameter that varies according to the measurement design (for further details, see Marcoulides & Drezner, 1993, 1995, 1997a). The actual values of X (i.e., the observed values on the latent trait of interest) are determined by calculating the eigenvectors of the second smallest eigenvalues of a matrix S (whose elements are defined as $s_{ii} = \sum_j w_{ij}$ and $s_{ij} = -w_{ij}$). The eigenvectors associated with the second and third smallest eigenvalues of S also provide coordinates of a diagnostic scatter plot for examining the various observations and conditions within a facet in any measurement design.

Figures 6.1, 6.2, and 6.3 present plots provided by the Marcoulides and Drezner (MD) model and the FACETS model (Linacre, 1988). Although the plots merely highlight results from more detailed analyses generated by each

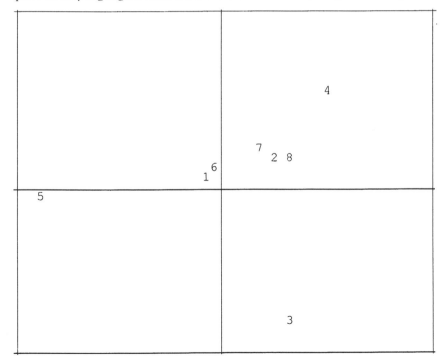

FIG. 6.1. MD plot for observed teachers in example study.

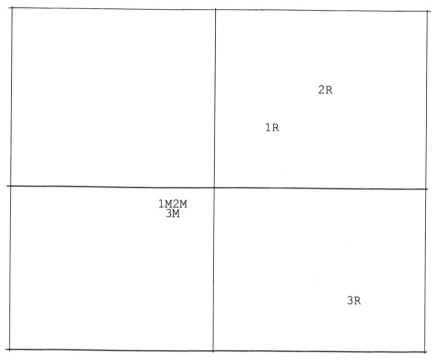

FIG. 6.2. MD plot for judge ratings in example study.

method (see discussion later this chapter), the plots or maps can be used to visualize the distribution of teacher performances and the rating patterns of the judges in the subject areas. As can be seen in Fig. 6.1, teachers are spread out in ability, and one can quickly identify that teacher #3 (as previously indicated), teacher #4, and teacher #5 are exhibiting unusual performances. Although it may not be clear from the plot what the unusual performances represent, there is no doubt that these teachers will require further study.

Figure 6.2 presents a plot of the judges rating patterns generated by the MD model. The judges are numbered 1 through 3 accompanied by the subject area letter (M or R). As can be seen by examining Fig. 6.2, the judges rating patterns appear identical in Mathematics and somewhat different in Reading.

Figure 6.3 presents the plot generated by the FACETS model. As can be seen in Fig. 6.3, the plot corroborates the information provided by the previously examined MD plot concerning teacher #4 and teacher #5. However, the FACETS plot reveals nothing unusual about teacher #3. In fact, in the FACETS plot, teacher #3 appears as part of the middle group of teachers. As it turns out, with the FACETS plot one also cannot discern any information concerning potential differences among the judges on each subject area.

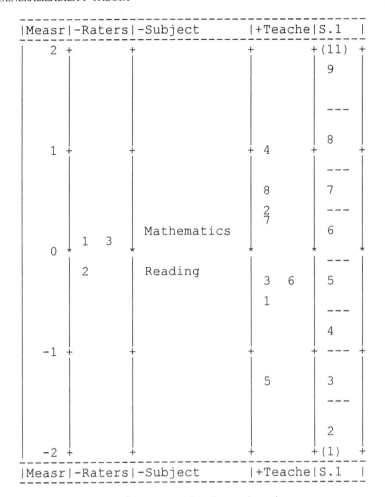

FIG. 6.3. FACETS plot of example study.

As previously mentioned, the MD model and the FACETS model also provide information concerning examinee ability or proficiency and rater severity. It is important to note that both models can be extended to include any other latent traits of interest depending on the facets included in the original measurement study. For example, if each teacher in this example study had been rated using some set of items, then an item difficulty estimate could also be determined and examined.

Table 6.7 and Table 6.8 provide the estimated ability measures for each examinee and the severity estimates for each judge generated by the MD and FACETS models. Marcoulides and Drezner (1997a) referred to the ability measure for each examinee (Se) as the Index of Examinees (the ability estimate is generally represented as θ in traditional IRT models), and the

TABLE 6.7
Teacher Ability Estimates Generated
by the MD Method and FACETS

Teacher	MD Method	FACETS*
1	−0.07	−0.31
2	0.14	0.44
3	0.25	−0.12
4	0.31	0.99
5	−0.88	−1.07
6	−0.01	−0.12
7	0.08	0.31
8	0.18	0.63

*In the FACETS model the unit of measurement is the log-odds unit or logits.

TABLE 6.8
Judge Severity Estimates Generated by the MD Method and FACETS

Judge	MD Method		FACETS
	Math.	Reading	
1	−0.39	0.14	0.05
2	−0.39	0.44	−0.17
3	−0.39	0.58	0.12

severity estimate for each judge (S_j) as the Index for Judges. It is important to note that the MD model (somewhat similar to FACETS) independently calibrates the examinees and judges so that all observations are positioned on the same scale: the scales range from +1 to −1. Thus, negative values of the Index of Examinees indicate less able examinees and positive values more able. Similarly, negative values of the Index for Judges indicate lenient judges and positive values severe judges.

An examination of the teacher ability estimates generated by the MD and FACETS models in Table 6.7 reveals that teacher #5 is the least able and teacher #4 the most able examinee. Interestingly, with the exception of teacher #3, the teacher ability estimates generated by each model are identical with respect to the rank ordering of each observed teacher. For teacher #3, the MD model generates an ability estimate that places this teacher second in terms of ability. In constrast, the FACETS model generates an ability estimate that places this teacher tied at the bottom in terms of ability. Perhaps the fact that teacher #3 was ranked first in mathematics is given more consideration in the MD model than the FACETS model. Further research will need to be conducted to investigate the various conditions under which the two models differ and the reasons they differ. Nevertheless, the similarity between all the other teacher ability estimates clearly supports the assertion that the MD model can accurately estimate latent traits of interest.

The judge severity estimates generated by the MD and FACETS models are presented in Table 6.8. The results of the FACETS analysis indicate that the judges performed in a relatively similar manner in both subjects. According to the results generated by the MD model, the judges' rating patterns are identical in mathematics and relatively similar in reading. Thus, based on the results of the MD model, it appears that judge #1 is slightly more lenient than judge #2 and judge #3. These same results are corroborated when using the traditional G theory analysis. For example, as presented in Table 6.6, it was determined that judges graded each teacher's performance somewhat inconsistently (the teacher by judge interaction was found to be approximately 10%).

There is no doubt that there are considerable similarities between the G theory latent trait model introduced by Marcoulides and Drezner (1995, 1997a) and the FACETS model (Linacre, 1988, 1989). As such, the assertion that the MD model can accurately estimate latent traits of interest is supported. Nevertheless, as observed in the previous example, there are cases when the two models generate slightly different ability and severity estimates. Perhaps, one reason for the earlier discrepancy between the two models is the way differences in performance ratings are treated (Marcoulides, 1997b). For example, in the FACETS model, "severity is the term used to encompass all of the factors that influence the way a judge grades performance" (Lunz, Stahl, & Wright, 1994, p. 918). In the MD model, however, the factors that are considered potential sources of variation that may influence the dependability of the measurement of teacher performance include both rater severity and rater inconsistency (Marcoulides, 1997b). Thus, the MD model follows Longford's (1994) assertion that there are two distinct ways in which raters can differ. Raters may vary in their severity (i.e., some raters tend to give higher scores and other give lower scores), and in terms of inconsistency (i.e., raters may disagree on the relative merits of responses—judge #2 may rate teacher #2 higher than teacher #1 in reading, disagreeing with judge #3 who rates teacher #1 higher than teacher #2). Because rater inconsistency is the principal cause of low score reliability in measurement designs and, "identification of these components is essential for improved calibration of readers . . . estimation of examinees' . . . scores" (Longford, 1994, p. 176), perhaps only models that incorporate these aspects can provide accurate estimates of the latent traits.

CONCLUSION

Generalizability theory is clearly a comprehensive method for designing, assessing, and impoving the dependability of measurement procedures. As illustrated in this chapter, the results obtained from a traditional generalizability analysis are essential for determining information concerning the psychometric properties of a measurement study. Generalizability analysis is also essential for determining what modifications can or should be made to a measurement procedure. With the added latent trait G theory model described earlier in this chapter, researchers will also be able to examine the latent traits embedded in a measurement procedure. Although the example cases illustrated throughout this chapter were purposely kept simple, it should be emphasized that G theory models can be adapted to all types of measurement designs that might be encountered in practical applications. G theory models can even be generalized to multivariate designs in which multiple scores are used in order to describe individuals' aptitude or skills (Marcoulides, 1994; Marcoulides & Hershberger, 1997; Webb, Shavelson, & Maddahian, 1983).

REFERENCES

Andrich, D. (1978). A rating formulation for ordered response categories. *Psychometrika, 43,* 561–573.
Bachman, L., Boodoo, G., Linacre, J. M., Lunz, M. E., Marcoulides, G. A., & Myford, C. (1993, April). *Generalizability theory and many-faceted Rasch modeling.* Invited presentation at the joint annual meeting of the American Educational Research Association and the National Council on Measurement in Education, Atlanta, GA.
Bejar, I. I. (1983). Achievement testing: Recent advances. In J. L. Sullivan & R. G. Niemi (Eds.), *Quantitative applications in the social sciences* (pp. 70–96). Beverly Hills, CA: Sage.
Brennan, R. L. (1983). *Elements of generalizability theory.* Iowa City, IA: American College Testing.
Brennan, R. L., & Kane, M. T. (1977a). An index of dependability for mastery of tests. *Journal of Educational Measurement, 14,* 277–289.
Brennan, R. L., & Kane, M. T. (1977b). Signal/noise ratios for domain-referenced tests. *Psychometrika, 42,* 609–625.
Cardinet, J., Tourneur, Y., & Allal, L. (1976). The symmetry of generalizability theory: Application to educational measurement. *Journal of Educational Measurement, 13,* 119–135.
Cleary, T. A., & Linn, R. L. (1969). Error of measurement and the power of a statistical test. *British Journal of Mathematical and Statistical Psychology, 22,* 49–55.
Cronbach, L. J., Gleser, G. C., Nanda, H., & Rajaratnam, N. (1972). *The dependability of behavioral measurements: Theory of generalizability scores and profiles.* New York: Wiley.
Cronbach, L. J., Rajaratnam, N., & Gleser, G. C. (1963). Theory of generalizability: A liberization of reliability theory. *British Journal of Statistical Psychology, 16,* 137–163.
Gleser, G. C., Cronbach, L. J., & Rajaratnam, N. (1965). Generalizability of scores influenced by multiple sources of variance. *Psychometrika, 30*(4), 395–418.
Goldstein, Z., & Marcoulides, G. A. (1991). Maximizing the coefficient of generalizability in decision studies. *Educational and Psychological Measurement, 51*(1), 55–65.
Linacre, J. M. (1988). *FACETS.* Chicago: MESA Press.
Linacre, J. M. (1989). *Multi-faceted Rasch measurement.* Chicago: MESA Press.
Longford, N. T. (1994). Reliability of essay rating and score adjustment. *Journal of Educational and Behavioral Statistics, 19*(3), 171–200.

Lunz, M. E., & Linacre, J. M. (1998). Measurement designs using multi-facet Rasch modeling. In G. A. Marcoulides (Ed.), *Modern methods for business research* (pp. 47–77). Mahwah, NJ: Lawrence Erlbaum Associates.

Lunz, M. E., Stahl, J. A., & Wright, B. D. (1994). Interjudge reliability and decision reproducibility. *Educational and Psychological Measurement, 54*(4), 913–925.

Marcoulides, G. A. (1987). *An alternative method for variance component estimation: Applications to generalizability theory.* Unpublished doctoral dissertation, University of California, Los Angeles, CA.

Marcoulides, G. A. (1988, January). *The use of generalizability analysis in observational studies.* Paper presented at the Annual Meeting of the Hawaii Educational Research Association, Honolulu, HI.

Marcoulides, G. A. (1989a). The application of generalizability theory to observational studies. *Quality & Quantity, 23*(2), 115–127.

Marcoulides, G. A. (1989b). From hands-on measurement to job performance: Issues of dependability. *Journal of Business and Society, 1*(2), 1–20.

Marcoulides, G. A. (1989c). The estimation of variance components in generalizability studies: A resampling approach. *Psychological Reports, 65,* 883–889.

Marcoulides, G. A. (1990). An alternative method for estimating variance components in generalizability theory. *Psychological Reports, 66*(2), 102–109.

Marcoulides, G. A. (1993). Maximizing power in generalizability studies under budget constraints. *Journal of Educational Statistics, 18*(2), 197–206.

Marcoulides, G. A. (1994). Selecting weighting schemes in multivariate generalizability studies. *Educational and Psychological Measurement, 54*(1), 3–7.

Marcoulides, G. A. (1995a). Designing measurement studies under budget constraints: Controlling error of measurement and power. *Educational and Psychological Measurement, 55*(3), 423–428.

Marcoulides, G. A. (1995b, March). *Generalizability theory: Applications and techniques.* Invited workshop presented at the 17th Language Testing Research Colloquium, Long Beach, CA.

Marcoulides, G. A. (1996). Estimating variance components in generalizability theory: The covariance structure analysis approach. *Structural Equation Modeling, 3*(3), 290–299.

Marcoulides, G. A. (1997a, March). *Generalizability theory: Models and applications.* Invited session at the Annual Meeting of the American Educational Research Association, Chicago, IL.

Marcoulides, G. A. (1997b). Optimizing measurement designs with budget constraints: The variable cost case. *Educational and Psychological Measurement, 57*(5), 808–812.

Marcoulides, G. A. (1998). Applied generalizability theory models. In G. A. Marcoulides (Ed.), *Modern methods for business research* (pp. 1–21). Mahwah, NJ: Lawrence Erlbaum Associates.

Marcoulides, G. A., & Drezner, Z. (1993). A procedure for transforming points in multidimensional space to a two-dimensional representation. *Educational and Psychological Measurement, 53*(4), 933–940.

Marcoulides, G. A., & Drezner, Z. (1995, April). *A new method for analyzing performance assessments.* Paper presented at the Eighth International Objective Measurement Workshop, Berkeley, CA.

Marcoulides, G. A., & Drezner, Z. (1997a). A method for analyzing performance assessments. In M. Wilson, K. Draney, & G. Engelhard, Jr. (Eds.), *Objective measurement: Theory into practice* (pp. 261–277). Norwood, NJ: Ablex.

Marcoulides, G. A., & Drezner, Z. (1997b, March). *A procedure for detecting pattern clustering in measurement designs.* Paper presented at the Ninth International Objective Measurement Workshop, Chicago, IL.

Marcoulides, G. A., & Goldstein, Z. (1990). The optimization of generalizability studies with resource constraints. *Educational and Psychological Measurement, 50*(4), 782–789.

Marcoulides, G. A., & Goldstein, Z. (1991). Selecting the number of observations in multivariate measurement designs under budget constraints. *Educational and Psychological Measurement, 51*(4), 573–584.

Marcoulides, G. A., & Goldstein, Z. (1992a). The optimization of multivariate generalizability studies under budget constraints. *Educational and Psychological Measurement, 52*(3), 301–308.

Marcoulides, G. A., & Goldstein, Z. (1992b). Maximizing the reliability of marketing measures under budget constraints. *SPOUDAI: The Journal of Economic, Business, Statistics and Operations Research, 42*(3–4), 208–229.

Marcoulides, G. A., & Hershberger, S. L. (1997). *Multivariate statistical methods: A first course.* Mahwah, NJ: Lawrence Erlbaum Associates.

Marcoulides, G. A., & Mills, R. B. (1988). Employee performance appraisals: A new technique. *Review of Public Personnel Administration, 9*(4), 105–113.

Marcoulides, G. A., & Schumacker, R. E. (1996). *Advanced structural equation modeling: Issues and techniques.* Mahwah, NJ: Lawrence Erlbaum Associates.

Masters, G. N., & Wright, B. D. (1984). The essential process in a family of measurement models. *Psychometrika, 49*, 529–544.

Muthén, L. (1983). *The estimation of variance components for dichotomous dependent variables: Applications to test theory.* Unpublished doctoral dissertation, University of California, Los Angeles, CA.

Rasch, G. (1960/1980). *Probabilistic models for some intelligence and attainment tests.* Chicago: University of Chicago Press.

Schmidt-McCollam, K. M. (1998). Latent trait and latent class models. In G. A. Marcoulides (Ed.), *Modern methods for business research* (pp. 23–46). Mahwah, NJ: Lawrence Erlbaum Associates.

Shavelson, R. J., & Webb, N. M. (1981). Generalizability theory: 1973–1980. *British Journal of Mathematical and Statistical Psychology, 34*, 133–166.

Shavelson, R. J., & Webb, N. M. (1991). *Generalizability theory: A primer.* Newbury Park, CA: Sage.

Shavelson, R. J., Webb, N. M., & Burstein, L. (1986). Measurement of teaching. In M. C. Wittrock (Ed.), *Handbook of research on teaching* (pp. 50–91). New York: Macmillan.

Shavelson, R. J., Webb, N. M., & Rowley, G. L. (1989). Generalizability theory. *American Psychologist, 44*(6), 922–932.

Stahl, J. A. (1994). What does generalizability theory offer that many-facet Rasch measurement cannot duplicate? *Rasch Measurement Transactions, 8*(1), 342–343.

Stahl, J. A., & Lunz, M. E. (1993, March). *A comparison of generalizability theory and multifaceted Rasch measurement.* Paper presented at the Annual Meeting of the American Educational Research Association, Atlanta, GA.

Suen, H. K. (1990). *Principles of test theories.* Hillsdale, NJ: Lawrence Erlbaum Associates.

Webb, N. M., Rowley, G. L., & Shavelson, R. J. (1988). Using generalizability theory in counseling and development. *Measurement and Evaluation in Counseling and Development, 21*, 81–90.

Webb, N. M., Shavelson, R. J., & Maddahian, E. (1983). Multivariate generalizability theory. In L. J. Fyans, Jr. (Ed.), *Generalizability theory: Inferences and practical applications* (pp. 67–81). San Francisco, CA: Jossey-Bass.

Wilson, M. (1989, March). *An extension of the partial credit model to incorporate diagnostic information.* Paper presented at the Fifth International Objective Measurement Workshop, Berkeley, CA.

Wright, B. D., & Panchapakesan, N. (1969). A procedure for sample-free item analysis. *Educational and Psychological Measurement, 29*, 23–48.

CHAPTER SEVEN

Introduction to Personality Measurement

Scott L. Hershberger
California State University—Long Beach

Although the previous part of this volume has been concerned with testing issues related to cognitive ability assessment, the remainder of this volume will be concerned with testing issues related to personality assessment. The separation of cognitive ability from personality assessment does not imply that many of the same testing issues are not relevant to both. As just one example, IRT has played an important role in the construction of both contemporary cognitive ability and personality tests. In the area of computer adaptive testing, IRT has been usefully and frequently applied to cognitive ability assessment; somewhat less frequently to personality assessment, however. In chapter 9, Waller provides a strong argument for the computer adaptive administration on the MMPI. IRT has also proven to be valuable to personality test development in other ways. In chapter 10, Reise will, for example, describe how several person–fit measures derived through IRT have been helpful in determining whether, in fact, a particular personality trait as measured by a test is appropriate for describing an individual.

This chapter is organized around three themes that are common to the three chapters in this section. The first theme concerns the importance of construct validity and how evidence of construct validity may be obtained. The second theme concerns whether standing on a trait is best described as a position on a dimensional continuum of individual differences or a membership in a discrete, taxonomic class. Designation of a trait as dimensional or taxonomic has profound implications for its assessment. The third theme concerns individual differences in the appropriateness or relevancy

of trait labels. Some people are simply more traited than others. The identification of three separate themes is not meant to imply that no relationship
exists among them. To the contrary, an intimate relationship exists among
whether a trait is dimensional or taxonomic, how construct validity evidence
is collected, and whether the trait is appropriate for describing a person.
Dimensional traits will require different types of construct validity evidence
than taxonomic traits. Our decision as to whether a person is traited or not
will also depend greatly on our conceptualization of the trait as dimensional
or taxonomic.

CONSTRUCT VALIDITY

It has been written many, many times before but it nonetheless bears repeating: Construct validity evidence is absolutely critical for our acceptance
of a test as measuring a particular trait. What is construct validity and why
is it so important? The construct validity of a test is the extent to which the
test may be said to measure a theoretical construct or trait. Examples of
personality constructs are extraversion, agreeableness, sociability, and conscientiousness. A construct is developed to explain and organize the observed response consistencies on personality test items. Furthermore, a construct is the organizing force underlying item responses—without it, the item
responses are at best unilluminating and at worst meaningless. An appropriate definition of the construct measured by a test is critical for our interpreting and understanding the responses given to the test.

How has construct validity evidence been traditionally obtained? One
method is through examining developmental changes on the test. Many
cognitive ability tests are checked against age to determine whether the scores
show a progressive increase with age. Although this criterion has been most
helpful in cognitive ability testing, it is not without merit in personality
assessment. For example, scores on many measures of temperament are
expected to change with age as the child matures. Another method of
obtaining construct validity evidence is through correlating the test with similar
earlier tests. If, in fact, we are confident that the earlier tests are measuring the
construct of interest, the new test's significant correlations with these earlier
tests may give us some confidence that the new test is measuring the same
construct also. A generalization and decided improvement over this method
is the construction of a multitrait-multimethod matrix. In the paradigmatic
example of this approach, several different measures of the same trait are
correlated among themselves and with several different measures of another
trait. By "different measures of the same trait," I explicitly mean the measurement of the same trait using different methods of assessment, such as
observational methods versus questionnaire measures versus peer ratings. In

the ideal case, we want measures of the same construct to intercorrelate highly; we also want measures of different constructs to not correlate at all. In addition, measures of different constructs should not correlate simply because the same method of response is used for both (resulting in so-called method variance). In the past, the usefulness of the multitrait-multimethod approach was limited by the somewhat subjective interpretation required from the test developer of the correlational patterns. Recently, test developers have used methods from structural equation modeling to substantially reduce the subjectivity involved by explicitly defining a model in which a specific pattern of correlations is expected. Yet another approach to construct validation involves comparing groups on a measure that we would expect to differ on the construct. For example, if we can assume librarians are more shy than salespersons, there should be a significant mean difference between the two occupational groups on a test purported to measures shyness. Perhaps the most common method of construct validation is through factor analysis: Do the item-factor loadings conform to the pattern expected? Thus, the variety of approaches used to gather construct validity evidence suggests that any data throwing light on the nature of the trait under consideration is appropriately labeled construct validity evidence.

Each of the chapter authors addresses the issue of construct validity. For example, Exner has developed special scores for the Rorschach that were not part of the original Comprehensive System. These special scores were developed to better understand certain aspects of personality and to quantify response features that in the past were more qualitatively examined. Exner's chapter describes how construct validity evidence was gathered for several of these special scores. Waller's chapter extensively reviews factor analytic studies of the MMPI, and the construction of two scales, Beta-f and Beta-m, based on their association with a frequently occurring second MMPI factor. Among the many IRT issues addressed in Reise's chapter is the identification of the correct construct dimensionality of the test under examination. Determining whether a test measures one or more constructs is vitally important for the correct interpretation of the IRT results.

DIMENSIONS VERSUS TAXA

When a personality trait is conceptualized as a taxon, persons are considered to have the trait when one or more indicators of the trait are present; the trait is absent when these indicators are absent. In contrast, when a personality trait is conceptualized as dimensional, persons vary on trait extremity, implying that all persons can be ordered on this trait. Whether a trait is conceptualized as taxonomic or dimensional will have a number of implications for how a test assessing the trait is developed. Perhaps the most important implication concerns the expected correlations among the test's items: Under a taxonomic model, no correlation is expected, whereas under a dimensional model, significant correlations are expected. Thus, under the empirical criterion keying used for the development of the original MMPI, items were retained if they distinguished groups of psychiatric patients from nonpsychiatric controls. This method of item selection implies a categorical conceptualization of psychiatric status: Either you are afflicted with a personality disorder or you are not. Notably, correlations among items selected in this way are not high.

The chapter authors take differing views toward the profitability of conceptualizing most personality traits as either taxonomic or dimensional. Exner has cautioned against using the Rorshach as a tool for identifying personality types; that is, he has cautioned against searching for a mythical profile of data that will lead to a homogeneous diagnostic category (Exner, 1995). Waller has noted that normal levels of a personality trait can be conceptualized as dimensional but that some pathological or abnormal personality states are better thought of as categorical (Waller, Putnam, & Carlson, 1996). For example, a normal dissociative state is daydreaming, and all people do vary in their level of daydreaming. This is a dimensional conceptualization. On the other hand, dissociative states that involve a loss of memory are not characteristic of most people: Either a person does or does not suffer from this. Here, dissociation is best conceptualized as categorical. Reise's application of IRT to personality tests explicitly assumes a dimensional model of traits.

What types of evidence can we use to determine if a trait is best thought of as taxonomic or dimensional? We can look at the distribution of the trait. If it is dimensional, the distribution should be fairly continuous; if it is taxonomic, it should be discontinuous or multimodal. We can also use the statistical techniques developed by Waller, in collaboration with Meehl, to determine if a trait is taxonomic or dimensional (Waller & Meehl, 1997). These techniques differ in certain ways but all require a specific correlational pattern among the indicators of the trait if the trait is categorical. Behavioral genetic methods have also been useful in this regard. One can calculate the heritability of a personality trait or disorder in a sample considered extreme on this trait, and on the population at large. If the two heritabilities differ, this implies that the distribution of genetic factors differs between the two groups, thus indicating a categorical personality trait.

TRAIT RELEVANCY

A third theme underlying this section's chapters are the individual differences that exist for the relevancy of certain traits for describing certain people. Bem and Allen (1974) and others noted that if a person is behavorially consistent across situations, the personality trait responsible for the behavior may be more relevant to this person than to a behaviorally inconsistent person. As one measure of consistency, Bem and Allen calculated an ipsatized variance index, or the variance of item responses on one trait scale divided by the total variance across all items on several trait scales. In Bem and Allen's classic study, the ipsatized variance index proved successful in differentiating individuals who were cross-situationally consistent from those who were inconsistent in conscientiousness, but it was not successful for the trait of friendliness. Baumeister and Tice (1988) later proposed the term *metatrait* to describe that trait of having versus not having a particular trait. Baumeister and Tice replaced the ipsatized variance index by the simple standard deviation of an individual's item responses. Both the ipsatized variance index and the Baumeister and Tice alternative has come under some attack. Some researchers (e.g., Paunonen & Jackson, 1985) pointed to statistical difficulties with the ipsatized index, among which is the confounding of item variance caused by the trait with the interitem variance of all other measures. Others (e.g., Burke, Kraut, & Dworkin, 1984) have claimed that measures of consistency possess little discriminant validity from total scale scores. Yet another problem exists with the correlation between the total scale score and consistency measures, which is frequently not linear but curvilinear because of the restrictions placed on the extremity of the total scale scores of inconsistently responding persons.

Few personality researchers doubt the importance of measuring the relevancy of a trait to an individual; the question is how can this be accomplished in a psychometrically sound way? In his current chapter and elsewhere, Exner pointed out that one of the Rorschach's greatest strengths lies in its ability to obtain an idiographic personality profile of a person. Exner cautions against the nomothetic interpretation of the results of an individual's Rorschach responses—to generalize them to some fictional homogenous group. This is consistent with his view that traits are most often best conceptualized as dimensional. The MMPI, as described by Waller, can be used for both nomothetic and idiographic purposes. It is possible to obtain a score on each MMPI factor for a person (a nomothetic perspective) while simultaneously plotting these scores to obtain a unique profile for that person (an idiographic perspective). Elevated or unusual profiles are also used to classify individuals into psychiatric categories (a taxonomic perspective). Reise directly addresses the assessment of traitedness by describing measures of person-fit calculable from the results of an IRT analysis. These measures of person-fit assess the degree to which a person is scalable on a trait dimension. If a person's responses are scalable, the responses are consistent; if they are not consistent, the person is not scalable. Thus if the person is not scalable, evidence exists that the trait dimension is not relevant to this person. Perhaps the most common type of inconsistent item response pattern results when a person passes harder (less frequently endorsed) items and fails easier (more frequently endorsed) items.

In summary, the chapters in this section address some of the most critical issues in personality testing: construct validity, dimensional versus taxonomic classification, and trait relevancy. What will be the future of personality testing? With the influence and assistance of IRT in particular, the future of personality testing looks bright. Up until the present, IRT has been notably underused in the construction and interpretation of tests. As personality psychologists recognize how IRT can be used profitably to address these three issues, and others, IRT will gain a stronger footing. One direct example that is discussed by Reise is the use of person-fit indices to assess trait relevancy for an individual. Many other examples pertinent to construct validity and dimensional/taxonomic classification issues could also be mentioned. To name just one, the ability scores that result from an IRT analysis provide excellent data to perform construct validity and dimensional/taxonomic analyses.

REFERENCES

Baumeister, R. E., & Tice, D. M. (1988). Metatraits. *Journal of Personality, 56,* 571–598.
Bem, D. J., & Allen, A. (1974). On predicting some of the people some of the time: The search for cross-situational consistencies in behavior. *Psychological Review, 81,* 506–520.
Burke, P. A., Kraut, R. E., & Dworkin, R. H. (1984). Traits, consistency, and self-schemata: What do our methods measure? *Journal of Personality and Social Psychology, 47,* 568–579.
Exner, J. E., Jr. (1995). Introduction. In I. B. Weiner (Ed.), *Issues and methods in Rorschach research* (pp. 1–24). Mahwah, NJ: Lawrence Erlbaum Associates.
Paunonen, S. V., & Jackson, D. N. (1985). Idiographic measurement strategies for personality and prediction: Some unredeemed promissory notes. *Psychological Review, 92,* 486–511.
Waller, N. G., & Meehl, P. W. (1997). *Multivariate taxometric procedures: Distinguishing types from continuua.* Thousand Oaks, CA: Sage.
Waller, N. G., Putnam, F. W., & Carlson, E. B. (1996). Types of dissociation and dissociative types: A taxometric analysis of dissociative experiences. *Psychological Methods, 1,* 300–321.

CHAPTER EIGHT

The Rorschach: Measurement Concepts and Issues of Validity

John E. Exner, Jr.
Rorschach Workshops

Since its publication in 1921, a large segment of Rorschach history, mainly from the late 1940s through the mid-1970s, was often marked by considerable criticism based largely on arguments that convincing evidence for the reliability and/or validity of the test had not been established. Some, such as Cronbach (1949) pointed out that many Rorschach scores do not have the psychometric characteristics that are common for most psychological tests because they are not normally distributed. Others, such as Holtzman, Thorpe, Swartz, and Herron (1961) noted that this problem is made even more complex by the fact that the test is open-ended; that is, all protocols do not contain the same number of answers. Holtzman argued that the variability in the number of responses makes systematic research concerning the test difficult at best, and the application of basic measurement principles and/or the serious application of statistical analyses virtually impossible.

The breadth of these criticisms caused some to disavow the use of the word *test* when discussing the Rorschach and substitute nomenclatures such as technique or method (Klopfer & Kelley, 1942), or even describe it as a form of unstructured interview (Zubin, Eron, & Schumer, 1965). Many advocates of the test have countered with the argument that specific measurement principles might not be applicable to its study because the Rorschach yield can only be understood in a clinically global interpretive framework (Holt, 1958, 1970). In effect, those on both sides of the Rorschach argument appear to have been influenced substantially by attitudinal sets about the test, or theories concerning it that generated positions often based much more on opinion than on carefully analyzed data from well designed investigations. It also seems important to note that much early Rorschach research, especially during the 1940s and 1950s, was marked by designs that were overly simplistic or confounded and by approaches to data analysis that would be judged as very primitive by contemporary standards.

RORSCHACH MEASUREMENT METHODS

In retrospect, it seems that many criticisms of, and claims on behalf of, the Rorschach were fomented by a lack of understanding about the nature of the test, and confounded even more by a misuse or overgeneralization of the term *score* by those responsible for the early development of the test. Traditionally, the procedure of translating Rorschach responses into Rorschach symbols has been called scoring. Unfortunately, the use of the word *score* carries with it concepts of measurement that are not always useful or appropriate to the Rorschach.

Actually, once a protocol has been collected from a subject, each response is not really scored. Rather, it is coded. Although historically the coding has been called scoring, most of the codes assigned to a response do not involve numbers and the codes are not scores in the traditional sense of the word. In effect, the coding procedure reduces the response into a logically systematic format; that is, a special Rorschach language. It is not really very different than the application of coding symbols that might be used during behavioral observations to record the occurrence of specific events. Table 8.1 illustrates the codings that have been assigned for an 18-response record.

The codes that are used in the Comprehensive System represent a combination of those derived from earlier systems for which some empirical usefulness has been established, plus new codings that have evolved as the System has matured. Each answer is coded for a minimum of five categories: (a) location (what part of the blot has been used), (b) developmental quality (how has the blot area been used), (c) determinant(s) (what about the blot, i.e. color, form, shading, symmetry, etc. contributes to the response), (d) form quality (to what extent is the answer conventional, unconventional but consistent with contours, or involves a distortion of contours, and (e) content (the categorization of the specific object reported).

Some responses also are coded for as many as four additional categories, which include (a) pairs (answers in which two identical objects are reported because of the blot symmetry), (b) Popular answers (those that occur at least once in every three records), (c) *z* scores (a weighted score assigned to some answers based on blot complexity), and (d) Special (codes) Scores (assigned to identify unusual verbal material or specific response features).

TABLE 8.1
Sequence of Scores (Codes) for a 41-Year-Old Female

CARD	NO	LOC	#	DETERMINANT(S)	(2)	CONTENTS(S)	POP	Z	SPECIAL SCORES
I	1	Wo	1	FMao		A	P	1.0	INC2
	2	Wo	1	FMao		Ad		1.0	INC2,MOR
	3	W+	1	mp.FYo		Art,(A)		4.0	
	4	W+	1	Mp.ma.FYo		Hd,Cg		4.0	MOR,INC2
II	5	W+	1	mp.CFo	2	Ad,Bl	P	4.5	MOR
III	6	W+	1	Ma.C.FDo	2	H,Cg,Hh,Art	P	5.5	COP
IV	7	Wo	1	FD.FTo		(H),Id	P	2.0	
V	8	Wo	1	Fo		A	P	1.0	PER
	9	Wo	1	FMao		A	P	1.0	
VI	10	W+	1	mp.FTo		Ad	P	2.5	PER,MOR,DR
	11	D+	1	Mpu	2	H		2.5	MOR
VII	12	W+	1	Mau	2	H,Cg		2.5	COP
VIII	13	W+	1	FC-		An,Sx		4.5	PER,INC2,MOR
	14	Do	1	Fo	2	A	P		
IX	15	W/	1	ma.YF.CFo		Na,Cl		5.5	
	16	Ddo	99	FT.FC.FY-		An			MOR
X	17	W+	1	F-		An,Sx		5.5	
	18	Wv	1	C		Art			

The lexicon of codes, excluding the weighted z scores, includes 84 items, 6 for location, 4 for developmental quality, 23 for determinants, 4 for form quality, 1 for pairs, 27 for contents, 1 for Popular answers, and 18 for Special Scores. The codes have been selected because there are data to suggest that each, in some way, reflects a psychological feature or operation. None, taken alone, have interpretive meaning and it is only in an extremely rare instance that a code for any single answer becomes interpretively important. The Rorschach coding format, or Rorschach language, permits those using the test to recognize the same characteristics in a single record and across records, but more importantly, the codes form the basis for the actual Rorschach scores.

In that Rorschach approaches to measurement are a bit different than for most tests, four primary issues become very important to those using or studying the Rorschach. First, are the criteria for the codes used sufficiently specific to insure that they are applied uniformly across coders; that is, are data regarding intercoder or interscorer agreement satisfactory? Second, does the variability in the number of responses given create significant variability in the frequencies by which the codes occur? Third, does the frequency of response components identified by the codes appear consistently in retests, or, stated differently, to what extent do the frequency data for each of the codes manifest retest reliability? Finally, and most important, to what extent do the frequency data for the various codes, or the scores derived from them, provide interpretively valid information? The question here is not whether the Rorschach is valid, but whether any of the data derived from it have a valid usefulness. Any of these four issues can be elaborated at length. However, as the main focus of this chapter concerns issues of validity, the first two (interscorer reliability and variability for the number of responses) are addressed briefly and the second two (retest reliability and validity) are discussed more extensively.

INTERCODER RELIABILITY

During the first few years when the Comprehensive System was being developed, a correlational formula was used to reflect intercoder (interscorer) reliability and data were reported for the various codes in which the correlations ranged from .78 to .98. Beginning in the early 1980s, an approach was initiated by which intercoder data have been calculated in terms of percentage of correct agreement, response by response. The reason for the shift to a percentage of correct agreement is the fact that none of the correlational approaches can be used easily to identify the extent to which the entries of several coders, coding the same group of responses, are correct.

Rorschach coding or scoring should not be subject to chance. For almost all responses, the coding entered is either correct or incorrect. There are instances in which coders may legitimately disagree about some determinants or special scores because of insufficient or unclear verbiage, but these are relatively isolated and, even for poorly taken records, probably constitute no more than 10% of the answers. Similarly, some disagreements may occur when extrapolation is required to determine form quality but, again, this constitutes a small proportion of answers. There should be no disagreement for the other scoring components such as location, developmental quality, pairs, contents, Populars, or z scores. They are simple straightforward codes and, for each, a code is either right or wrong.

Correlational approaches such as *kappa* do provide useful information about intercoder consistency and are appropriate when that issue is relevant, such as in some research projects, especially those involving many coders and a large number of subjects. However, the matter of coding accuracy can also be very important in research and becomes even more so when small samples are involved. It is important because the validity of interpretations or conclusions is dependent on the assumption that the frequencies, ratios, percentages, and so forth have been calculated from correct codes or scores.

When the percentages of correct agreement, response by response, for each of the nine possible scoring (coding) categories were calculated for 15 coders across 400 answers, and 20 scorers across 500 answers, the results range from approximately 89% to 98% correct agreement for the 18 Special

Scores and between 87% and 97% correct agreement for the 23 determinants (Exner, 1993).

VARIABILITY OF *R*

The relationship between the number of responses (*R*) given and most variables is not nearly as direct as was often thought to be the case. Table 8.2 (Exner, 1992) shows the correlations between *R* and 14 parametric variables for four groups. The groups were randomly selected from much larger samples.

The data in Table 8.2 do not provide any absolute answers about whether it might be necessary to partial or control for *R* when analyzing Rorschach data, however, collectively they suggest that concerns about variations in *R* may have been overemphasized. They also offer some clues about when

TABLE 8.2
Correlations Between R and 17 Other Rorschach Variables
for Four Groups of Randomly Selected Subjects

Variable	Nonpatient Males $N = 70a$	Nonpatient Females $N = 125b$	Inpatient Schizophrenic $N = 100c$	Inpatient Depressive $N = 125b$
Range of R	14–30	15–34	14–31	14–28
Correlations of R With				
W	.3098*	.3106*	.0139	−.1637
D	.6171**	.5252**	.4245**	.8721**
M	.0377	.1314	.1207	.1490
FM+m	.2199	.2299*	.2573*	.2807*
Pair	.2356	.0771	.2073	.2765*
Popular	.2597	−.0172	.1184	.1155
Zf	.3800**	.3135*	.2794*	.1279
Blends	.3168*	.2522*	.3338**	.1331
Color resp	.2593	.1537	.2474	.2888*
EA	.3259*	.2174	.2173	.2168
es	.2699	.2070	.2794	.2505*
Afr	.1816	.0951	.0910	.1049
3r+(2)/R	−.0930	−.1139	.1357	−.0659
Lambda	.0536	.0800	−.0904	−.0316
X+%	−.1932	−.2057	−.1397	−.2081
Xu%	.3009	.2413*	.2072	.1265
X−%	.0113	−.0052	.2082	.2501*

* = significant, $p < .01$; ** = significant, $p < .001$
a = *r* of .302 is significant at .01, *r* of .379 is significant at .001
b = *r* of .228 is significant at .01, *r* of .314 is significant at .001
c = *r* of .254 is significant at .01, *r* of .321 is significant at .001

partialing might or might not be important, especially when considered in terms of power estimates. Obviously, R does correlate with some variables at statistically significant levels for some groups, but a close examination of the correlations reveals that only those related to D (common location area) consistently account for more than 10% of the variance. Any researcher should always be concerned about whether differences in R across groups affect the frequency distributions for any of the various codes, thereby requiring some form of partialing or normalizing for purposes of data analyses. However, this usually will not be an issue of major importance.

RETEST RELIABILITY

The Rorschach scores that are used to form a basis for interpretation include frequency data for specific variables plus numerous percentages, ratios, and other derivations that are calculated from them. Collectively, they represent the Structural Summary of a record. A sample Structural Summary, derived from the codings for the Rorschach protocol shown in Table 8.1, is shown as Table 8.3.

The top portion of the Structural Summary consists mainly of the frequency data for each of the codes. These frequencies are then used for the creation of 49 variables and six indices, presented as ratios, percentages, frequencies, and derivations shown in the lower portion of the Structural Summary. This collective of variables relates to various response styles and other features of the individual that generally fall into seven broad categories related to psychological organization and/or functioning. They include (a) the capacity for control and tolerance for stress, (b) ways in which the subject handles emotion, (c) characteristics of processing new information, (d) the manner in which new information is translated, (e) the manner in which new information is conceptualized, (f) issues of self-perception, and (g) issues of interpersonal perception and behavior.

The diverse nature of these data pose numerous questions concerning the reliability of the test. Most psychological tests are expected to demonstrate some sort of internal consistency. That is not possible for the Rorschach, and attempts to confirm an internal consistency of Rorschach codes have yielded rather dismal results. This is because it is impossible to equate the complexity, simplicity, or difficulty levels of the various blots. The stimulus characteristics of each blot differ substantially from those in all of the other blots. Thus, the issue of test reliability has been addressed through studies concerning temporal consistency or test–retest reliability. Therefore, the issue of temporal consistency has a very important relationship to issues of validation.

TABLE 8.3
Structural Summary for a 41-Year-Old Female

Location Features	Determinants Blends	Single	Contents	S-Constellation
Zf = 15	m.FY	M = 2	H = 3, 0	NO . . FV+VF+V+FD>2
ZSum = 47.0	M.m.FY	FM = 3	(H) = 1, 0	YES . . Col-Shd Bl>0
ZEst = 49.0	m.CF	m = 0	Hd = 1, 0	YES . . Ego<.31,>.44
	M.C.FD	FC = 1	(Hd) = 0, 0	YES . . MOR > 3
	FD.FT	CF = 0	Hx = 0, 0	NO . . Zd > +- 3.5
W = 15	m.FT	C = 1	A = 4, 0	YES . . es > EA
(Wv = 1)	m.YF.CF	Cn = 0	(A) = 0, 1	YES . . CF+C > FC
D = 2	FT.FC.FY	FC′ = 0	Ad = 3, 0	YES . . X+% < .70
Dd = 1		C′F = 0	(Ad) = 0, 0	NO . . S > 3
S = 0		C′ = 0	An = 3, 0	NO . . P < 3 or > 8
		FT = 0	Art = 2, 1	NO . . Pure H < 2
		TF = 0	Ay = 0, 0	NO . . R < 17
DQ		T = 0	Bl = 0, 1	6 . . . . . TOTAL
. . . . . . (FQ-)		FV = 0	Bt = 0, 0	
+ = 9 (2)		VF = 0	Cg = 0, 3	Special Scorings
o = 7 (1)		V = 0	Cl = 0, 1	
v/+ = 1 (0)		FY = 0	Ex = 0, 0	Lv1 Lv2
v = 1 (0)		YF = 0	Fd = 0, 0	DV = 0x1 0x2
		Y = 0	Fi = 0, 0	INC = 0x2 4x4
		Fr = 0	Ge = 0, 0	DR = 1x3 0x6
		rF = 0	Hh = 0, 1	FAB = 0x4 0x7
		FD = 0	Ls = 0, 0	ALOG = 0x5
Form Quality		F = 3	Na = 1, 0	CON = 0x7
			Sc = 0, 0	Raw Sum6 = 5
FQx FQf MQual SQx			Sx = 0, 2	Wgtd Sum6 = 19
+ = 0 0 0 0			Xy = 0, 0	
o = 12 2 2 0			Id = 0, 1	AB = 0 CP = 0
u = 2 0 2 0				AG = 0 MOR = 7
- = 3 1 0 0				CFB = 0 PER = 3
none = 1 — 0 0		(2) = 5		COP = 2 PSV = 0

Ratios, Percentages, and Derivations

R = 18	L = 0.20		FC:CF+C = 2: 4	COP = 2 AG = 0
			Pure C = 2	Food = 0
EB = 4: 6.0	EA = 10.0	EBPer = 1.5	SumC′:WSumC = 0:6.0	Isolate/R = 0.22
eb = 8: 7	es = 15	D = -1	Afr = 0.50	H: (H)Hd(Hd) = 3: 2
	Adj es = 8	Adj D = 0	S = 0	(HHd) : (AAd) = 1: 1
			Blends:R = 8:18	H+A:Hd+Ad = 9: 4
FM = 3 : C′ = 0	T = 3		CP = 0	

			P = 8	Zf = 15	3r+(2)/R = 0.28
a:p = 7: 5	Sum6 = 5		X+% = 0.67	Zd = -2.0	Fr+rF = 0
Ma:Mp = 2: 2	Lv2 = 4		F+% = 0.67	W:D:Dd = 15: 2: 1	FD = 2
2AB+Art+Ay = 3	WSum6 = 19		X-% = 0.17	W:M = 15: 4	An+Xy = 3
M- = 0	Mnone = 0		S-% = 0.00	DQ+ = 9	MOR = 7
			Xu% = 0.11	DQv = 1	

SCZI = 2	DEPI = 3	CDI = 1	S-CON = 6	HVI = No	OBS = No

Table 8.4 provides data from two temporal consistency studies of Rorschach codes (Exner, 1993). It includes retest data for two groups of nonpatient adults. One group of 35 subjects was retested 3 weeks after the baseline test. The second group of 50 subjects was retested after 1 year. It will be noted that the retest reliability data are substantial for most of the variables but very low for five. It is reasonable to argue that, hypothetically, codes manifesting retest coefficients greater than .70 in both studies probably reflect some trait-like feature. Conversely, where the retest data in either study produce coefficients less than .71, the question has been whether to

TABLE 8.4

Correlation Coefficients for 26 Variables or Variable Combinations for Two
Groups of Nonpatient Adults Retested After 3 Weeks and 1 Year

Variable	Description	35 Adults 3 Week Retest *r*	50 Adults 1 Year Retest *r*
R	No. Responses	.84	.86
Codes			
P	Popular Responses	.81	.83
Zf	Z frequency	.89	.85
F	Pure Form	.76	.74
M	Human Movement	.83	.84
FM	Animal Movement	.72	.77
m	Inanimate Movement	.34*	.26*
a	Active Movement	.87	.83
p	Passive Movement	.85	.72
FC	Form Color Responses	.92	.86
CF	Color Form Responses	.68*	.58*
C	Pure Color Responses	.59*	.56*
CF+C	Color Dominant Responses	.83	.81
SumT	Texture Responses	.96	.91
SumC'	Achromatic Color Responses	.67*	.73
SumY	Diffuse Shading Responses	.41*	.31*
SumV	Vista Responses	.89	.87
FD	Dimension Responses	.90	.88
Fr+rF	Reflection Responses	.89	.82
(2)	Pair Responses	.83	.81
Special Scores (Codes)			
DV+DR	Deviant Responses	.86	.82
INC+FAB	Inappropriate Combinations	.92	.89
ALOG	Faulty Judgement	.93	.90
COP	Cooperative Movement	.88	.81
AG	Aggressive Movement	.86	.82
MOR	Morbid Content	.83	.71

* indicates that this variable is temporally inconsistent

discard these codes or to study their possible validity as state-related variables. This issue has been addressed by studying the actual scores derived from the codes. Table 8.5 provides data concerning the same two temporal consistency studies for various Rorschach scores that are derived from the frequency data.

It will be noted that the distribution of scores for 14 of the 15 scores appear to be reasonably consistent over both the short- and long-term retest intervals. The fifteenth, *es*, is considerably less stable over both the short and long intervals, a finding that is not surprising because the *es* includes the coding variables *m* and *Y*, both of which are temporally inconsistent.

Another approach to studying the temporal consistency of Rorschach codes and scores is by categorization. Table 8.6 provides data for the same 85 adult subjects for 14 scores.

The categories shown are defined in terms of validation data; that is, they are selected in terms of cut-off scores to study the issue of whether a second test yields a code frequency or a score for a particular variable that remains in the same interpretive range as was found in the first test. It will be noted from examination of Table 8.6 that more than 90% of the subjects in each group have ratios or scores in their second record for the variables listed that fall into the same range as for the first test. In fact, the baseline and retest distributions are identical for 4 of the 14 variables in the short-term retest group and 3 of the 14 variables for the long-term retest group.

TABLE 8.5
Correlation Coefficients for 15 Rorschach Scores for Two Groups
of Nonpatient Adults Retested After 3 Weeks and 1 Year

Variable	Description	35 Adults 3 Week Retest r	50 Adults 1 Year Retest r
EA	Experience Actual	.84	.83
es	Experience Stimulation	.59*	.64*
Adjes	Adjusted es	.85	.82
L	Lambda	.76	.78
X+%	Conventional Form Use	.87	.86
Xu%	Unconventional Form Use	.89	.85
X–%	Distorted Form Use	.88	.92
WSumC	Weighted Sum Color	.83	.82
Afr	Affective Ratio	.85	.82
Blends	Multiple Determinants	.71	.74
Sum6	Sum Special Scores	.81	.81
WSum6	Weighted Sum Special Scores	.86	.86
Intell	Intellectualization Index	.88	.84
3r+(2)/R	Egocentricity Index	.90	.89
Isolate/R	Isolation Index	.83	.84

* indicates that this variable is temporally inconsistent

TABLE 8.6

Categorial Consistency by Subject for 14 Rorschach Scores for Two Groups of Nonpatient Adults Retested After 3 Weeks and 1 Year With Superscript Indicating Number of Subjects Shifting Categories

Variable	Categories (A)	Categories (B)	35 Adults Baseline (A)	35 Adults Baseline (B)	35 Adults 3 Week Retest (A)	35 Adults 3 Week Retest (B)	50 Adults Baseline (A)	50 Adults Baseline (B)	50 Adults 1 Year Retest (A)	50 Adults 1 Year Retest (B)
EB[a]	Introversive	Extratensive	16	13	16	13	22	18	21^1	18
L	< 1.0	> 0.99	28	7	30^2	5^2	42	8	43^1	7^1
EA	> 6 & < 11	>10	21	8	19^2	10^2	35	11	33^2	13^2
EA	< 6.5	> 6	6	29	5^1	30^1	4	46	4	46
es[b]	> 3 & < 10	> 9	25	6	23^2	8^2	43	5	42^1	6^1
Adjes[b]	> 3 & < 10	> 9	32	2	32	2	46	3	43^3	6^3
FC:CF+C	FC≥CF+C	CF+C>FC	19	16	20^1	15^1	27	23	26^1	24^1
Afr	< .55	> .54	6	29	7^1	28^1	7	43	9^2	41^2
X+%	> 59%	< 60%	31	4	32^1	3^1	47	3	47	3
Xu%	< 21%	> 20%	19	16	18^1	17^1	38	12	36^2	14^2
X–%	< 20%	> 19%	32	3	29^3	6^3	44	6	43^1	7^1
a:p	a+1 ≥ p	p > a+1	33	2	33	2	47	3	46^1	4^1
WSum6	< 7.0	> 6.5	29	6	30^1	5^1	43	7	43	7
COP	0 or 1	> 1	12	23	11^1	24^1	17	33	18^1	32^1
MOR	< 3	> 2	31	4	32^1	3^1	44	6	46^2	4^2
3r+(2)/R[c]	> .32 & < .44	> .43	22	9	22	9	31	10	32^1	9^1
3r+(2)/R	< .33	> .32	4	31	4	31	6	44	4^2	46^2

Totals less than N because: [a] = ambitents are excluded; [b] = values less than 4 are excluded; [c] = values < .33 are excluded

These findings are not very surprising when considered in light of results from two other short-term retest studies. In each, subjects were retested after a 3 or 4 day interval and a random half of the subjects were asked to remember the responses that they gave in the first test and avoid giving those responses in the second test. One consisted of retesting of 60 8-year-old nonpatient children (Exner, 1980), and the second involved the retesting of 50 first admission adults with preliminary diagnoses of affective disorder (Haller & Exner, 1985). A comparison of responses in the retest with those given in the first test reveal that the 30 children asked to avoid repeating responses did give about 75% of different responses in the second test than those in the first test, whereas the 30 control children repeated more than 80% of their first test answers. The 25 adult subjects asked to avoid repeating answers gave approximately 65% different answers in the second test, whereas the 25 control subjects repeated about two thirds of their answers.

The retest correlations for both the experimental and control groups in each of these studies are very similar to the retest correlations shown in Tables 8.4 and 8.5, and categorical data for both groups in each study are very similar to the data shown in Table 8.6. In other words, even when different responses are given, the retest data, whether studied correlationally or categorically, show very little change. These findings suggest that most of these scores are, in some way, representative of enduring features.

ISSUES OF VALIDITY

In that most of the codes and derived scores manifest a respectable temporal consistency, the issue of what characteristics are being measured by these codes or scores becomes central to any evaluation of the Rorschach. As mentioned earlier, the composite of Rorschach scores and frequencies seem to relate to seven different aspects of psychological functioning. It is impractical to discuss all of the variables related to each but, for purposes of illustration, it seems appropriate to describe some of the validity studies related to three different types of structural variables that appear to be related to trait-like features. One is a simple variable consisting of frequency data. The second is a ratio based on frequency data, and the third is a numerical score.

COOPERATIVE MOVEMENT RESPONSES (COP)

The first is the special score (code) COP, which is used to identify cooperative movement responses. COP is coded for any movement answer in which the interaction between two or more humans or animals is unequivocally positive or cooperative, such as men trying to lift something, people dancing, children playing, a bird feeding her young, wolves attacking another animal, and so forth. Cooperative movement answers appear at least once in almost 80% of adult nonpatient records, in about two thirds of outpatient protocols, about 50% of the records from inpatient schizophrenics and depressives, and less than 40% of the protocols from character disorders.

Cooperative movement is not easily reported on some cards. It is almost nonexistent in responses to Cards IV and VI and has a very low frequency in responses to Card V. It occurs in about 15% to 20% of the movement responses on Cards I, VIII, IX, and X. It occurs most frequently in responses to Cards II, III, and VII.

The frequency of COP responses appears to provide some important information concerning an attitude or orientation that the subject may have concerning interactions between people. Table 8.7 provides an abbreviated summary of some studies related to cooperative movement responses.

The first investigation concerning the interpretive usefulness of the COP Special Score was a sociometric study (Exner & Farber, 1983). Peer nominations were collected from 25 third-year high-school students and 35 female college freshmen living in the same dormitory. Analysis of the data revealed that the 16 subjects who gave more than two COP answers were nominated significantly more often than any other subjects for three items: (a) is the most fun to be with, (b) is the easiest to be around, and (c) is the most trustworthy. Nine subjects whose records contained no COP responses were never nominated by any of their peers for any those three items. However, those nine subjects did receive the most nominations for three relatively negative items: (a) is the person I know least about, (b) is a person who does not seem to have many friends, and (c) I would probably not vote for this person for a class office.

COP also appears to relate to group therapy interactions (Exner, 1988). A review of audio recordings of 17 subjects in two groups, taken in three group therapy sessions, reveals that the four participants who gave more than two COP responses in their Rorschachs talked more frequently, for longer intervals, and directed remarks more to other group members than did the other 13 subjects in the groups. Six subjects with no COP responses in their Rorschachs talked least frequently and directed remarks to the therapists more often than to others in the groups.

Another study regarding the interpretive meaningfulness of COP responses focused on interpersonal adjustment following termination from treatment (Exner, 1988). It involved a stratified random sample of 70 outpatients drawn from a pool of subjects who volunteered to participate in multiple retest study. The criteria for selection was fourfold: (a) that each entered treatment because of interpersonal problems, (b) that each participated in the retest study for at least 2 years, (c) that each had terminated treatment before the 18th month, and (d) that the pretreatment protocol contained no more than one COP

TABLE 8.7

A Summary of Studies Regarding Cooperative Movement (COP) Responses

Design	Subjects	Findings
Peer Nominations (Exner & Farber, 1983)	25 High School and 35 1st Year College Students	1. COP > 2 (N = 16) Most nominations as: "more fun to be with," "easiest to be around," "most trustworthy" 2. COP = 0 (N = 9) Most nominations as: "the person I know least," "a person who does not seem to have many friends," "a person I probably would not vote for class office"
Audio Recordings of group therapy interaction (Exner, 1988)	17 adult outpatients in two groups recorded during 3 sessions	1. COP > 2 (N = 4) a. Talked most frequently b. Talked for longer intervals c. Talked most frequently to other group members 2. COP = 0 (N = 6) a. talked less frequently than other group members b. talked to therapist more frequently than others
Posttreatment Adjustment Retest 18 to 20 mos. after pretreatment test IP adjustment judged by self-report (Exner, 1988)	70 outpatients treated for interpersonal (IP) problems. All had terminated treatment.	1. Pretreatment COP Frequencies & Self Report Data a. COP = 0 (N = 31) Mean IP Adjustment Rating = 3.5 (Range 1.0 to 6.0) b. COP = 1 (N = 39) Mean IP Adjustment Rating = 4.5 (Range 0.5 to 6.5) 2. Posttreatment COP Frequencies & Self Report Data a. COP = 0 (N = 18) Mean IP Adjustment Rating = 5.0 (Range 2.5 to 7.5 with 8 rating less than 5.0 & 5 of the 8 reentered treatment)

TABLE 8.7 (*Continued*)

171

Study	Sample	Results
Posttreatment Adjustment—Retest at discharge, 21 to 45 days after admission Adjustment by self-report 9 to 10 mos postdischarge on an 8-point scale (KAS) (Exner, 1991)	100 first admission adults diagnosed as affective disorder	b. COP = 1 (N = 15) Mean IP Adjustment Rating = 6.0 (Range 4.0 to 8.5 with 3 rating less than 5.0 & 1 of the 3 reentered treatment) c. COP > 1 (N = 37) Mean IP Adjustment Rating = 7.5 (Range 5.5 to 9.0) Post Discharge COP Frequencies & Self-Report 1. COP = 0 (N = 34) Mean Adjustment Rating = 3.1 (Range 1.5 to 6.0 with 16 rating less than 4.0 & 9 of the 16 rehospitalized) 2. COP = 1 (N = 29) Mean Adjustment Rating = 3.8 (Range 1.0 to 7.0 with 10 rating less than 4.0 & 6 of the 10 rehospitalized) 3. COP > 1 (N = 37) Mean Adjustment Rating = 4.9 (Range 2.5 to 7.5 with 7 rating less than 4.0 & 3 of the 7 rehospitalized)
Observed Prosocial Behaviors: picking up books, sitting closest to examiner, help moving chairs (Alexander, 1993)	50 nonpatient adults	1. COP = 0 (N = 15) Mean Prosocial Behavior Score = 0.8 (Range 0 to 2) 2. COP = 1 (N = 19) Mean Prosocial Behavior Score = 1.7 (Range 1 to 3) 2. COP > 1 (N = 16) Mean Prosocial Behavior Score = 2.4 (Range 2 to 3)
Early Termination (Exner, 1995)	168 outpatients	COP > 1 plus AG (aggressive movement) = 0 loads positively as postdictor of early termination for patients in dynamic and cognitive therapy (N = 28)
Early Termination (Hilsenroth et al., 1995)	188 patients in university clinic	COP > 1 loads positively as a postdictor of early termination (N = 97)
Sexual Homocide (Gacono & Meloy, 1994)	20 Cases	1. COP = 0 (N = 6) 2. COP = 1 or 2 (N = 9) 3. COP > 2 (N = 5)

response. Actually, 31 pretreatment protocols contained no COP and 39 protocols contained one COP response. In the second retest in this study, taken between the 18th and 20th month after the onset of treatment and at a time when all had terminated treatment, 37 of the 70 subjects gave at least two COP responses in their Rorschachs and 29 of the 37 gave more than two COP answers. Fifteen of the subjects had one COP response in their second retest and the remaining 18 had no COP responses, and none of those 18 had COP responses in their pretreatment record.

The Katz Adjustment Scale (KAS–S), modified to include a 10-point self-rating concerning interpersonal adjustment (IP), was administered prior to treatment and concurrently with each of the retests. The mean pretreatment IP rating for those with no COP in their baseline Rorschachs was 3.5 and 4.5 for those with one COP in their baseline records. After 18 to 20 months, the mean IP rating for 37 subjects with two or more COP responses in their retest was 7.5 as contrasted with a mean IP of 6.0 for 15 subjects having one COP response in their retest, and a mean IP of 5.0 for 18 participants having no COP in their retest. None of the 37 having more than one COP in their retest had reentered treatment and all gave IP ratings greater than 5.0. Three of the 15 having only one COP had IP ratings less than 5.0 and one of the three had reentered treatment. Eight of the 18 having no COP had IP ratings of less than 5.0 and five had reentered treatment.

Another treatment affects study concerning cooperative movement involved follow-up data for 100 first admission inpatient affective disorders (Exner, 1991). A review of the pretreatment Rorschach records for this group indicate that 31 contained two or more COP responses, 36 contained one COP response, and 33 had no COP answers. At discharge (21 to 45 days after admission), all subjects were retested and 37 retest records contained two or more COP responses, 29 had one COP, and 34 had no COP responses. Adjustment at between 9 and 10 months following discharge was evaluated using the KAS-S, modified to include an eight-point scale concerning overall adjustment (OA). The mean OA rating for the 37 subjects who had two or more COP responses at discharge was 4.9 with seven of the 37 rating themselves less than 4.0. Three of those seven had been rehospitalized. The mean OA rating for the 29 subjects having one COP in their discharge records was 3.8 with 10 rating less than 4.0 and six of those 10 had been rehospitalized. The mean OA rating for the 34 participants with no COP answers in their discharge records was 3.1 with 16 rating themselves less than 4.0 and nine of the 16 had been rehospitalized.

Alexander (1993) recorded prosocial behaviors; that is, instances in which each of 50 subjects manifest positive and/or cooperative behaviors in each of three contrived interpersonal situations. In one, a confederate feigned distress and/or helplessness after dropping a pile of books. The second involved whether the participant elected to sit closer or further away from an examiner during testing, and the third focused on whether the participant assisted in rearranging chairs after testing was completed. The 50 subjects, ranging in age from 18 to 65, included 36 undergraduate students from two universities plus 14 nonstudent adults from various middle and upper-middle class occupational groups. Seven tests were administered, including the Rorschach. Sixteen gave Rorschachs that contained more than one COP response, 19 gave one COP answer, and the remaining 15 gave no COP. The maximum possible score for prosocial behaviors was 3. The 16 participants who had given more than one COP averaged 2.4, those who gave one COP averaged 1.7, and those with no COP averaged 0.8. Alexander also reported that COP is highly correlated with self-reported empathy and self-reported altruism.

Although the results of these studies suggest that the presence of cooperative movement in a Rorschach is a favorable finding related to interpersonal attitudes or behaviors, other data suggest that it is unwise to interpret COP as an isolated variable. For instance, ongoing research (Shaffer & Erdberg, 1996) suggests that some types of COP responses should be regarded much less favorably than others, and in fact, the presence or absence of several other variables in the Rorschach all might well alter the seemingly positive finding even if two or more COP appear in a record. Two studies indicate that COP seems related to premature termination from treatment. The first (Exner, 1995) is a treatment effects study of 168 outpatients in cognitive or dynamic therapy, 41 of whom terminated prematurely (prior to the eighth week of treatment). The combination of more than two pure Human responses, more than one COP response, and the absence of aggressive movement responses appears in the protocols of 28 of the 41 early terminators. The second (Hilsenroth, Handler, Toman, & Padawar, 1995) is an archival study of 188 patients at a university clinic, including 97 who terminated treatment prematurely (fewer than eight sessions). The early terminators averaged more than twice as many COP responses in their Rorschachs when compared to a group of 81 patients who remained in treatment until termination was mutually agreed.

Possibly the most striking findings that caution against casually interpreting the presence of COP answers in a positive framework are those published by Gacano and Meloy (1994). They studied the Rorschachs of 20 individuals adjudicated for sexual homocide and found that only six contained no COP responses, nine contained one or two COP answers, and five gave protocols with more than two COP responses.

ACTIVE–PASSIVE MOVEMENT RATIO ($a:p$)

Rorschach (1921) postulated that differences in the type of movement answers could be used to discriminate features of personality. He suggested a differentiation of flexion or extension, the former being defined as those in which the action is toward the center of the blot, the latter for those in which the action pulled away from the center axis of the blot. He hypothesized that extensor movement answers reflect assertiveness, whereas flexor answers indicate submissiveness of compliance. Two studies reported during the 1950s (Hammer & Jacks, 1955; Mirin, 1955) offered some modest support for his hypothesis, however, both Beck, Beck, Levitt, and Molish (1961) and Piotrowski (1957) warned about the limitations of approaching movement answers using Rorschach's flexor–extensor concept. Beck correctly pointed out that many movement answers do not meet either of those criteria because they are static, such as a person standing, sleeping, or looking, whereas Piotrowski proposed a broader differentiation of movement answers using categories such as cooperativeness, lack of restraint, confident postures, assertiveness, and passivity. Piotrowski demonstrated that these categories, especially assertiveness and passivity in human movement answers, enabled a differentiation between effective and nonadaptive parole conduct of released army prisoners and successful versus unsuccessful business executives. The Piotrowski findings were quite influential to the decision to use the superscripts a and p to differentiate active and passive movement answers in the coding format of the Comprehensive System.

Some early research findings, derived from modest-size samples, indicated that substantially greater proportions of active movement appear in the records of acute schizophrenics and subjects with a history of assaultiveness, however, those findings have not replicated in larger-size samples. In fact, numerous investigations designed to study the relation between active movement and various behaviors have yielded negative findings. In other words, a high frequency of active movement responses does not equate with an unusual frequency of active behaviors, or with any special class of behaviors. This is apparently because most people give more active than passive movement responses, as will be noted in some descriptive statistics for 11 groups shown in Table 8.8.

Adult nonpatients tend to give about twice as many active movement answers as passive responses and only about 2% are positive when the criterion of $p > a + 1$ is applied. The proportion of nonpatient children who have $a:p$ ratios in which $p > a + 1$ range from 2 to 12%, depending on the age group. As is noted from Table 8.8, patient groups tend to have higher proportions of subjects for whom the frequency of passive movement is greater than the frequency of active movement plus 1. This finding is positive for about 19% of first admission schizophrenics and about 23% of first admission depressives and a group of character disorders.

There are three groups shown in Table 8.8 for which the $p > a + 1$ criterion is positive for a very substantial proportion of subjects. They are introversive outpatients, passive–dependent personality disorders, and outpatients described by their therapist as being excessively passive. The find-

TABLE 8.8
Some Descriptive Statistics Concerning Active & Passive
Movement and the a:p Ratio for 11 Groups

Group	N	Active Mean	Active SD	Passive Mean	Passive SD	$p > a + 1$ N	$p > a + 1$ %
Nonpatient Adults Introversive*	150	7.9	2.1	3.6	1.6	4	2%
Nonpatient Adults Extratensive*	150	5.4	1.6	2.1	1.1	3	2%
Nonpatient Adults Ambitent*	150	6.2	1.9	2.5	1.5	2	1%
First Admission Schizophrenics	320	5.5	3.9	4.3	3.2	60	19%
First Admission Inpatient Depressives	315	4.8	3.1	3.7	2.5	72	23%
Adult Character Disorders	180	2.8	2.3	2.4	1.9	42	23%
Outpatients Introversive*	154	4.7	2.4	5.2	2.3	81	53%
Outpatients Extratensive*	168	4.2	1.5	1.9	1.8	12	7%
Outpatients Ambitent*	173	3.9	2.6	2.7	2.0	37	21%
Outpatients—Passive Dependent Personality	54	3.3	1.9	4.6	2.0	41	79%
Outpatients described by therapists as excessively passive	79	3.6	1.8	4.4	2.1	56	71%

*Excludes subjects with Lambda > 0.99

ings for the latter two groups led to the postulate that the criterion $p > a + 1$ reflects a critical cutoff for the *a:p* ratio from which a stylistic response tendency appears to be identified. Essentially, if the value for passive movement exceeds the value for active movement by more than one point, it indicates that the subject generally will assume a more passive, although not necessarily submissive, role in interpersonal relations.

Findings indicate that people with this feature usually prefer to avoid responsibility for decision making and are less prone to search out new solutions to problems or initiate new patterns of behavior. An abbreviated summary of some of these findings is shown in Table 8.9.

The first test of this hypothesis involved a study (Exner, 1974) in which 34 adult females were paid to induce a 10-minute period of daydreaming on each of 25 consecutive days and to record those daydreams in a diary. The activity of the central figure in the daydream was scored as being active or passive, for whether a shift from one characteristic to the other occurred and whether the central figure was responsible for the outcome. Those scores were then compared with the data from the *a:p* ratios in the Rorschachs of the participants that had been collected prior to the onset of the daydream routine. Twenty of the 34 subjects had *a:p* ratios in which the value for active movement plus 1 was equal or greater than the value for passive movement. Nearly 75% of the daydreams of these subjects included a central figure in the daydream who tended to be active, and the outcome was usually the result of the action of the central subject. The remaining 14

TABLE 8.9

A Summary of Studies Regarding the Active:Passive (a:p) Ratio When p > a + 1

Design	Subjects	Findings
10 minute deliberate daydreams recorded for 25 days & central figure scored for being active or passive & outcome involvement (Exner, 1974)	34 adult females who had taken the Rorschach as part of a standardization sample	1. a + 1 ≥ p (N = 20) 366 of the 500 (73%) daydreams were marked by an active central figure who was responsible for the outcome 2. p + 1 > a (N = 14) 224 of the 350 (64%) daydreams were marked by a passive central figure. Other characters in the daydream were responsible for the outcome in 202 (91%) of the 224
Completion of 6 TAT stories which were scored for outcome, new people included, who was responsible for outcome (Exner, Armbruster, & Wylie, 1976)	25 nonpatient adults (12 male, 13 female) who had taken the Rorschach as part of a standardization sample	1. a + 1 ≥ p (N = 13) a. 70 of 78 outcomes positive b. In 17 of 78 (22%) stories, new characters were added c. 21 of 78 (27%) outcomes initiated by person other than central character 2. p + 1 > a (N = 12) a. 69 of the 72 outcomes positive b. In 38 of 72 (53%) stories, new characters were added c. 49 of 72 (68%) outcomes initiated by person other than central character
Behavioral passivity ratings by significant others (KAS) (Exner, 1978)	166 outpatients in treatment effects study	1. a + 1 ≥ p (N = 83) Mean KAS Rating for behavioral passivity = 5.3 (SD = 3.3) 2. p > a + 1 (N = 83) Mean KAS Rating for behavioral passivity = 11.6 (SD = 4.2)
Ratings for verbal and nonverbal dependency behaviors from videos of two assertiveness training sessions (Exner & Kazaoka, 1978)	16 adults who voluntarily entered assertiveness training	1. a + 1 ≥ p (N = 9) a. Mean verbal dependency gestures = 6.3 (SD = 3.1) b. Mean nonverbal dependency gestures = 3.9 (SD = 2.2) 2. p > a + 1 (N = 7) a. Mean verbal dependency gestures = 10.6 (SD = 3.9) b. Mean nonverbal dependency gestures = 5.8 (SD = 3.2)

177

participants had $a{:}p$ ratios in which the value for passive movement was greater than the value of active movement plus 1. About 64% of the day-dreams recorded by these women included a central figure clearly described in a passive role, and more than 90% of the outcomes were typically attributed to the actions of other characters in the daydream.

A variation of this design was used in a study (Exner, Armbruster, & Wylie, 1976) involving 24 nonpatient adults who had been administered Rorschachs for the normative sample. Each had given at least nine movement responses, and 12 had given more active than M passive movement, whereas the remaining 12 had given more passive than active movement. They were asked to write endings for each of six TAT stories that had been created to present dilemma situations. For example, the figure in Card 3BM was featured as having lost a job, the boy in 13B was described as having wandered away from a picnic and was lost, and so on. The story endings were scored for (a) positive or negative outcome, (b) outcomes involving new people injected into the story, and (c) outcomes initiated by the central figure of the story versus those contingent on the actions of someone else. The majority of the outcomes were positive (88%) and did not differentiate the two groups. The 12 participants with more passive movement added new people to 38 of the 72 endings (53%), whereas those with more active movement added new people to only 17 of their endings (24%). The most striking difference concerned the initiation of outcomes. Forty nine of the 72 outcomes given by the high passive movement group (68%) were initiated by someone other than the central figure of the story. The high active movement group did this in only 21 (29%) of their endings (p < .01).

In another study (Exner, 1978) an index of behavioral passivity was devised using 20 items in the Katz Adjustment Scale, Form R. The entire KAS–R was completed for 279 outpatients by a significant other of the patient 9 months after treatment had been initiated. All subjects were volunteers in a long-term treatment effects study, the design of which required psychological testing and behavioral evaluations at 9-month intervals for at least 3 years, regardless of whether treatment had terminated. Examination of the Rorschachs collected at the 9-month interval revealed that 83 of the 279 subjects had $a{:}p$ ratios in which p exceeded a by more than 1. Their mean score for the KAS–R passivity index was 11.6 (SD = 4.2). A comparison group of 83 other patients was randomly drawn from the remaining 196 subjects. The mean passivity score for that group was 5.3 (SD = 3.3), reflecting a very substantial difference between the groups (p < .001).

In another related study (Exner & Kazaoka, 1978), videotapes were recorded for the first two sessions of two groups of eight subjects participating in assertiveness training. Rorschachs were administered prior to the training, and revealed that 7 of the 16 trainees had $a{:}p$ ratios in which p exceeded a by more than 1. The videotapes were scored for the frequencies of verbal and nonverbal dependency gestures by subject, by two groups of three raters each. One group of raters scored only the audio segment of the tapes, whereas the second group scored using both the audio and visual data. The seven subjects who began the training with the passive $a{:}p$ ratios were scored for nearly twice as many verbal dependency statements and approximately the same number of nonverbal dependency gestures during the two sessions, as were the other 11 subjects.

As with the COP response, it is important to note that the $a{:}p$ ratio data should not be interpreted in isolation. Findings for other variables are often important in attempting to discern how the passive style is most commonly manifest in behavior and whether it should be regarded as a liability in the context of the overall adjustment of the individual.

CRITICAL SPECIAL SCORES: SUM6 AND WSUM6

During the early 1970s, after the basic coding format for the Comprehensive System had been selected, a series of projects were undertaken to focus on the possible use of so-called Special Scores; that is, codes that could be applied systematically to identify special features of responses about which intelligently thought-through hypotheses had been put forth, such as cooperative movement answers discussed earlier. Among the more important of these was a project designed to sort through a substantial number of suggested codes that might be used to identify instances in which some difficulty occurred in various aspects of thinking.

Rapaport, Gill, and Schafer (1946), and Weiner (1961) had suggested more than 20 such codes, however, the criteria often overlapped and a simple pilot study indicated major problems concerning intercoder reliability. Gradually, most were discarded but six were redefined and retained (Exner, Weiner, & Schuyler, 1976). They include: (a) Deviant Verbalization (DV), assigned when an incorrect word, neologism, or redundant wording is used; (b) Deviant Response (DR), assigned for strange or peculiar wording that involves inappropriate phrasing or circumstantiality; (c) Incongruous Combinations (INCOM) assigned for instances in which implausible characteristics are attributed to a single object; (d) Fabulized Combinations (FABCOM) assigned when an implausible relationship between two or more objects is reported; (e) Autistic Logic (ALOG) assigned when, without prompting, strained reasoning is used to justify an answer; and (f) Contamination (CONTAM), assigned when two or more impressions are fused in a single response in a manner that clearly violates reality.

A major objective related to the selection of these Special Scores concerned the correct identification of schizophrenia. It was postulated that, because that condition is marked by serious problems in thinking, the records of schizophrenics would include significantly more of these six Special Scores

(Sum6), and especially the three that, at face value, reflect more serious forms of cognitive mismanagement or dysfunctioning; that is, FABCOM, ALOG, and CONTAM answers. During the next few years, a substantial number of protocols collected from adult patients tended to support that proposition and, in fact, a five-variable Schizophrenia Index (SCZI) was created (Exner, 1983). Two of the five variables (Sum6 > 4; Sum FABCOM + ALOG + CONTAM > Sum DV + DR + INCOM) related directly to these six Special Scores. However, as the number of records from inpatient affective disorders and both patient and nonpatient children accumulated, serious challenges concerning the diagnostic efficacy of the SCZI evolved. The data in Table 8.10 can be used to illustrate the sources of some of these challenges.

It will be noted that the mean, median, and mode for the Sum6 is actually greater for 5- to 8-year-old nonpatient children than the schizophrenic group, and the mean, median, and mode for 9- to 12-year-old nonpatient children is almost the same as for schizophrenics. Similarly, the means for Sum6 for both outpatients and first admission depressives are not enormously different than for schizophrenics and, in fact, the frequency range for outpatients is actually greater than for schizophrenics.

Another source of challenge to the SCZI appeared when the frequencies of the three more serious Special Scores, FABCOM, ALOG, and CONTAM were reviewed in a new schizophrenia sample and compared to two large samples of affective disorder records. It was found that they occurred among the affective disorders almost as often as among the schizophrenia group. This raised a question about the breadth of responses being coded in each of the six Special Score categories.

TABLE 8.10
Descriptive Statistics Concerning the Frequency of
Critical Special Scores* (Sum6) for Eight Groups

Group	N	Mean	SUM6 SD	Range	Median	Mode
NONPATIENTS						
Nonpatient Adults	700	1.59	1.3	0–7	1	1
Nonpatient Children (Ages 5 to 8)	410	6.39	2.2	2–10	6	5
Nonpatient Children (Ages 9 to 12)	515	4.88	1.4	2–9	4	4
Nonpatient Children (Ages 13 to 16)	465	2.60	1.4	0–9	3	2
PATIENTS						
Adult Character Disorders	180	2.62	2.1	0–9	2	2
Outpatients	440	3.48	3.0	0–21	3	2
First Admission Inpatient Depressives	315	3.40	2.2	1–9	3	3
First Admission Schizophrenics	320	5.07	3.2	0–15	5	4

*Includes Deviant Verbalizations (DV), Deviant Response (DR), Incongruous Combinations (INCOM), Fabulized Combinations (FABCOM), Autistic Logic (ALOG), and Contaminations (CONTAM).

This issue was studied by using 600 responses that had been coded for at least one of the six Special Scores reviewed. Two hundred of the responses were from schizophrenic records, 200 were from the protocols of affective disorder patients, and 200 were from the records of nonpatient children, ages 5 to 12. This review indicated that four of the Special Score Categories (DV, DR, INCOM, and FABCOM) include answers that varied considerably in terms of apparent dysfunction. For instance, INCOM was being assigned to such disparate responses as "a bat flying with his antennae out" and "a man with three and a half heads." The second reflects much more cognitive mismanagement than the first. Similarly, "two dogs kissing" seems much less bizarre than "an elephant having intercourse with a butterfly," both of which were correctly scored as FABCOM. Clearly, the criteria were too broad and not accurately accounting for degrees of dysfunctioning.

A twofold solution was devised (Exner, 1991). First, the codings for the four Special Scores DV, DR, INCOM, and FABCOM were revised to include a second level. In other words, the criteria, as originally stated, would continue to be applied; however, they would be coded as Level 1 if they reflect only a mild or modest instance of illogical, fluid, peculiar, or circumstantial thinking, and coded as Level 2 if the answer clearly reflects the presence of a much more severe instance of dissociated, illogical, fluid, or circumstantial thinking, such as "the public arch of a woman" (DV2), "it looks like the face of Clinton if you're a democrat" (DR2), "a marvelous penis with wings" (INCOM2), or "the head of a rabbit with satanic smoke coming from its eyes" (FABCOM2). Figure 8.1 displays a conceptualization of the two-tier coding format in relation to issues of cognitive mismanagement or dysfunctioning.

The recoding of the 600 responses using this two-tier format revealed that Level 2 Special Scores appear in schizophrenic records nearly five times as often as in the records of affective disorders or nonpatient children.

In addition to the two-tier format, a system of weighting (WSum6) was devised for the six Special Scores with values of 1, 2, 3, and 4 assigned to Level 1 DV, INCOM, DR, and FABCOM answers respectively, values of 2, 4, 5, and 7 assigned to Level 2 DV, INCOM, DR, and FABCOM answers respectively, a value of 5 assigned to all ALOG answers, and a value of 7 assigned to all CONTAM responses. Some data concerning the sum of weighted Special Scores is shown in Table 8.11.

It will be noted that the mean WSum6 values for the nonpatient children are considerably less than depressives or schizophrenics and a much more marked differentiation exists across the four patient groups.

DV1 INCOM1 DR1	DV2 FABCOM1 INCOM2 ALOG	DR2 FABCOM2 CONTAM
MILD	MODERATE TO SERIOUS	SEVERE

FIG. 8.1. A continuum illustrating the extent of cognitive mismanagement or dysfunction represented by six special scores with four differentiated into two levels.

TABLE 8.11
Descriptive Statistics Concerning Weighted Scores (WSum6)
Derived From Six Critical Special Scores for Eight Groups

Group	N	Mean	WSUM6 SD	Range	Median	Mode
NONPATIENTS						
Nonpatient Adults	700	3.28	2.9	0–15	3	1
Nonpatient Children (Ages 5 to 8)	410	13.67	4.9	1–29	13	10
Nonpatient Children (Ages 9 to 12)	515	10.27	3.9	2–26	9	7
Nonpatient Children (Ages 13 to 16)	465	6.06	4.8	0–40	5	3
PATIENTS						
Adult Character Disorders	180	11.31	9.9	0–48	8	7
Outpatients	440	9.59	9.8	0–97	8	4
First Admission Inpatient Depressives	315	18.20	13.6	1–55	16	6
First Admission Schizophrenics	320	44.69	35.4	0–173	32	32

CLOSING REMARKS

It is hoped that this brief discourse on approaches to measurement, as used for the Rorschach, adequately differentiates the procedures of Rorschach coding from Rorschach scores or scoring and clarifies the various kinds of scores that form the interpretive nucleus for Rorschach interpretation. It is important to note that the three variables that have been described are by no means the sturdiest in terms of validation data when compared to the remaining 46 variables included in the bottom portion of the Structural Summary. In fact, if the accumulated validation data for some of the other 46 were to be used as a standard, these three might be considered as lightweights in the total group. Nonetheless, each of the three appear sufficiently sturdy to provide some useful information concerning features of the individual. Most of the codes and scores used in the Comprehensive System continue to be studied and it seems reasonable to predict that, as more information concerning the nature of the test and the process of forming responses unfolds, many aspects of Rorschach measurement will become much more precise.

REFERENCES

Alexander, S. E. (1993). *Cooperative movement responses in Rorschach protocols as related to cooperative behavior and self-reported measures of related constructs.* Unpublished doctoral dissertation, Columbia University, New York, NY.

Beck, S. J., Beck, A. G., Levitt, E. E., & Molish, H. B. (1961). *Rorschach's test: Basic processes.* New York: Grune & Stratton.

Cronbach, L. J. (1949). Statistical methods applied to Rorschach scores: A review. *Psychological Bulletin, 46,* 393–429.

Exner, J. E. (1974). *The Rorschach: A comprehensive system* (Vol. 1). New York: Wiley.

Exner, J. E. (1978). *The Rorschach: A comprehensive system* (Vol. 2). *Current research and advanced interpretation.* New York: Wiley.

Exner, J. E. (1980). But it's only an inkblot. *Journal of Personality Assessment, 44,* 562–577.

Exner, J. E. (1983). Additions to the Structural Summary. *Alumni Newsletter.* Asheville, NC: Rorschach Workshops.

Exner, J. E. (1988). Research findings. *Alumni Newsletter.* Asheville, NC: Rorschach Workshops.

Exner, J. E. (1991). *The Rorschach: A comprehensive system* (Vol. 2). *Interpretation* (2nd ed.). New York: Wiley.

Exner, J. E. (1992). *R* in Rorschach research—A ghost revisited. *Journal of Personality Assessment, 58,* 245–251.

Exner, J. E. (1993). *The Rorschach: A comprehensive system* (Vol. 1). *Basic foundations* (3rd ed.). New York: Wiley.

Exner, J. E. (1995). Recent research. *Alumni Newsletter.* Asheville, NC: Rorschach Workshops.

Exner, J. E., Armbruster, G. L., & Wylie, J. R. (1976). *TAT stories and the* M^d:M^p *ratio.* Workshops study 225 (unpublished). Bayville, NY: Rorschach Workshops.

Exner, J. E., & Farber, J. G. (1983). *Peer nominations among female college students living in a dormitory setting.* Workshops study 290 (unpublished). Bayville, NY: Rorschach Workshops.

Exner, J. E., & Kazaoka, K. (1978). *Dependency gestures of 16 assertiveness trainees as related to Rorschach movement responses.* Workshops study 261 (unpublished). Bayville, NY: Rorschach Workshops.

Exner, J. E., Weiner, I. B., & Schuyler, W. (1976). *A Rorschach workbook for the comprehensive system.* Bayville, NY: Rorschach Workshops.

Gacano, C. B., & Meloy, J. R. (1994). *The Rorschach assessment of aggressive and psychopathic personalities.* Hillsdale, NJ: Lawrence Erlbaum Associates.

Hammer, E. F., & Jacks, I. (1955). A Rorschach study of flexor and extensor human movement responses. *Journal of Clinical Psychology, 11,* 63–67.

Haller, N., & Exner, J. E. (1985). The reliability of Rorschach variables for inpatients presenting symptoms of depression and/or helplessness. *Journal of Personality Assessment, 49,* 516–521.

Hilsenroth, M. J., Handler, L., Toman, K. M., & Padawer, J. R. (1995). Rorschach and MMPI-2 indices of early psychotherapy termination. *Journal of Consulting and Clinical Psychology, 63,* 956–965.

Holt, R. R. (1958). Clinical and statistical prediction: A reformulation and some new data. *Journal of Abnormal and Social Psychology, 56,* 1–12.

Holt, R. R. (1970). Yet another look at clinical and statistical prediction: Or, is clinical psychology worthwhile? *American Psychologist, 25,* 337–349.

Holtzman, W. H., Thorpe, J. S., Swartz, J. D., & Herron, E. W. (1961). *Inkblot perception and personality.* Austin: University of Texas Press.

Klopfer, B., & Kelley, D. (1942). *The Rorschach technique.* Yonkers, NY: World Book.

Mirin, B. (1955). The Rorschach human movement response and role taking behavior. *Journal of Nervous and Mental Disorders, 122,* 270–275.

Piotrowski, Z. (1957). *Perceptanalysis.* New York: Macmillan.

Rapaport, D., Gill, M., & Schafer, R. (1946). *Diagnostic psychological testing* (Vol. 2). Chicago: Yearbook.

Rorschach, H. (1921). *Psychodiagnostik.* Bern, Switzerland: Bircher.

Shaffer, T. W., & Erdberg, P. (1996, July). *Cooperative movement in the Rorschach response: A qualitative approach.* 15th International Congress of Rorschach and Projective Methods, Boston, MA.

Weiner, I. B. (1961). *Psychodiagnosis in schizophrenia.* New York: Wiley.

Zubin, J., Eron, L. D., & Schumer, F. (1965). *An experimental approach to projective techniques.* New York: Wiley.

CHAPTER NINE

Searching for Structure in the MMPI

Niels G. Waller

University of California, Davis

The Minnesota Multiphasic Personality Inventory, the MMPI (Hathaway & McKinley, 1940, 1983), and its recent offspring, the MMPI–2 (Butcher, Dahlstrom, Graham, Tellegen, & Kaemmer, 1989), are the most widely used psychopathology measures in the world (Butcher & Rouse, 1996; Lubin, Larsen, Matarazzo, & Seever, 1985). With item pools of unparalleled richness for characterizing psychopathology and many normal-range personality traits, these inventories are the questionnaires of choice in numerous clinical and research contexts (Ben-Porath & Waller, 1992). For these reasons psychologists are keenly interested in the underlying factor structure of the MMPI item pool. Although many have tried to uncover this structure (e.g., Archer & Klinefelter, 1991; Comrey, 1957a, 1957b, 1957c, 1958a, 1958b, 1958c, 1958d; Costa, Zonderman, & Williams, 1985; Johnson, Null, Butcher, & Johnson, 1984; Reddon, Marceau, & Jackson, 1982) a replicable factor structure for the MMPI has yet to be found.

My goals in this chapter are to summarize the literature on the MMPI dimensional structure and to critically evaluate this literature in light of the new rules of measurement that are described in this book. Readers will learn how these psychometric principles can be effectively used to elucidate a psychologically meaningful and psychometrically unbiased structure for the MMPI. To accomplish these goals, I demonstrate how traditional factor methods—as implemented in standard statistical packages such as SAS (SAS Institute, 1989) or SPSS (SPSS Inc., 1994)—produce spurious (artefactual, biased, noncontent-based) factors when applied to inventories such as the

MMPI or MMPI–2 (cf. Waller, Tellegen, McDonald, & Lykken, 1996). Standard factor models and programs produce spurious factors when item responses can be efficiently modeled by Item Response Theory (IRT; Hambleton & Swaminathan, 1985; Hambleton, Swaminathan, & Rogers, 1991; McDonald & Ahlawat, 1974; Reise & Waller, 1990) and the items differ widely in difficulty values (as they do in the MMPI). Analyses presented later in the chapter demonstrate that the two-parameter logistic IRT model (Birnbaum, 1968; also see Panter, Swygert, & Dahlstrom, 1997) can be profitably used to characterize item response behavior on the MMPI. In a major section of the chapter, I report the results of an item factor analysis of more than 28,000 MMPI protocols. These findings were generated using a psychometrically defensible method for item-level factor analysis (Waller, 1995). On the basis of these results, I describe 16 content-homogeneous factor scales for the MMPI. Focusing on one of these scales, labeled Physical Complaints, I demonstrate how the MMPI can be administered via IRT-based computerized adaptive testing (Wainer, 1990; Waller & Reise, 1989). The chapter ends with some general thoughts on the development of IRT-based computerized adaptive versions of the MMPI and MMPI–2.

THE DEVELOPMENT OF THE MINNESOTA
MULTIPHASIC PERSONALITY INVENTORY

Pinpointing the precise birth date of the so-called multiphasic personality schedule (Hathaway & McKinley, 1940) is difficult because the original MMPI scales were developed over a number of years. Suffice it to say that sometime during the 1930s, Hathaway and McKinley collected items for their diagnostic inventory from "various textbooks of psychiatry, from certain of the directions for case taking in medicine and neurology and from the earlier published scales of personal and social attitudes" (Hathaway & McKinley, 1940, p. 249). These clinician/researchers eventually identified more than 1,000 diagnostic statements, an unwieldy collection that was soon winnowed to a more manageable pool of 504 items. The official MMPI item pool was later expanded to its current size of 550 items (the MMPI–2 contains 567 items).

In the MMPI's inaugural publication, Hathaway and McKinley (1940) suggested that their collection of self-descriptive statements could be rationally divided into 25 content-homogeneous categories: General Health; General Neurologic; Cranial Nerves; Motility and Coordination; Sensibility; Vasomotor, Trophic, Speech, Secretory; Cardiorespiratory; Gastrointestinal; Genitourinary; Habits; Family and Marital; Occupational; Educational; Sexual Attitudes; Religious Attitudes; Political Attitudes—Law and Order; Social Attitudes; Affect, Depressive; Affect, Manic; Obsessive, Compulsive; Delusions, Hallucinations, Illusions, Ideas of Reference; Phobias; Sadistic, Masochistic; Morale; and items suggesting whether an individual is trying to place himself in an improbably acceptable light.

Interestingly, Hathaway and McKinley purposely ignored these content categories when they developed the original MMPI scales. Instead, these dust-bowl empiricists relied almost exclusively on empirical keying (i.e., the method of contrasted groups) to develop scales that could identify the major psychiatric syndromes in the then-popular Kraepelian nosology. The original scales (still in use today) included measures of hypochondriasis (Hs), depression (D), hysteria (Hy), psychopathic deviance (Pd), paranoia (Pa), psychasthenia (Pt), schizophrenia (Sc), and hypomania (Ma). Later, scales were added to distinguish homosexual men from heterosexual men (Mf) and to measure social introversion (Si) (see Dahlstrom, Welsh, & Dahlstrom, 1972, for a thorough discussion of MMPI scale development).

Hathaway and McKinley noted that:

> The problems to be solved by the scales of the MMPI are frankly those of detecting and evaluating typical and commonly recognized forms of major psychological abnormality. (a) The terminology and classification system are largely drawn from preliminary psychiatric practice. (b) Where there are correlations between clinical syndromes, the scales tend to show correlation; where the clinically recognized diagnosis is impure the scales will tend to be impure. (c) These are usually, therefore, not statistically true scales. They often contain deliberately diverse types of items. One additional point should be especially stressed. (d) Every item finally chosen differentiates between criterion and normal groups and that is the reason for acceptance or rejection of the items. (e) They are not selected for their content or theoretical import. (f) Frequently, the authors can see no possible rationale to an item in a given scale; it is nevertheless accepted if it appears to differentiate. (McKinley & Hathaway, 1944, reprinted in Welsh & Dahlstrom, 1956, pp. 87–88; letters added for emphasis)

Statements a and b in this passage remind us that the MMPI scales were originally developed to measure membership status in clinical syndromes or psychiatric classes. Stated otherwise, the scales were not developed to measure individual differences on orthogonal latent dimensions or factors, and in many samples the clinical scales correlate as highly as .60 or greater (e.g., Sc & Pd; see Appendix F, Butcher et al., 1989). Moreover, as noted in Statement c, no attempt was made to construct unidimensional scales; single items were frequently scored on more than one scale (thus allowing shared measurement error to inflate the scale correlations). For instance, Item 32, "I find it hard to keep my mind on a task or job," is currently scored on six clinical scales (D, Hy, Pd, Pt, Sc, & Si).

Item selection was guided by the fundamental rule of empirical keying. Accordingly, each item had to discriminate (by differential item endorsements) individuals in the target group from both the Minnesota Normals and from persons in other diagnostic categories (Statement d). Items were not required to be face valid (Statement e), and in some cases an item was included on a scale despite the fact that the scale authors could find no theoretical reason for the item's discriminatory success (Statement f; see Hollrah, Schlottmann, Scott, & Brunetti, 1995, for a review of the so-called subtle items).

THE INTERNAL STRUCTURE OF THE MMPI

The phrase *blind empiricism* is sometimes used to describe Hathaway and McKinley's philosophy of scale development. When used pejoratively, the phrase implies an unabashed disregard for item content. Hathaway and McKinley certainly paid less attention to item content than is currently fashionable (e.g., Jackson, 1971). Yet to claim that they ignored content would be misleading. On the contrary, before developing any scales, the MMPI authors assembled a highly diverse and content-heterogeneous item pool. Due to the richness of their item pool, Hathaway and McKinley could comfortably rely on their data—rather than on their preconceived notions—to guide item selection for their empirically keyed scales.

In later years, researchers would pay far more attention to content considerations when developing MMPI scales (see Koss, 1979, for an overview). Wiggins (1966), for example, relied on Hathaway and McKinley's rationally derived content categories when he developed his widely used content scales. More recently, Butcher, Graham, Williams, and Ben-Porath (1990) used rationally derived item groupings to develop the new content scales for the MMPI–2. Although the efforts of Hathaway and McKinley (1940), Wiggins (1966), and Butcher et al. (1990), have undeniably extended our knowledge of the internal structures of the MMPI and MMPI–2, these authors have not offered empirically generated structures for these instruments.

Ironically, a strength of the MMPI—its large number of items—was a handicap when researchers first used multivariate statistics to understand the structural properties of the item pool. Recall that when Hathaway and McKinley constructed the MMPI, the word computer referred to a human being rather than to a machine. Consequently, early multivariate analyses of MMPI items were necessarily conducted on reduced item pools rather than on the full set.

In an early series of studies, Comrey factor analyzed the items of the individual clinical and validity scales (Comrey, 1957a, 1957b; Comrey, 1958a, 1958b, 1958c, 1958d, 1958e, 1958f; Comrey & Marggraff, 1958). Even with these modest aims, however, Comrey ran into difficulties. Due to limited computing power, Comrey was unable to analyze all 78 items of the Schizophrenia scale. Nevertheless, Comrey's work holds an important place in the history of MMPI research because it firmly established the multidimensional structure of the clinical scales. It also showed that similar factors could be recovered in scales that putatively measure diagnostically distinct syndromes. For example, Comrey found a Psychotic Tendencies factor when he separately factor analyzed the Psychasthenia (Comrey, 1958e) and Schizophrenia (Comrey & Marggraff, 1958) scales.

Rapid advancements in computer technology eventually allowed researchers to analyze larger and larger collections of MMPI items. Twenty five years ago researchers could move beyond the clinical scales and factor analyze the items of MMPI short forms (Barker, Fowler, & Peterson, 1971; Overall, Hunter, & Butcher, 1973). One researcher (Lushene, 1967) during this period analyzed the full item pool, although his findings were of questionable value due to the paucity of subjects in his samples (189 males and 253 females).

More recently there have been at least five factor analyses of the entire MMPI item pool.[1] The major findings of these studies are summarized in Table 9.1.[2] Even a cursory glance at these findings reveals that a replicable factor structure for the MMPI item pool has yet to be found. Consider, for instance, the different number of factors that were reported in the four summarized studies. At the extremes, Reddon et al. (1982) claimed that six factors are needed to account for the major sources of variance in the MMPI, whereas Johnson et al. (1984) claimed that at least 21 factors could be meaningfully interpreted.

For several reasons, we should not expect these studies to reveal similar factor structures. One reason concerns the lack of comparability of the four samples. For instance, two samples are unusually homogenous (Costa et al., 1985; Reddon et al., 1982). Sample homogeneity is problematic here because it is likely that neither prison inmates (Reddon et al., 1982) nor coronary patients (Costa et al., 1985) express the full range of symptoms that are measured by an omnibus psychiatric inventory. Thus we should not be surprised if some factors fail to emerge in these samples.

A closer look at the studies summarized in Table 9.1 reveals additional puzzling findings. For instance, in their original report, Reddon et al. (1982) claimed that the highest marker of Severe Maladjustment is Item 512, "I dislike a bath." According to Archer and Klinefelter (1991) Item 23, "I am troubled by attacks of nausea and vomiting," is a potent marker of Psychoticism. Johnson et al. (1984) suggested that Item 60, "I do not read every editorial," is a valid marker of Denial of Somatic Complaints. These investigators are apparently honoring the long-standing MMPI tradition of including subtle items (Hollrah et al., 1995) in their scales.

---

[1]There have also been some noteworthy analyses of the 399 items that make up the validity and clinical scales; *see* Beck, McRae, Henrichs, Sneider, Horwitz, Rennier, Thomas, and Hedlund (1989).

[2]Only four studies are summarized in Table 9.1 because I was unable to obtain a copy of Stewart (1974).

TABLE 9.1
Previous Factor Analyses of the Full MMPI Item Pool

Study	1	2	3	4
Authors	Reddon et al.	Johnson et al.	Costa et al.	Archer & Klinefelter
Publication date	1982	1984	1985	1991
Sample characteristics	prison inmates	psychiatric inpatients & outpatients	coronary patients	Adolescents receiving psychiatric services
Sample Size	682	5,506; 5,632	1,576	1,762
Methodology	PC of phi coefficients[1]	PC of phi coefficients	PC of phi coefficients	Principal factors of phi coefficients
Rotation	Varimax	Varimax	Varimax	Varimax
		Factor Names		
1	General-Maladjustment	Neuroticism	Neuroticism	Neuroticism
2	Somatic-Complaints	Psychoticism	Psychoticism/infrequency	Psychoticism
3	Impulse-Expression	Cynicism	Masculinity vs. femininity	Somatization
4	Cynical Outlook	Denial of Somatic Problems	Extraversion	Cynicism
5	Religiosity	Social-Extroversion	Religious orthodoxy	Phobias/Fearfulness
6	Severe-Maladjustment	Stereotypic-Femininity	Somatic complaints	Extroversion
7		Aggressive-Hostility	Inadequacy	Masculinity
8		Psychotic-Paranoia	Cynicism	Femininity
9		Depression	Intellectual interests	Delinquency
10		Delinquency		Hostility
11		Inner-Directedness		Familial Discord
12		Assertiveness		Denial of Somatic-Concerns
13		Stereotypic-Masculinity		Self-Esteem
14		Neurasthenic-Somatization		Denial
15		Phobias		Mania
16		Family-Attachment		Self-Consciousness
17		Well-Being—Health		Religiosity
18		Intellectual-Interests		
19		Religious-Fundamentalism		
20		Sexual-Adjustment		
21		Dreaming		

[1]PC = principal components.

Readers should also be warned that several factor names in Table 9.1 are misleading. Consider the factors labeled Denial of Somatic Problems by Johnson et al. (1984) and Denial of Somatic Concerns by Archer and Klinefelter (1991). Relying on their labels, you might conclude that these factors measure similar constructs. However, you would be wrong. Only four items are scored on both scales.

ITEM-TRAIT REGRESSIONS AND BINARY
ITEM FACTOR ANALYSIS

Table 9.1 indicates that phi coefficients (Pearson product moment correlations between binary variables) were analyzed in all previous factor analyses of the MMPI item pool. In this section, I discuss the appropriateness of this coefficient for MMPI research by considering the dimensional structure of the MMPI physical complaint items.

Recall from Table 9.1 that Archer and Klinefelter (1991) and Johnson et al. (1984) recovered two physical health factors from the MMPI item pool. One factor was labeled Denial of Somatic Problems (Factor 4; Johnson et al., 1984)/Denial of Somatic Concerns (Factor 12; Archer & Klinefelter, 1991), whereas the other was called Neurasthenic Somatization (Factor 14; Johnson et al., 1984)/Somatization (Factor 3; Archer & Klinefelter, 1991). This apparent replication of a two-dimensional structure might seem reassuring until we recall that the other studies in Table 9.1 found evidence for only one somatic factor. In other words, when considered together, the four studies leave us wondering whether a one- or two-dimensional model better represents the MMPI somatic complaint items.

One clue that only a single dimension is needed to represent the underlying structure of these items is illustrated in Fig. 9.1. These side-by-side boxplots summarize the item difficulties (endorsement frequencies) for the markers of the Denial of Somatic Problems and Neurasthenic Somatization factors from the Johnson et al. (1984) study. The plots were generated using data from 28,390 MMPI protocols, which are included in the Hathaway Data Bank. This sizable and highly diverse collection of MMPI data will be described more fully in a later section.

Notice in Fig. 9.1 that the boxplots show no overlap. In words, these graphical summaries are telling us that the Denial of Somatic Problems items are considerably easier—in the sense that they are endorsed more frequently—than the markers of Neurasthenic Somatization.

Consider what happens when both scales are keyed such that high values represent physical health. Under this condition, all items on the first scale (Denial of Somatic Problems) are keyed True and all items on the second scale (reversed Neurasthenic Somatization) are keyed False. This finding,

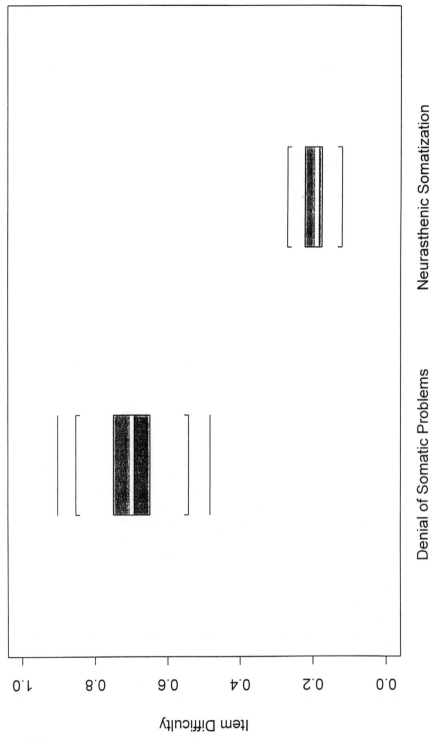

Denial of Somatic Problems   Neurasthenic Somatization

FIG. 9.1.   Item difficulties for two MMPI factor scales of Somatic Complaints.

when considered with the boxplots in Fig. 9.1, suggests that one of these factors may be spurious—a so-called difficulty factor (Bernstein & Teng, 1989; McDonald & Ahlawat, 1974; Mislevy, 1986; Waller, Tellegen, McDonald, & Lykken, 1996). I shortly test this hypothesis with the tools of item response theory (Lord, 1980). First, I present some historical background on the concept of difficulty factors.

Many years ago methodologists (e.g., Ferguson, 1941; Guilford, 1941; Wherry & Gaylord, 1944) suggested that phi coefficients should not be used in item-level factor analyses. These researchers noted that the empirical range of phi rarely equals that of a product moment correlation between continuous variables (i.e., −1.00 to 1.00). Furthermore, because the maximum value of phi is a function of the item thresholds (endorsement frequencies), phi is rarely 1.00 even when two variables measure the identical construct (the maximum value is unity only when the marginal distributions are identical).

These psychometric properties of phi are said to be the underlying cause of difficulty factors. A difficulty factor is an artefactual or construct heterogeneous factor that is characterized by a high correlation between its factor loadings and the item endorsement frequencies (i.e., classical item difficulties) of the factor-defining markers.

Researchers were advised to avoid difficulty factors by avoiding their cause, the maligned phi coefficient. In place of phi coefficients, they were told to use tetrachoric correlations. Unfortunately, until recently, few applied researchers had the computational means to calculate tetrachoric correlations, and the advice of the methodologists has generally fallen on deaf ears.

To better understand these notions, consider the findings in Table 9.2. In this table I report classical item difficulties (i.e., endorsement frequencies) for the 35 physical health items from the Johnson et al. (1984) factors. I also report the results of two principal components analyses of these items. A total of 28,390 MMPI protocols were used in these analyses.

In the first solution, I extracted two principal components from a 35 by 35 matrix of phi coefficients. I then rotated the components to maximize the Varimax criterion. Johnson et al. (1984) also extracted Varimax rotated components from phi coefficients, and the results in Table 9.2 show that I have replicated their main findings. As reported in Table 9.2, these findings exhibit a clear simple structure with Items 1 through 25 (from the Denial of Somatic Problems factor) and Items 26 through 35 (from the Neurasthenic Somatization factor) defining two orthogonal components.

At first glance, this two-dimensional structure seems plausible. But two observations should raise concerns in our minds. The first is that the item difficulties (i.e., the proportion of responses in the keyed direction) correlate −.80 with the loadings on the first rotated component and .93 with the loadings on the second rotated component. These correlations suggest (but do not prove) that we may be faced with difficulty factors. The second cause

TABLE 9.2
Two Alternative Structures for MMPI Somatization Items

MMPI Item Number and Abbreviated Content	Item Means	Principal Components (phis)		Principal Component (tetrachorics)
		I	II	I
1 55. No heart or chest pains.	.69	−.36	.29	.58
2 60. Do not read every editorial.	.90	.04	.35	.32
3 63. No problems with bowel movements.	.67	−.26	.31	.50
4 68. No pain in back of neck.	.62	−.39	.30	.63
5 103. No muscle twitches.	.67	−.31	.39	.60
6 130. Never vomited or coughed blood.	.74	−.06	.45	.43
7 154. No fits or convulsions.	.77	.00	.43	.36
8 174. No fainting spells.	.48	−.13	.30	.37
9 175. No dizzy spells.	.66	−.38	.35	.65
10 187. Hands not clumsy.	.71	−.20	.40	.52
11 192. No difficulty keeping balance.	.69	−.26	.41	.58
12 193. No hay fever or asthma.	.75	−.01	.35	.32
13 214. Skin doesn't break out.	.55	−.06	.27	.28
14 243. Few or no pains.	.58	−.40	.27	.60
15 281. No ear ringing.	.73	−.23	.36	.53
16 302. No trouble because of sex behavior.	.54	.00	.05	.05
17 330. Never been paralyzed.	.59	−.11	.48	.48
18 405. No trouble swallowing.	.84	−.29	.32	.60
19 462. No difficulty holding my urine.	.72	−.19	.38	.50
20 464. Never seen a vision.	.74	−.04	.41	.40
21 486. No blood in urine.	.81	−.01	.44	.40
22 496. Never seen things doubled.	.70	−.06	.45	.42
23 533. Not bothered by stomach gas.	.68	−.36	.22	.53
24 540. Face never been paralyzed.	.85	.00	.48	.44
25 542. No tarry-looking bowel movements.	.64	−.10	.38	.40
26 10. Often have lump in throat.	.12	.46	−.05	−.56
27 23. I have attacks of nausea and vomiting.	.13	.48	−.05	−.57
28 29. Bothered by acid stomach.	.22	.59	.03	−.55
29 44. Head often hurts all over.	.17	.56	−.08	−.64
30 47. Often feel hot for no cause.	.20	.50	−.08	−.57
31 72. Often have discomfort in pit of stomach.	.22	.67	.04	−.61
32 108. Fullness in my head or nose.	.18	.52	−.05	−.57
33 114. Tight band around my head.	.18	.56	−.06	−.61
34 125. I have much stomach trouble.	.18	.62	.01	−.60
35 189. Often feel weak all over.	.26	.56	−.11	−.62

for concern stems from our analysis of the tetrachoric correlations. Notice that when we analyze tetrachorics, rather than phi coefficients, almost all of the items have high loadings on a single principal component. Item 302 is a notable exception, although the content of this item suggests that it is misplaced. To gain a better understanding of these findings requires that we consider the role of item-trait regression functions in binary-item factor analysis. One way to do so is to apply the new rules of measurement using IRT.

Current notions of difficulty factors have been greatly influenced in recent years by the insights of Roderick McDonald (1965; Fraser & McDonald, 1988; McDonald & Ahlawat, 1974; see also Mislevy, 1986). Starting from an IRT perspective, McDonald showed that difficulty factors are actually not due to item difficulties, per se. Rather, they stem from nonlinear item-trait regression functions. To fully understand McDonald's arguments requires a hefty background in mathematics. Waller et al. (1996) provided a nontechnical discussion of the main ideas. The gist of the argument is that difficulty factors—McDonald prefers the descriptively more accurate phrase *curvature factors*—can arise when item response data are well described by a two-parameter IRT model and the items have widely different difficulty parameters and/or very high discrimination parameters.

To illustrate these ideas, I have estimated IRT parameters for 33 of the 35 previously mentioned physical health items from the MMPI (Items 60 and 302 were not analyzed because they do not refer to physical health). The parameter estimates from the IRT analyses are reported in Table 9.3. To generate these estimates I analyzed 1,000 randomly selected subjects from the Hathaway Data Bank. For these analyses I used marginal maximum likelihood algorithms as implemented in the BILOG 3 computer program (Mislevy & Bock, 1990).

Table 9.3 shows the estimated item discrimination parameters (α), item difficulty parameters (β) and chi-square (χ^2) goodness-of-fit values (with associated significance levels) for the physical health items. When looking at these estimates and fit values keep in mind that Johnson et al. (1984) claimed that the first 23 items and the last 10 items belong to orthogonal latent dimensions. In contrast, our IRT findings, which are based on a unidimensional model, provide cogent evidence that the physical complaint items can be effectively scaled on a single latent dimension. Further evidence for this view is provided by the item-trait regression lines that are shown in Figs. 9.2 and 9.3.

These figures illustrate representative item response curves for the MMPI physical health items (listed in Table 9.3). Figure 9.2 displays an item from the Denial of Somatic Problems factor, whereas Fig. 9.3 shows an item from the Neurasthenic Somatization factor.[3] These figures illustrate the types of information that can be gained from an IRT analysis. They also suggest that additional factor analytic work on the MMPI item pool is warranted. Findings from such work will be unenlightening, however, unless researchers use psychometrically defensible models for binary-item factor analysis.

---

[3]The blackened circles illustrate the Bayesian posterior probability estimates of a keyed response at several points along the trait continuum; the vertical lines represent the 95% tolerance limits of the item response curves.

TABLE 9.3
IRT Parameters for MMPI Somatization Items

	MMPI Item Number and Abbreviated Content	α	β	χ^2 (DF)	prob.
1	55. No heart or chest pains.	1.072	−.879	7.1 (8)	.530
2	63. No problems with bowel movements.	.883	−.840	6.0 (8)	.645
3	68. No pain in back of neck.	1.339	−.424	11.9 (8)	.154
4	103. No muscle twitches.	1.135	−.894	14.0 (8)	.082
5	130. Never vomited or coughed blood.	.825	−1.434	3.0 (8)	.931
6	154. No fits or convulsions.	.753	−1.719	12.4 (8)	.132
7	174. No fainting spells.	.739	.213	18.5 (9)	.030
8	175. No dizzy spells.	1.474	−.690	6.0 (7)	.550
9	187. Hands not clumsy.	.937	−1.163	7.7 (8)	.468
10	192. No difficulty keeping balance.	1.12	−.934	10.8 (8)	.215
11	193. No hay fever or asthma.	.568	−1.958	11.8 (9)	.225
12	214. Skin doesn't break out.	.384	−.611	11.9 (9)	.220
13	243. Few or no pains.	1.224	−.423	9.7 (7)	.207
14	281. No ear ringing.	.951	−1.255	4.6 (8)	.805
15	330. Never been paralyzed.	.858	−.385	12.8 (9)	.171
16	405. No trouble swallowing.	1.196	−1.790	7.9 (6)	.241
17	462. No difficulty holding my urine.	1.029	−1.101	3.8 (7)	.805
18	464. Never seen a vision.	.727	−1.859	5.0 (9)	.836
19	486. No blood in urine.	.883	−1.907	3.7 (8)	.883
20	496. Never seen things doubled.	.879	−1.025	6.6 (9)	.684
21	533. Not bothered by stomach gas.	1.067	−.764	12.9 (9)	.165
22	540. Face never been paralyzed.	.971	−2.128	7.0 (7)	.426
23	542. No tarry-looking bowel movements.	.671	−1.023	13.1 (8)	.109
24	10. Often have lump in throat.	1.119	−2.427	8.6 (6)	.195
25	23. I have attacks of nausea and vomiting.	1.157	−1.867	2.9 (6)	.820
26	29. Bothered by acid stomach.	1.321	−1.203	7.5 (6)	.275
27	44. Head often hurts all over.	1.369	−1.455	11.8 (6)	.066
28	47. Often feel hot for no cause.	1.350	−1.407	4.2 (6)	.671
29	72. Often have discomfort in pit of stomach.	1.216	−1.286	7.1 (7)	.415
30	108. Fullness in my head or nose.	.967	−1.665	2.0 (7)	.957
31	114. Tight band around my head.	1.292	−1.418	11.9 (7)	.104
32	125. I have much stomach trouble.	1.406	−1.415	9.2 (6)	.160
33	189. Often feel weak all over.	1.226	−1.142	6.4 (7)	.490

BINARY-ITEM FACTOR ANALYSIS

Several methods are available for binary-item factor analysis (Mislevy, 1986; Panter et al., 1997; Waller et al., 1996). Many methods use tetrachoric correlations (Christofferson, 1975; Muthén, 1978, 1989; Waller, 1995) rather than phi coefficients. The computationally more demanding methods are based on multidimensional IRT models (Bock & Aitken, 1981; Bock, Gibbons, & Muraki, 1988; Wilson, Wood, & Gibbons, 1991).

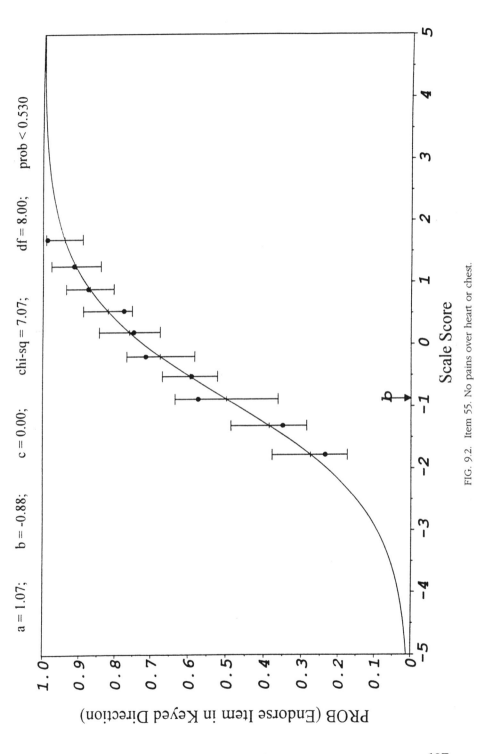

a = 1.07;   b = -0.88;   c = 0.00;   chi-sq = 7.07;   df = 8.00;   prob < 0.530

PROB (Endorse Item in Keyed Direction)

Scale Score

FIG. 9.2.   Item 55. No pains over heart or chest.

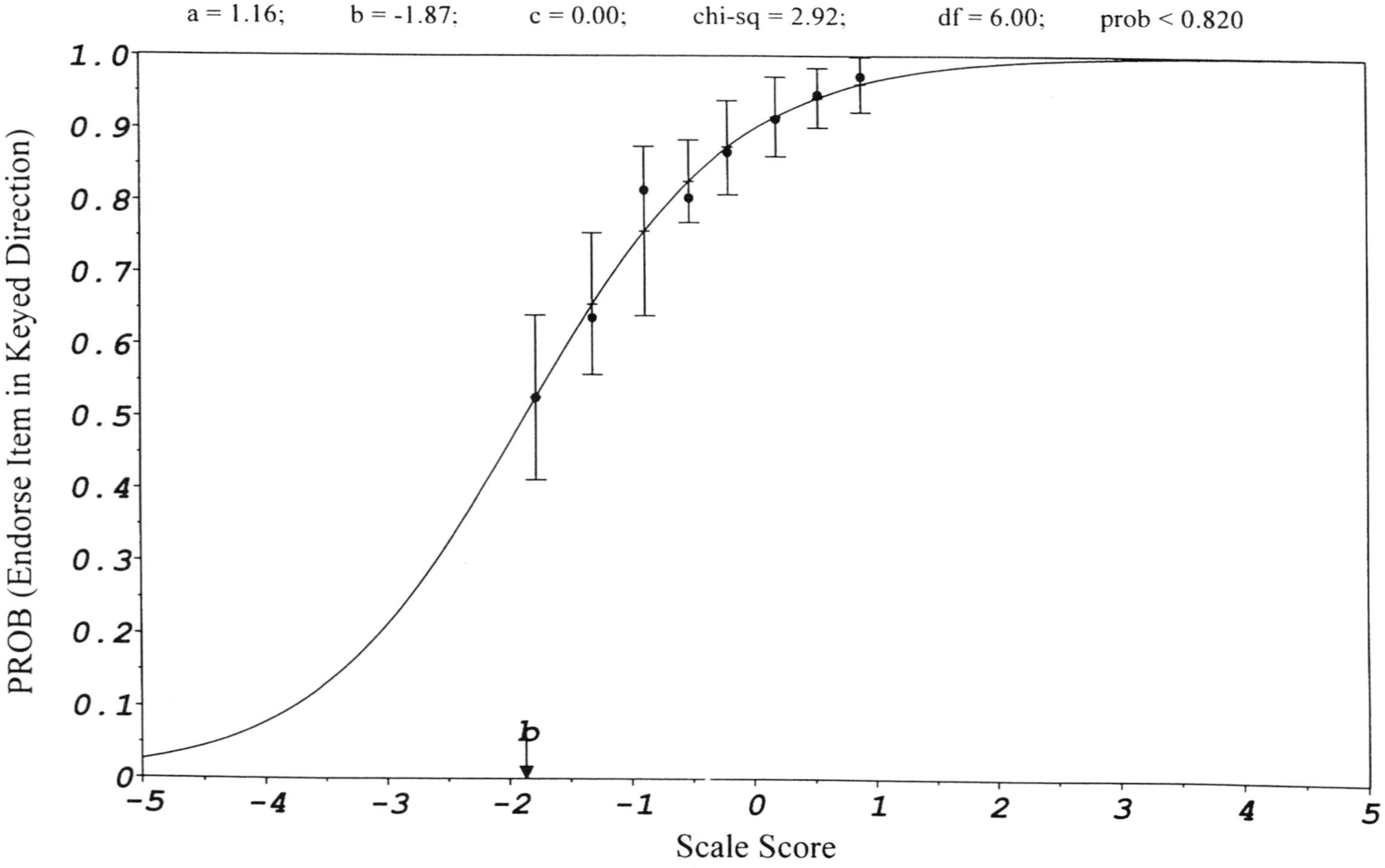

a = 1.16;   b = -1.87;   c = 0.00;   chi-sq = 2.92;   df = 6.00;   prob < 0.820

FIG. 9.3. Item 23. I have attacks of nausea and vomiting.

Knol and Berger (1988; see also Waller et al., 1996) recently compared the alternatives for binary-item factor analysis and concluded that "a common [iterated] factor analysis on the matrix of tetrachoric correlations yields the best estimates" (Knol & Berger, 1988, p. 1; see also Knol & Berger, 1991). The term *best* was defined in this study as the method that generated the smallest mean-squared error of parameter recovery. In their extensive Monte Carlo findings, Knol and Berger observed that the performance of a simple factor analysis of tetrachoric correlations improved as the number of items and dimensions increased. Because the MMPI is composed of hundreds of items, and potentially many factors, this latter finding is of particular interest.

Motivated by Knol and Berger's results, I conducted a large-scale study of the MMPI item-level factor structure by using iterated factor analyses on tetrachoric correlations. The data for these analyses were sampled from the Hathaway Data Bank.

The Hathaway Data Bank

The Hathaway Data Bank is undoubtedly one of the largest and most varied collections of MMPI records that have been assembled to date. At the time of this writing, the data bank contains MMPI data from 33,964 medical and psychiatric patients who were treated at the University of Minnesota Hospitals between 1940 and 1976. The data were originally culled from individual hospital units by Drs. Paul Meehl and Robert Golden. Patient files were aggregated from a diverse collection of settings, including (a) outpatient psychiatry; (b) physical medicine and rehabilitation; (c) heart clinic; (d) audiology; (e) orthopedics clinic; (f) medicine clinic; (g) neurology; (h) child psychiatry consultation; (i) pediatric clinic; (j) gynecology clinic; (k) skin clinic; (l) general medicine; (m) metabolism clinic; (n) ear, nose, and throat clinic; (o) urology; (p) surgery; (q) health services; (r) isolation clinic; (s) neurosurgery; (t) inpatient psychiatry; and (u) child psychiatry.

All records that satisfied purposely conservative inclusion criteria were selected for my final sample. The criteria used were (a) 30 or fewer missing values, (b) a raw F-K score of 15 or less, and (c) age greater than 16 and less than 88 at the time of testing. In addition, protocols were excluded if any of three problematic record flags were present in the original data files. These flags are included in the Hathaway Data Bank to identify possibly invalid records. The flags mark records with unusual properties such as subjects with last names of Doe or Smith and identification numbers of 0, or records with long strings of continuous True and/or False responses.

By adopting these criteria, I identified 28,390 MMPI records for the final sample. Sixty percent of the records were completed by females. At the time of testing, the examinees had an average age of 36.37 years (median age = 34, standard deviation = 14.33). Missing values were recoded True if a uniform random number was greater than .50; otherwise they were recoded False.

THE LATENT STRUCTURE OF THE MMPI

Based on previous considerations, iterated factor analyses of tetrachoric correlations were used to investigate the latent structure of the MMPI item pool. All of the analyses were carried out with MicroFACT (Waller, 1995), a computer program that performs factor analyses of ordered-categorical data (e.g., binary items, Likert items). Because MicroFACT uses virtual memory for dynamical array storage, it handles data sets of virtually any size. This feature of the program made it uniquely suited for a factor analysis of the MMPI item pool.

Both the Scree test (Cattell & Vogelman, 1977) and the results of prior factor analytic work (reviewed in Table 9.1) were used to suggest a plausible number of factors for the MMPI. Note that I did not consider the so-called *eigenvalues*-greater-than-one rule. This popular default in many statistical packages is not theoretically justifiable (Cliff, 1988), does not perform well in simulation studies (Zwick & Velicer, 1986) and, in the present case, would have resulted in a solution with more than 100 factors!

All together, I examined factor solutions from 6 to 25 factors, as well as many other solutions using just the female or male subjects. Because the gender-specific results were highly similar to those from the combined sample, in the remainder of this section I focus on the combined-sample results only.

The 16-factor solution appeared to provide the most psychologically meaningful and psychometrically justifiable representation of the MMPI item pool. The residuals (i.e., the difference between the observed and the model-implied correlations) for the 16-factor solution were uniformly small and centered at zero. The mean squared residual was only .0004 (standard deviation = .019) and the distribution of the residuals was markedly kurtotic (kurtosis = 61.37) although slightly skewed (skewness = 1.85). Over 50% of the residuals were less than .01 from their respective correlations. All told, these findings suggest that a 16-factor solution provides an accurate model for the major sources of covariance in the MMPI item pool.

I have provisionally labeled the 16 factors from these analyses as follows: General Maladjustment (Gm); Denial of Somatic Complaints (Sm); Cynicism (Cy); Antisocial Tendencies (At); Psychotic Ideation (Ps); Social Inhibition (So); Stereotypic Feminine Interests (Fe); Stereotypic Masculine Interests (Mc); Christian Fundamentalism (Cf); Extroversion (Ex); Phobias (Ph); Family Attachment (Fm); Assertiveness (As); Dream (Dr); Hypomania (Hm); and Hostility (Ho). Space limitations prevent me from reporting all 8,800 factor loadings of this structure. Nevertheless, the reader can gain some understanding of the psychological implications of these factors by referring to Tables 9.4 and 9.5 where I report clarifying information, such as (a) factor names, (b) representative items with factor loadings from the Varimax-rotated solution, and (c) alpha reliability coefficients for the 16 factor scales.

TABLE 9.4
Alpha Reliability and Highest Loading Items for 16 MMPI Factors

Factor	α	Item	Highest Loading Items (factor loading)
1. General Maladjustment	.96	301	Life is a strain for me much of the time. (.76)
		236	I brood a great deal. (.76)
2. Denial of Somatic Complaints	.88	243	I have few or no pains. (.67)
		51	I am in just as good physical health as most of my friends. (.63)
3. Cynicism	.86	124	Most people will use somewhat unfair means to gain profit or an advantage rather than lose it. (.62)
		117	Most people are honest chiefly through fear of being caught. (.59)
4. Antisocial Tendencies	.82	38	During one period when I was a youngster I engaged in petty thievery. (.61)
		277	At times I have been so entertained by the cleverness of a crook that I have hoped he would get by with it. (.61)
5. Psychotic Ideation	.80	151	Someone has been trying to poison me. (.80)
		123	I believe I am being followed. (.73)
6. Social Inhibition	.79	201	I wish I were not so shy. (.63)
		180	I find it hard to make talk when I meet new people. (.56)
7. Stereotypic Feminine Interests	.78	87	I would like to be a florist. (.61)
		78	I like poetry. (.61)
8. Stereotypic Masculine Interests	.75	1	I like mechanics magazines. (.66)
		552	I like to read about science. (.59)
9. Christian Fundamentalism	.72	483	Christ performed miracles such as changing water into wine. (.77)
		115	I believe in a life hereafter. (.77)
10. Extroversion	.74	547	I like parties and socials. (.69)
		450	I enjoy the excitement of a crowd. (.68)
11. Phobias	.71	367	I am not afraid of fire. (−.53)
		385	Lightning is one of my fears. (.48)
12. Family Attachment	.70	220	I loved my mother. (.57)
		17	My father was a good man. (.57)
13. Assertiveness	.63	502	I like to let people know where I stand on things. (.59)
		520	I strongly defend my own opinions as a rule. (.50)
14. Dream	.51	329	I almost never dream. (−.71)
		425	I dream frequently. (.58)
15. Hypomania	.50	296	I have periods in which I feel unusually cheerful without any special reason. (.46)
		134	At times my thoughts have raced ahead faster than I could speak them. (.42)
16. Hostility	.43	381	I am often said to be hotheaded. (.51)
		75	I get angry sometimes. (.46)

TABLE 9.5
Marker Items for 16 MMPI Factors From an Analysis of 28,390 Observations

Factor Name	Marker Items
1 General Maladjustment (148 items)	8F, 13, 15, 16, 20F, 21, 22, 24, 31, 32, 39, 40, 41, 43, 46F, 52, 54F, 61, 67, 76, 82, 84, 86, 88F, 94, 97, 100, 102, 104, 106, 107F, 109, 122F, 129, 138, 139, 142, 146, 147, 152F, 156, 157, 158, 159, 168, 170F, 178F, 179, 182, 186, 191, 198F, 212, 217, 228F, 236, 238, 239, 242F, 247, 252, 257F, 259, 262F, 264F, 266, 267, 278, 282, 284, 287F, 297, 299, 301, 303, 305, 307, 317, 322, 335, 336, 337, 338, 339, 340, 342, 343, 344, 345, 349, 351, 352, 355, 356, 357, 358, 359, 360, 361, 368, 369F, 371F, 375, 377, 379F, 382, 383, 384, 389, 396, 397, 398, 403F, 407F, 408, 411, 414, 416, 418, 421, 431, 439, 442, 443, 448, 459, 465, 468, 484, 487, 494, 499, 506, 509, 511, 517, 518, 526, 531, 536, 543, 549, 555, 559, 560, 564, 565
2 Denial of Somatic Complaints (51 items)	2, 3, 7, 9, 10F, 14F, 18, 23F, 29F, 36, 44F, 47F, 51, 55, 62F, 63, 68, 72F, 103, 108F, 114F, 119, 125F, 130, 153, 160, 161F, 163, 174, 175, 185, 187, 189F, 190, 192, 230, 243, 273F, 274, 281, 330, 332F, 405, 462, 474, 486, 496, 533, 535F, 542, 544F
3 Cynicism (36 items)	19, 26, 28, 59, 71, 89, 93, 117, 124, 136, 244, 250, 265, 271, 280, 298, 313, 316, 319, 348, 386, 390, 395, 404, 406, 410, 426, 436, 437, 438, 456, 469, 475, 485, 507, 558
4 Antisocial Tendencies (29 items)	6, 30, 38, 45, 56, 111F, 118, 135, 145, 150, 208, 215, 225, 231, 277, 285, 294F, 419, 427F, 430, 434, 446, 452, 457F, 470F, 481, 490F, 529, 548F
5 Psychotic Ideation (40 items)	11, 27, 33, 35, 48, 49, 50, 53, 66, 85, 110, 113F, 121, 123, 151, 184, 197, 200, 202, 205, 209, 210, 213, 218, 227, 256, 269, 275, 286, 291, 293, 334, 341, 350, 354, 364, 393, 420, 476, 514
6 Social Inhibition (16 items)	57F, 171, 172, 180, 201, 292, 304, 309F, 321, 353, 479F, 482F, 521F, 523F, 528F, 530
7 Stereotypic Feminine Interests (23 items)	4, 25, 70, 77, 78, 87, 92, 126, 132, 140, 149, 173, 203, 204, 261, 295, 300F, 429, 463, 538, 554, 557, 566
8 Stereotypic Masculine Interests (16 items)	1, 74F, 81, 144, 164, 219, 221, 223, 283, 423, 497, 537, 546, 550, 552, 563
9 Christian Fundamentalism (13 items)	58, 83, 95, 98, 115, 206, 249, 258, 373, 387F, 413, 483, 488
10 Extroversion (15 items)	99, 181, 207, 229, 254, 268, 312F, 391, 440, 445, 449, 450, 451, 473F, 547
11 Phobias (15 items)	128F, 131F, 166, 176F, 270F, 367F, 385, 388, 392, 401F, 480, 492, 522F, 525, 539F
12 Family Attachment (15 items)	17, 42F, 65, 96, 137, 177, 216F, 220, 224F, 226F, 237, 245F, 325F, 515, 527
13 Assertiveness (12 items)	112, 233, 380, 415, 417, 432, 444F, 447, 495, 502, 503F, 520
14 Dream (5 items)	241, 320, 329F, 425, 545
15 Hypomania (7 items)	134, 248, 272, 296, 409, 505, 534
16 Hostility (5 items)	75, 105, 234, 381, 399F

Note. Numbers followed by 'F' are keyed false.

The factors in these tables replicate earlier findings and offer novel perspectives of the MMPI panorama. In terms of replication, our findings contain well-defined measures of several factors that have been seen in almost all factor analyses of the MMPI item pool, such as neuroticism (here labeled General Maladjustment), cynicism, psychotic ideation, and religiosity. In terms of novelty, our solution clears away some spurious factors that have needlessly cluttered the MMPI landscape.

One region where the view is considerably clearer concerns the dimensional structure of the physical health or somatization items. For instance, the findings in Tables 9.4 and 9.5 provide ample evidence for a unitary dimension of somatic complaints. Notice that my Denial of Somatic Complaints factor subsumes three factors from the Johnson et al. (1984) study: (a) Denial of Somatic Problems, (b) Somatization, and (c) Well-Being Health. Earlier I discovered that the fractionation of this dimension was due to the use of phi coefficients on items with widely different thresholds and nonlinear item trait regression functions. Notice also that my findings include a Hypomania factor, a dimension that was mysteriously absent from previous MMPI factor structures (e.g., Johnson et al., 1984).[4]

The 16 factors of the current solution originate from a Varimax-rotated factor analysis of tetrachoric correlations. The fact that these dimensions are uncorrelated is not surprising. Varimax rotations impose orthogonality, they do not uncover it. Nevertheless, scales that measure Varimax factors can be correlated, especially if the scale scores are derived by summing items with high factor loadings. The scales in Table 9.5 fit this description and thus we can correlate the scores and possibly extract a higher-order factor structure. Alternatively, we could analyze the inter-factor correlations from an oblique factor solution.

Table 9.6 reports the interscale correlations for samples of 16,890 females and 11,297 males from the Hathaway Data Bank. Because the original (Varimax) solution had a well-defined, simple structure, we do not expect these scales to be highly correlated; and indeed they are not. The mean absolute correlation for females is only .18 (SD = .13), and for males it is .19 (SD = .12). Some correlations are noticeably higher, particularly those that include General Maladjustment.

The correlational patterns displayed in Table 9.6 suggest that meaningful higher-order factors may be lurking behind the scenes. To uncover these general dimensions, Scree plots were generated for both correlation matrices. On the basis of these plots, four Varimax-rotated (principal axis) factors were extracted from each matrix. The factor loadings from these analyses are reported in Table 9.7.

---

[4]It is noteworthy that my Hypomania scale does not include the general anxiety and nervousness items that are scored on the Wiggins' content scale of the same name.

TABLE 9.6
Correlations Among 16 MMPI Factor Scales

	Gm	Sm	Cy	At	Ps	So	Fe	Mc	Cf	Ex	Ph	Fm	As	Dr	Hm	Ho
Gm		.45	.53	.24	.48	.58	-.13	-.14	-.06	-.26	.35	-.53	-.02	.39	.16	.37
Sm	.45		.25	-.08	.32	.21	-.12	-.06	.10	-.18	.32	-.22	.02	.21	.06	.17
Cy	.52	.22		.18	.52	.25	-.04	.05	.02	.08	.27	-.32	.30	.29	.33	.29
At	.25	-.08	.23		.05	.00	.14	.13	-.34	.23	-.06	-.28	.23	.26	.25	.25
Ps	.49	.31	.49	.03		.21	-.02	.08	.08	-.05	.21	-.30	.16	.26	.21	.14
So	.59	.24	.24	.04	.22		-.22	-.17	-.03	-.39	.30	-.26	-.25	.19	-.02	.17
Fe	.06	-.04	.08	.07	.22	-.10		.36	.11	.39	-.06	.12	.22	.02	.21	-.04
Mc	-.19	-.08	.08	.13	-.06	-.19	.21		.03	.22	-.20	.01	.21	.02	.22	-.02
Cf	-.05	.07	.07	-.28	.12	-.08	.09	.17		.10	.13	.15	.02	-.05	.04	-.01
Ex	-.20	-.20	.15	.23	.02	-.39	.31	.32	.14		-.07	.12	.32	.00	.29	.05
Ph	.33	.33	.23	-.06	.26	.27	.06	-.14	.10	-.07		-.11	.01	.16	.05	.20
Fm	-.50	-.21	-.28	-.27	-.32	-.27	-.02	.16	.19	.13	-.13		-.08	-.25	-.11	-.25
As	.02	-.01	.29	.25	.13	-.23	.21	.22	.07	.34	.03	-.06		.10	.31	.20
Dr	.39	.19	.27	.21	.28	.18	.14	-.06	-.02	.03	.17	-.20	.10		.21	.20
Hm	.25	.04	.39	.30	.25	.00	.20	.17	.06	.28	.07	-.14	.32	.22		.19
Ho	.35	.19	.32	.27	.14	.16	-.05	.03	.04	.03	.16	-.20	.22	.17	.22	

Note. Gm = General Maladjustment, Sm = Somatic Complaints, Cy = Cynicism, At = Antisocial Tendencies, Ps = Psychotic Ideation, So = Social Inhibition, Fe = Stereotypic Feminine Interests, Mc = Stereotypic Masculine Interests, Cf = Christian Fundamentalism, Ex = Extroversion, Ph = Phobias, Fm = Family Attachment, As = Assertiveness, Dr = Dream, Hm = Hypomania, Ho = Hostility.

Below the diagonal N = 16,890 females; above the diagonal N = 11,297 males.

TABLE 9.7
Higher-Order Factors for 16 MMPI Factor Scales

Scales	Female Factors				Male Factors			
	I	*II*	*III*	*IV*	*I*	*II*	*III*	*IV*
Gm	**.86**	−.20	.17	.16	**.87**	−.13	.22	.16
Ps	**.65**	.07	−.14	−.12	**.68**	.16	−.08	−.17
At	.20	**.32**	**.68**	.02	.12	**.33**	**.65**	.20
Hm	**.30**	**.47**	.05	−.03	**.30**	**.48**	.14	.10
Sm	**.47**	−.11	−.19	.11	**.49**	−.14	−.17	.12
Fe	−.07	**.47**	−.04	−.20	.15	**.40**	−.00	**−.35**
Mc	.03	**.38**	.01	**−.47**	−.15	**.45**	−.07	.03
Ex	−.15	**.70**	.01	.04	−.14	**.70**	.03	−.10
Fm	**−.51**	.07	**−.30**	−.00	**−.47**	.08	**−.35**	−.03
Cf	.02	.12	**−.53**	.04	.06	.22	**−.54**	.04
Ph	**.37**	−.04	−.21	**.40**	**.44**	−.06	−.17	.06
So	**.47**	**−.42**	.04	.14	**.51**	**−.40**	.09	.14
Cy	**.67**	.23	−.01	.08	**.60**	**.33**	.05	.19
Dr	**.43**	.09	.15	.05	**.42**	.12	.15	−.01
Ho	**.37**	.15	.16	.26	**.31**	.18	.10	**.49**
As	.15	**.55**	.04	−.00	.09	**.57**	.06	.13

Note. Loadings ≥ | .30 | are printed in boldface. Gm = General Maladjustment, Sm = Somatic Complaints, Cy = Cynicism, At = Antisocial Tendencies, Ps = Psychotic Ideation, So = Social Inhibition, Fe = Stereotypic Feminine Interests, Mc = Stereotypic Masculine Interests, Cf = Christian Fundamentalism, Ex = Extroversion, Ph = Phobias, Fm = Family Attachment, As = Assertiveness, Dr = Dream, Hm = Hypomania, Ho = Hostility.

Before discussing these factors, it is worth noting how the present analyses compare to earlier attempts to elucidate higher-order MMPI factors. Specifically, most researchers (although see Edwards & Edwards, 1991) have factored the clinical and validity scales or purified subscales of the clinical scales (Block, 1965; Welsh, 1956; Wheeler, Little, & Lehner, 1951). Unfortunately, as noted by Guilford many years ago (1952; see also Shure & Rogers, 1965), the former approach is problematic. Guilford reminded us that many MMPI items are scored on multiple scales and thus the interscale correlations are artificially inflated due to correlated error variance.

In virtually all analyses of the MMPI clinical and validity scales, the first factor has been interpreted as a pervasive dimension of psychological maladjustment. Typically, all clinical scales, except Hy (Hysteria) and Mf (Masculinity–Femininity), have high loadings on this factor. The largest positive loadings (typically around .90) occur for Pt (Psychasthenia) and Sc (Schizophrenia), whereas the largest negative loading (−.80) occurs for K.

Welsh (1956) labeled the first MMPI factor *A*, believing that it measured general anxiety and poor psychological health. Edwards (1957) offered a different interpretation that emphasized response sets rather than substance, and suggested that the first factor was best conceived as a measure of Social

Desirability (SD). Block (1965) later proved that Edward's interpretation was implausible by showing that scores on the first factor have psychologically meaningful extra test correlates that cannot be explained by response set variance. Block named the first factor Ego-Resiliency (ER), preferring to focus on the healthy pole of the dimension.

Moving beyond this factor, there is little consensus on the meaning and correlates of the remaining higher-order dimensions. Preferences for two, three, and four higher-order factors have been expressed in the literature. After the first, the second dimension has received the most attention. Welsh (1956) labeled this general factor *R*, believing that it measures individual differences in Repression. Block (1965) uncovered a similar factor from purified MMPI scales but called his dimension Ego-Control (EC). In his view, the second MMPI factor measures individual differences in impulse expression and constraint.

From a psychometric perspective, my findings differ from those of earlier studies in at least one important respect. Specifically, because these findings are based on unidimensional factor scales, rather than on the multidimensional clinical and validity scales, they are not influenced by item overlap or correlated error. Thus, we can be reasonably certain that the factors in this solution represent substantive dimensions rather than psychometric artifacts.

Overall, the findings in Table 9.7 offer support for, and evidence against, prior interpretations of the MMPI higher-order factor structure. On the one hand, my findings offer strong support for previous interpretations of the first higher-order factor; on the other hand, they suggest that earlier interpretations of factors beyond the first should be modified. Beginning with Factor I, the pattern of loadings on the first factor supports the notion of a general psychological maladjustment dimension. Persons with high scores on this dimension reportedly experience intense and diffuse anxiety, paranoid and otherwise psychotic ideation, and generalized somatic complaints. They may hold cynical views about the motivations of others and, with little provocation, they express open hostility.

The scale correlates of the second factor suggest that, in both the female and male samples, this dimension influences a conjunction of lower-order traits that relate to interpersonal functioning. Persons with elevated scores on Factor II reportedly derive considerable comfort from the company of others. They are extroverted persons who are highly engaged in their social milieu where they enjoy stereotypically feminine and masculine pastimes. Some individuals with extreme scores on this dimension may be viewed as either socially dominant (i.e., excellent leaders) or socially domineering (i.e., excellent manipulators).

The third factor seemingly measures individual differences in social and behavioral constraint. Persons with elevated scores on Factor III describe childhoods that are filled with school suspensions, petty thievery, aggressive outbursts, and thrill-seeking and dangerous behaviors. Regardless of their gender, these persons deny interest in stereotypically feminine activities and, as a rule, they reject the beliefs, customs, and behavioral constraints of organized religion (or at least, Christian Fundamentalism). I do not discuss Factor IV except to say that it apparently differs across the two samples and in neither sample is it easily interpreted.

The psychological portraits that I have painted are based entirely on the pattern of factor loadings that are reported in Table 9.7. The factor scores from these dimensions can also be used to touch up these portraits.

Table 9.8 reports correlations between the (weighted least squares) factor scores on the MMPI higher-order factors and the original clinical and validity scales. The table also reports correlations for a number of supplementary

TABLE 9.8
Correlations of Validity, Clinical, and Supplementary
Scales With Four MMPI Higher-Order Factors

	Higher-Order MMPI Factor Scores							
	Females				Males			
	I	*II*	*III*	*IV*	*I*	*II*	*III*	*IV*
L	−**.32**	−.24	−**.54**	.06	−.24	−.27	−**.51**	−**.35**
F	**.70**	−.24	.15	.04	**.74**	−.14	.20	−.12
K	−**.80**	−.11	−.12	.12	−**.73**	−.22	−.19	−**.43**
Hs	**.49**	−.16	−.24	−.12	**.49**	−.16	−.22	.23
D	**.49**	−**.59**	−.02	−.24	**.50**	−**.58**	.01	.12
Hy	.12	−.28	−.14	−.11	.11	−**.35**	−.12	−.02
Pd	**.63**	−.18	**.35**	−.07	**.59**	−.12	**.41**	.10
Mf	−.04	−.08	.18	−.06	**.32**	−.17	**.33**	−.28
Pa	**.59**	−.25	.08	.01	**.61**	−.17	.12	−.10
Pt	**.88**	−**.30**	.13	−.19	**.89**	−.20	.19	.24
Sc	**.89**	−.21	.16	−.04	**.91**	−.12	.22	.08
Ma	**.57**	**.42**	.20	.17	**.54**	**.48**	.29	.03
Si	**.61**	−**.67**	−.05	−.22	**.62**	−**.62**	.00	.26
A	**.90**	−.25	.13	−.14	**.89**	−.14	.22	.23
R	−.25	−**.71**	−**.30**	−**.33**	−.19	−**.78**	−.27	−.07
ER	−**.86**	**.31**	−.09	.23	−**.86**	.24	−.15	−**.34**
EC-f	**.41**	−**.54**	−.08	−.27	**.43**	−**.51**	−.05	.25
EC-m	−.08	−**.74**	−**.50**	−.18	−.05	−**.72**	−**.53**	−.02
SD	−**.88**	**.32**	−.09	.17	−**.89**	.21	−.15	−.22
Beta-f	−.02	**.91**	.08	.28	.00	**.90**	.10	−.15
Beta-m	.01	**.92**	.07	**.33**	.00	**.93**	.05	−.05

Note. A = Factor dimension A (Welsh, 1956); R = Factor dimension R (Welsh, 1956); ER = Ego Resiliency (Block, 1965); EC-f = Ego-Control females (Block, 1965); EC-m = Ego-Control males (Block, 1965); SD = Social Desirability (Edwards, 1957); Beta-f and Beta-m are measures of the second MMPI higher-order factor that were developed in this study.

scales that were developed to measure the higher-order factors. Three scales were intended to measure the first higher-order factor: (a) Welsh's Anxiety scale (A), (b) Block's Ego Resiliency scale (ER), and (c) Edward's Social Desirability scale (SD). Three additional scales were designed to measure the second higher-order factor: (a) Welsh's Repression scale, (b) Block's Ego-Control scale for females (EC–f), and (c) Block's Ego-Control scale for males (EC–m). Table 9.8 also reports correlations for two new scales that will be described shortly. All of the correlations in this table are based on data from 16,890 females and 11,297 males.

Focusing on the top half of the table, we find remarkable similarities between the first column of correlations (in both samples) and the factor loadings from previous factor analyses of the MMPI (e.g., Wheeler, Little, & Lehner, 1951). These findings suggest that earlier interpretations of Factor I are both reliable and valid. This position receives further support from the findings in the bottom half of Table 9.8. Notice, for instance, that Welsh's *A* (1956) is an excellent marker of the general psychological maladjustment dimension (Factor I). Block's (1965) measure of Ego Resiliency, and Edward's Social Desirability scale, are also superb markers of Factor I.

The present findings also support my earlier contention that previous researchers have misinterpreted the second MMPI higher-order factor. Notice, for instance, that neither the correlations with the basic validity and clinical scales, nor the correlations with the supplementary scales, supports an interpretation of Factor II in terms of Welsh's Repression factor or Block's Ego Control dimension.

Based on these findings, it seemed desirable to develop more faithful measures of the second MMPI factor. The scales labeled Beta-f (females) and Beta-m (males) were developed to meet this need. The results in Table 9.8 indicate that our new scales have high correlations with their target factor and low correlations with the other factors. In other words, they possess impressive convergent and discriminant validities in these extremely large derivation samples. Because other researchers may wish to use these scales in different samples, I briefly describe their construction.

THE DEVELOPMENT OF BETA-F AND BETA-M

Beta-f and Beta-m were developed using MMPI data from 16,890 females and 11,297 males. Items were selected by inspecting the correlations between the 550 MMPI items and the (weighted least squares) factor scores of the first three MMPI higher-order factors. Polychoric correlations were used, rather than point biserial or biserial correlations, because (a) MMPI items have widely different threshold values and (b) the factor score distributions are differentially skewed. Had I ignored these characteristics, the psychometric biases that

TABLE 9.9
Item Composition of Gender-Specific Scales
for the Second Higher-Order Factor of the MMPI

Beta-f											
True											
25	46	73	77	99	126	143	164	181	196	203	204	207
228	229	248	254	268	272	296	372	380	391	400	415	429
432	440	445	449	450	451	482	495	497	502	520	534	566
False											
none											

Beta-m											
True											
12	73	77	83	99	112	126	140	143	144	164	181	196
207	219	223	228	229	254	268	272	283	296	372	380	391
400	410	415	417	426	429	432	440	445	449	450	451	482
495	497	502	520	534	537	547	550	554	561	566		
False											
none											

create difficulty (Carroll, 1945, 1961; Ferguson, 1941; Guilford, 1941) or curvature (McDonald & Ahlawat, 1974; Waller et al., 1996) factors could have influenced the item selection process. To avoid these biases, the factor scores were categorized into 7-point distributions (thresholds were determined such that the categorical factor scores approximated a uniform distribution). I then used MicroFACT (Waller, 1995) to correlate the binary MMPI items with the categorized factor scores. Finally, in each sample, I selected all items that met the following two criteria: (a) a polychoric correlation $\geq |.30|$ with the second MMPI factor, and (b) no correlations $\geq |.25|$ on Factors I or III. Using these criteria I was able to identify 39 and 50 univocal markers of the second higher-order factor in the female and male samples. A listing of these items is reported in Table 9.9.

ADMINISTERING THE MMPI
VIA COMPUTERIZED ADAPTIVE TESTING

The MMPI holds a prominent position in the history of computerized assessment (Butcher, 1987). Thirty five years ago, it was the first personality questionnaire to be computer scored and administered (Rome et al., 1962).

Several years later, one of earliest programs for automated test interpretation (Fowler, 1969) was written for the MMPI.

Despite these milestones, it is ironic that the most powerful method of computerized testing—namely, IRT-based computerized adaptive testing (CAT; Wainer, 1990; Weiss, 1978, 1980, 1985)—has rarely been applied to the MMPI. Although several researchers have fit IRT models to individual MMPI scales (Carter & Wilkinson, 1984) or subscales (Panter, Swygert, & Dahlstrom, 1997), their results have not been encouraging. Furthermore, some researchers doubt that IRT can be applied to the MMPI (or MMPI–2) because the clinical and validity scales do not meet the unidimensionality assumptions of popular IRT models (Butcher, Keller, & Bacon, 1985; Roper, Ben-Porath, & Butcher, 1991, 1995).

An important theme of this book is that IRT can be used to enhance test results in a wide variety of psychological and educational settings. It is fitting, therefore, to conclude this chapter by showing that the MMPI is an appropriate questionnaire for an IRT analysis. The following paragraphs demonstrate, through example, that it is possible, and indeed preferable, to administer the MMPI and MMPI–2 with IRT-based CAT.

Previous applications of IRT with the MMPI have floundered because researchers have mistakenly focused their attentions on the multidimensional clinical and validity scales. A better approach, in my opinion, is to focus on the underlying factors of the MMPI. The factor scales that are described in this chapter measure unidimensional constructs; thus IRT parameter estimates for the items of these scales should be easily generated. Once in hand, these estimates can be used to develop an IRT-based computerized adaptive version of the MMPI.

To demonstrate the feasibility of these ideas, I have estimated IRT parameters for the 51 items of the Denial of Somatic Complaints scale (described in Table 9.5). For purposes of illustration, the scale was reverse-keyed so that higher scores correspond to greater degrees of psychopathology. Item parameter estimates for the two-parameter logistic model were obtained with BILOG 3 (using program defaults, Mislevy & Bock, 1990). It is noteworthy that only records with zero missing data were included in these analyses so that the randomly generated replacement values would not influence the IRT results. The final samples included data from 12,823 females and 8,865 males.

Table 9.10 presents the IRT item parameter estimates for the 51 somatic complaint items. Notice that across the two samples the estimates are similar but not equivalent. The few discrepancies may imply some interesting psychological and physiological differences between the sexes. The reader is encouraged to generate his or her own hypotheses.

For each sample, a real-data simulation (Waller & Reise, 1989) was conducted to investigate the utility of IRT-based CAT with the 51 MMPI items.

TABLE 9.10
IRT Parameters for 51 Physical Complaint Items From the MMPI

Item Number	Abbreviated Item Content	Females α	Females β	Males α	Males β
2	Have a good appetite. F	0.888	1.768	0.983	2.099
3	Wake up fresh and rested. F	1.144	−0.116	0.965	0.216
7	Hands and feet warm enough. F	0.831	0.790	1.039	1.867
9	Able to work as ever. F	1.178	0.090	1.320	0.083
10	Often have lump in throat. T	1.348	1.970	1.217	2.512
14	Often have diarrhea. T	0.729	2.283	0.775	2.537
18	Seldom constipated. F	0.755	0.980	0.795	1.873
23	I have attacks of nausea and vomiting. T	1.351	1.625	1.190	2.552
29	Bothered by acid stomach. T	1.228	1.269	0.980	1.525
36	Seldom worry about my health. F	0.959	−0.054	1.041	0.163
44	Head often hurts all over. T	1.541	1.286	1.663	1.652
47	Often feel hot for no cause. T	1.321	1.245	1.302	1.959
51	Physical health good as friends. F	1.291	0.344	1.588	0.396
55	No heart or chest pains. F	1.083	1.075	1.057	1.078
62	Body parts burning, tingling or crawling. T	1.423	0.303	1.347	0.410
63	No problems with bowel movements. F	0.944	0.692	0.961	1.359
68	No pain in back of neck. F	1.216	0.365	1.174	0.643
72	Often have discomfort in pit of stomach. T	1.385	1.199	1.314	1.488
103	No muscle twitches. F	1.181	0.854	1.360	0.752
108	Fullness in my head or nose. T	1.347	1.510	1.109	1.715
114	Tight band around my head. T	1.453	1.323	1.500	1.725
119	Speech the same as always (no slurring). F	0.968	1.147	0.822	1.347
125	I have much stomach trouble. T	1.442	1.305	1.355	1.643
130	Never vomited or coughed blood. F	0.604	1.957	0.612	1.779
153	Past few years I've been well. F	1.122	0.319	1.297	0.725
160	Never felt better in my life. F	1.007	−1.864	1.075	−1.592
161	Top of head feels tender. T	1.215	1.323	1.193	1.774
163	Do not tire quickly. F	1.219	−0.349	1.278	0.344
174	No fainting spells. F	0.465	−0.675	0.600	0.533
175	No dizzy spells. F	1.274	0.688	1.190	1.1052
185	Hearing as good as most people. F	0.662	3.291	0.565	3.034
187	Hands not clumsy. F	0.950	1.109	1.019	1.360
189	Often feel weak all over. T	1.803	0.908	1.744	1.181
190	Very few headaches. F	1.075	0.263	1.174	0.920
192	No difficulty keeping balance. F	1.278	0.740	1.267	0.991
230	Heart doesn't pound; seldom breathless. F	1.155	0.294	1.085	0.456
243	No or few pains. F	1.580	0.180	1.492	0.323
273	Numbness in my skin. T	1.127	1.269	1.093	1.193
274	Eyesight is good. F	0.723	0.434	0.625	0.811
281	No ear ringing. F	0.922	1.352	0.804	1.472
330	Never been paralyzed. F	0.838	0.478	0.938	0.513
332	My voice changes. T	0.871	1.472	0.755	1.997
405	No trouble swallowing. F	1.281	1.664	1.091	2.310
462	No difficulty holding my urine. F	0.973	1.182	0.920	1.529
474	Urinate no more often than others. F	0.672	1.423	0.665	1.957
486	No blood in urine. F	0.513	2.682	0.602	3.096

(Continued)

TABLE 9.10
(Continued)

Item Number	Abbreviated Item Content	Females		Males	
		α	β	α	β
496	Never seen things doubled. F	0.595	1.481	0.599	1.615
533	Not bothered by stomach gas. F	0.882	1.082	0.745	1.240
535	Mouth feels dry. T	1.075	1.587	0.985	2.301
542	No tarry-looking bowel movements. F	0.562	1.120	0.561	1.326
544	I often feel tired. T	1.438	−0.252	1.234	0.220

In these analyses, the computer uses previously collected data to identify items that would have been administered had the subjects been given an adaptive test. To simulate the test, a small FORTRAN program was written with the following structure.

The computer uses the ordinate of a Gaussian distribution as a prior estimate of a subject's theta level (i.e., their estimated trait level). Formal testing begins by administering the item with the median difficulty. The item is scored (from the previously obtained response vector) and the theta estimate is updated by multiplying the item response function with the normal prior. After the new theta estimate is calculated, the computer selects the item with the highest information function at the appropriate point along the theta continuum. The next item is administered, scored, and the cycle of (a) theta estimation, (b) maximum-information item selection, and (c) item scoring is repeated until two termination criteria are satisfied. First, each subject receives a minimum of 20 items. This rule was adopted to insure that all theta estimates were accurately estimated. Second, items were administered until the conditional item information in the next item fell below a threshold value of .10. Preliminary results with these data suggested that this cutoff was reasonable. Other values may work better in different settings. For further information on the logic and implementation of computerized adaptive testing, readers can consult the tutorial article by Waller and Reise (1989) or the edited book by Wainer (1990).

A summary of the real-data simulations for the female and male samples is presented in Table 9.11. Recall that each subject received a minimum of 20 items. Remarkably, 53% of females and 63% of males finished the test after taking only 20 items. For these subjects, the test was effectively shortened by 61%. Overall, testing time was reduced for all subjects; no person answered more than 44 items (from a total of 51 items).

It is apparent these findings are worthless unless the adaptively generated scores are strongly correlated with the full-scale theta estimates and the full-scale raw scores. Impressively, the relevant correlations are large. In

TABLE 9.11
Number of Items Administered in a Real-Data Simulation
of CAT With a 51-Item Physical Complaints Scale

		Females		Males	
Number of Items	% Decrease in Scale Length	Frequency	Cumulative Percentage	Frequency	Cumulative Percentage
20	61	6756	53	5586	63
21	59	413	56	251	66
22	57	377	59	277	69
23	55	171	60	104	70
24	53	242	62	134	72
25	51	166	63	60	72
26	49	267	65	156	74
27	47	192	67	119	75
28	45	91	68	47	76
29	43	123	69	99	77
30	41	87	69	44	78
31	39	37	70	19	78
32	37	133	71	67	79
33	35	245	73	129	80
34	33	457	76	242	83
35	31	442	79	243	85
36	29	535	84	242	88
37	27	440	87	301	92
38	25	174	88	81	93
39	24	429	92	174	94
40	22	354	95	195	97
41	20	221	96	92	98
42	18	286	99	100	99
43	16	167	100	85	100
44	14	18	100	18	100

both the female and male samples, the adaptive theta estimates correlate
.95 with both the raw scores (from the 51-item scale) and full-scale theta
estimates. If future studies obtain similar results with other MMPI factor
scales, then it would seem highly desirable to develop IRT-based computerized adaptive versions of the MMPI and MMPI–2.

The new rules of measurement that are described in this chapter are in fact
not really new. Appropriate methods for binary-item factor analysis and IRT
have been available for decades. Nevertheless, these methods are novelties in
many applied areas of research. An important goal of this chapter was to
introduce these tools to clinicians and other psychologists who may use
questionnaires such as the MMPI and MMPI–2 in their day-to-day activities. If
this chapter convinces them to incorporate the new rules of measurement into
their methodological toolbox, it will have achieved its goals.

REFERENCES

Archer, R. P., & Klinefelter, D. (1991). MMPI factor analytic findings for adolescents: Item- and scale-level factor structures. *Journal of Personality Assessment, 57*, 356–367.

Barker, H. R., Fowler, R. D., & Peterson, L. P. (1971). Factor analytic structure of the short form MMPI items in a VA Hospital population. *Journal of Clinical Psychology, 27*, 228–233.

Beck, N. C., McRae, C., Henrichs, T. F., Sneider, L., Horwitz, B., Rennier, G., Thomas, S., & Hedlund, J. (1989). Replicated item level factor structure of the MMPI: Racial and sexual differences. *Journal of Clinical Psychology, 45*, 553–560.

Ben-Porath, Y. S., & Waller, N. G. (1992). "Normal" personality inventories in clinical assessment: General requirements and the potential for using the NEO personality inventory. *Psychological Assessment, 4*, 14–19.

Bernstein, I. H., & Teng, G. (1989). Factoring items and factor scales are different: Spurious evidence for multidimensionality due to item categorizations. *Psychological Bulletin, 105*, 467–477.

Birnbaum, A. (1968). Some latent trait models and their use in inferring an examinee's ability. In F. M. Lord & M. R. Novick (Eds.), *Statistical theories of mental test scores* (pp. 397–472). Reading, MA: Addison-Wesley.

Block, J. (1965). *The challenge of response sets.* New York: Appleton-Century-Crofts.

Bock, R. D., & Aitken, M. (1981). Marginal maximum likelihood estimation of item parameters: An application of an EM algorithm. *Psychometrika, 46*, 443–459.

Bock, R. D., Gibbons, R. D., & Muraki, E. (1988). Full-information factor analysis. *Applied Psychological Measurement, 12*, 261–280.

Butcher, J. N. (1987). *Computerized psychological assessment: A practitioner's guide.* New York: Basic Books.

Butcher, J., Dahlstrom, G. W., Graham, J. R., Tellegen, A., & Kaemmer, B. (1989). *Minnesota Multiphasic Personality Inventory (MMPI–2). Manual for administration and scoring.* Minneapolis: University of Minnesota Press.

Butcher, J. N., Graham, J. R., Williams, C. L., & Ben-Porath, Y. S. (1990). *Development and use of the MMPI–2 content scales.* Minneapolis: University of Minnesota Press.

Butcher, J. N., Keller, L. S., & Bacon, S. F. (1985). Current developments and future directions in computerized personality assessment. *Journal of Consulting and Clinical Psychology, 53*, 803–815.

Butcher, J. N., & Rouse, S. V. (1996). PERSONALITY: Individual differences and clinical assessment. *Annual Review of Psychology, 47*, 87–111.

Carroll, J. B. (1945). The effect of difficulty and chance success on correlations between items or between tests. *Psychometrika, 10*, 1–19.

Carroll, J. B. (1961). The nature of data, or how to choose a correlation coefficient. *Psychometrika, 26*, 347–372.

Carter, J. E., & Wilkinson, L. (1984). A latent trait analysis of the MMPI. *Multivariate Behavioral Research, 19*, 385–407.

Cattell, R. B., & Vogelman, S. (1977). A comprehensive trial of the scree and KG criteria for determining the number of factors. *Multivariate Behavioral Research, 12*, 289–325.

Christofferson, A. (1975). Factor analysis of dichotomized variables. *Psychometrika*, 5–32.

Cliff, N. (1988). The eigenvalue greater than one rule and the reliability of components. *Psychological Bulletin, 103*, 276–279.

Comrey, A. L. (1957a). A factor analysis of items on the MMPI hypochondriasis scale. *Educational and Psychological Measurement, 17*, 568–577.

Comrey, A. L. (1957b). A factor analysis of items on the MMPI depression scale. *Educational and Psychological Measurement, 17*, 568–585.

Comrey, A. L. (1957c). A factor analysis of items on the MMPI hysteria scale. *Educational and Psychological Measurement, 17,* 586–592.

Comrey, A. L. (1958a). A factor analysis of items on the F scale of the MMPI. *Educational and Psychological Measurement, 18,* 621–632.

Comrey, A. L. (1958b). A factor analysis of items on the K scale of the MMPI. *Educational and Psychological Measurement, 18,* 633–639.

Comrey, A. L. (1958c). A factor analysis of items on the MMPI psychopathic deviate scale. *Educational and Psychological Measurement, 18,* 91–98.

Comrey, A. L. (1958d). A factor analysis of items on the MMPI paranoia scale. *Educational and Psychological Measurement, 18,* 99–107.

Comrey, A. L. (1958e). A factor analysis of items on the MMPI psychasthenia scale. *Educational and Psychological Measurement, 18,* 293–300.

Comrey, A. L. (1958f). A factor analysis of items on the MMPI hypomania scale. *Educational and Psychological Measurement, 18,* 313–323.

Comrey, A. L., & Levonian, E. (1958). A comparison of three point coefficients in factor analyses of MMPI items. *Educational and Psychological Measurement, 18,* 739–755.

Comrey, A. L., & Marggraff, W. M. (1958). A factor analysis of items on the MMPI schizophrenia scale. *Educational and Psychological Measurement, XVIII,* 301–311.

Costa, P. T., Zonderman, A. B., & Williams, R. B. (1985). Content and comprehensiveness in the MMPI: An item factor analysis in a normal adult sample. *Journal of Personality and Social Psychology, 48,* 925–933.

Dahlstrom, G. W., Welsh, G. S., & Dahlstrom, L. (1972). *An MMPI handbook, Volume I: Clinical Interpretation.* Minneapolis: University of Minnesota Press.

Edwards, A. L. (1957). *The social desirability variable in personality assessment and research.* New York: Dryden.

Edwards, L. K., & Edwards, A. L. (1991). A principal-components analysis of the Minnesota Multiphasic Personality Inventory factor scales. *Journal of Personality and Social Psychology, 60,* 766–772.

Ferguson, G. A. (1941). The factorial interpretation of test difficulty. *Psychometrika, 6,* 323–329.

Fowler, R. D. (1969). Automated interpretation of personality test data. In J. N. Butcher (Ed.), *MMPI: Research developments and clinical applications* (pp. 105–126). New York: McGraw-Hill.

Fraser, C., & McDonald, R. P. (1988). NOHARM: Least squares item factor analysis. *Multivariate Behavioral Research, 23,* 267–269.

Guilford, J. P. (1941). The difficulty of a test and its factor composition. *Psychometrika, 6,* 67–77.

Guilford, J. P. (1952). When not to factor analyze. *Psychological Bulletin, 49,* 26–37.

Hambleton, R. K., & Swaminathan, H. (1985). *Item response theory: Principles and applications.* Boston: Kluwer-Nijhoff.

Hambleton, R. K., Swaminathan, H., & Rogers, H. J. (1991). *Fundamentals of item response theory.* Newbury Park, CA: Sage.

Hathaway, S. R., & McKinley, J. C. (1940). A multiphasic personality schedule (Minnesota): I. Construction of the schedule. *Journal of Psychology, 10,* 249–254.

Hathaway, S. R., & McKinley, J. C. (1983). *The Minnesota Multiphasic Personality Inventory manual.* New York: Psychological Corporation.

Hollrah, J. L., Schlottman, R. S., Scott, A. B., & Brunetti, D. G. (1995). Validity of the MMPI subtle items. *Journal of Personality Assessment, 65,* 278–299.

Jackson, D. N. (1971). The dynamics of structured personality tests: 1971. *Psychological Review, 78,* 229–248.

Johnson, J. H., Null, C., Butcher, J. N., & Johnson, K. N. (1984). Replicated item level factor analysis of the full MMPI. *Journal of Personality and Social Psychology, 47,* 105–114.

Knol, D. L., & Berger, M. P. F. (1988). *Empirical comparison between factor analysis and item response models*. Research Report 88–11, Department of Education: Division of Educational Measurement and Data Analysis: University of Twente.

Knol, D. L., & Berger, M. P. F. (1991). Empirical comparison between factor analysis and multidimensional item response models. *Multivariate Behavioral Research, 26*, 457–477.

Koss, M. P. (1979). MMPI item content: Recurring issues. In J. N. Butcher (Ed.), *New developments in the use of the MMPI* (pp. 3–38). Minneapolis: University of Minnesota Press.

Lord, F. M. (1980). *Applications of item response theory to practical testing problems*. Hillsdale, NJ: Lawrence Erlbaum Associates.

Lubin, B. B., Larsen, R. M., Matarazzo, J. D., & Seever, M. (1985). Psychological test usage patterns in five professional settings. *American Psychologist, 40*, 857–861.

Lushene, R. E. (1967). *Factor structure of the MMPI item pool*. Unpublished master's thesis, Florida State University, Tallahassee, FL.

McDonald, R. P. (1965). Difficulty factors and nonlinear factor analysis. *British Journal of Mathematical and Statistical Psychology, 18*, 11–23.

McDonald, R. P., & Ahlawat, K. S. (1974). Difficulty factors in binary data. *British Journal of Mathematical and Statistical Psychology, 27*, 82–99.

McKinley, J. C., & Hathaway, S. R. (1944). The MMPI: V. Hysteria, hypomania, and psychopathic deviate. *Journal of Applied Psychology, 28*, 153–174.

Mislevy, R. J. (1986). Recent developments in the factor analysis of categorical variables. *Journal of Educational Statistics, 11*, 3–31.

Mislevy, R. J., & Bock, R. D. (1990). *BILOG 3: Item analysis and test scoring with binary logistic models*. Chicago: Scientific Software International.

Muthén, B. (1978). Contributions to factor analysis of dichotomous variables. *Psychometrika, 43*, 551–560.

Muthén, B. (1989). Dichotomous factor analysis of symptom data. *Sociological Methods and Research, 18*, 19–65.

Overall, J. E., Hunter, S., & Butcher, J. N. (1973). Factor structure of the MMPI–168 in a psychiatric population. *Journal of Consulting and Clinical Psychology, 41*, 284–286.

Panter, A. T., Swygert, K. A., & Dahlstrom, W. G. (1997). Factor analytic approaches to personality item-level data. *Journal of Personality Assessment, 68*, 561–589.

Reddon, J. R., Marceau, R., & Jackson, D. N. (1982). An application of singular value decomposition to the factor analysis of MMPI items. *Applied Psychological Measurement, 6*, 275–283.

Reise, S., & Waller, N. G. (1990). Fitting the two-parameter model to personality data. *Applied Psychological Measurement, 14*, 45–58.

Rome, H. P., Swenson, W. M., Mataya, P., McCarthy, C. E., Pearson, J. S., Keating, F. R., & Hathaway, S. R. (1962). Symposium on automation technics in personality assessment. *Proceedings of the Staff Meetings of the Mayo Clinic, 37*, 61–82.

Roper, B. L., Ben-Porath, Y. S., & Butcher, J. N. (1991). Comparability of computerized adaptive and conventional testing with the MMPI–2. *Journal of Personality Assessment, 57*, 278–290.

Roper, B. L., Ben-Porath, Y. S., & Butcher, J. N. (1995). Comparability and validity of computerized adaptive testing with the MMPI–2. *Journal of Personality Assessment, 65*, 358–371.

SAS Institute. (1989). *SAS/STAT user's guide* (Version 6, 4th ed.). Cary, NC: Author.

SPSS, Inc. (1994). *SPSS Advanced Statistics*. Chicago: Author.

Stewart, R. A. C. (1974). Factor Analysis and rotation of the 566 MMPI items. *Social Behavior and Personality, 2*, 147–156.

Shure, G. H., & Rogers, M. S. (1965). Note of caution on the factor analysis of the MMPI. *Psychological Bulletin, 63*, 14–18.

Wainer, H. (1990). *Computerized adaptive testing: A primer*. Hillsdale, NJ: Lawrence Erlbaum Associates.

Waller, N. G. (1995). MicroFACT 1.1 [computer program]. Assessment Systems Corporation, St. Paul, MN 55114.

Waller, N. G., & Reise, S. (1989). Computerized adaptive personality assessment: An illustration with the Absorption scale. *Journal of Personality and Social Psychology, 57*, 1051–1058.

Waller, N. G., Tellegen, A., McDonald, R., & Lykken, D. T. (1996). Exploring nonlinear models in personality assessment: Development and preliminary validation of a Negative Emotionality Scale. *Journal of Personality, 64*, 545–576.

Weiss, D. J. (1978). *Proceedings of the 1977 Computerized Adaptive Testing Conference.* Minneapolis: University of Minnesota.

Weiss, D. J. (1980). *Proceedings of the 1979 Computerized Adaptive Testing Conference.* Minneapolis: University of Minnesota.

Weiss, D. J. (1985). *Proceedings of the 1982 Computerized Adaptive Testing Conference.* Minneapolis: University of Minnesota.

Welsh, G. S. (1956). Factor dimensions *A* and *R*. In G. S. Welsh & W. G. Dahlstrom (Eds.), *Basic reading on the MMPI in psychology and medicine* (pp. 264–281). Minneapolis: University of Minnesota Press.

Welsh, G. S., & Dahlstrom, G. W. (1956). *Basic readings on the MMPI in psychology and medicine.* Minneapolis: University of Minnesota Press.

Wheeler, W. M., Little, K. B., & Lehner, G. F. J. (1951). The internal structure of the MMPI. *Journal of Consulting Psychology, 15*, 134–141.

Wherry, R. I., & Gaylord, R. H. (1944). Factor pattern of test items and tests as a function of the correlation coefficient. *Psychometrika, 9*, 237–244.

Wiggins, J. S. (1966). Content dimensions in the MMPI. In J. N. Butcher (Ed.), *MMPI: Research developments and clinical applications* (pp. 127–180). New York: McGraw Hill.

Wilson, D., Wood, R., & Gibbons, R. D. (1991). *TESTFACT: Test scoring, item statistics, and item factor analysis.* Chicago: Scientific Software.

Zwick, W. R., & Velicer, W. F. (1986). Comparison of five rules for determining the number of components to retain. *Psychological Bulletin, 99*, 432–442.

CHAPTER TEN

Personality Measurement Issues Viewed Through the Eyes of IRT

Steven P. Reise
University of California, Los Angeles

The term *item response theory* (IRT) refers to a set of psychometric proce-dures that serve as an alternative to traditional classical test theory (CTT) methods of analyzing psychological tests and test items. In educational and aptitude testing, IRT procedures are well known and well established. This fact can be validated by pointing to the existence of several introductory texts on IRT (e.g., Hambleton, Swaminathan, & Rogers, 1991; Lord, 1980) and through examining the preponderance of IRT-based research in journals such as *Applied Psychological Measurement* or the *Journal of Educational Measurement.* Despite its proliferation in educational assessment, only re-cently has IRT been applied in the domain of typical performance or per-sonality assessment (cf. Steinberg & Thissen, 1995). The goal of this chapter, therefore, is to describe and discuss some applications of IRT measurement models in personality assessment and to highlight advantages and disadvan-tages that might be accrued through such application. In the subsequent section, a brief introduction to IRT models as they may be applied to un-derstanding the psychometric properties of personality tests and test items is provided.

INTRODUCTION TO IRT MEASUREMENT MODELS

IRT measurement models are nonlinear mathematical functions that are used to describe the relationship between test item responses and an examinee's position on a latent trait variable, which in turn is assumed to underlie test performance. IRT measurement models represent a class of logistic functions, called item characteristic curves (ICCs), that describe how the probability of responding to an item in a specific way changes as a function of an examinee's position on a latent trait variable. There are a variety of alternative IRT models, or equivalently, different functional forms for the item characteristic curve that are applicable under different testing contexts. An IRT model that some researchers have found useful for analyzing dichotomously scored (true/false) personality questionnaire items is the 2-parameter logistic function (2PL) shown in Equation 10.1 (Birnbaum, 1968). It is important to note that Equation 10.1 is a unidimensional model in that only a single common latent variable is assumed to underlie item responses and to account for the covariation among test items.

$$P \mid \Theta = \{1 + EXP(-\alpha(\Theta - \beta))\}^{-1} \qquad (10.1)$$

Where,

$P \mid \Theta$ = the conditional probability of item endorsement

Θ = the examinee trait level parameter (typically expressed on a 0,1 scale)

α = the item discrimination parameter

β = the item difficulty parameter (typically expressed on a 0,1 scale)

To flesh out the meaning of these parameters, Figs. 10.1 and 10.2 display four item-characteristic curves that were estimated for items taken from the 26-item Stress Reaction scale of the Multidimensional Personality Questionnaire (MPQ; Tellegen, 1982). In both Figs. 10.1 and 10.2, examinee trait level is on the x axis and note that the scale range is similar to a z-score metric. It is a common practice in IRT modeling to identify the latent trait scale (Θ) by fixing it to have a mean of zero and a standard deviation of 1.0. Thus, assuming normality of the latent trait, it is appropriate to consider a Θ score of zero as being about average in the examinee population and a Θ score of + or −1.5 as being rather high or low on the trait, respectively.

In the 2-parameter logistic model, the α parameter (discrimination) represents the steepness of the item characteristic curve and the β parameter (difficulty) represents the point on the latent trait continuum where the examinee has a .50 probability of responding to an item in the keyed direction (i.e., endorsing the item). Figure 10.1 displays two Stress Reaction scale items that differ in both discrimination and difficulty; Item #1 has a discrimination of 1.67 and difficulty of −0.32, whereas Item #7 has a discrimination of 0.82 and a difficulty of 1.31. Notice how the response probabilities change more rapidly for Item #1 as opposed to Item #7. In Fig. 10.2 the two Stress Reaction items differ widely in difficulty but are equal in

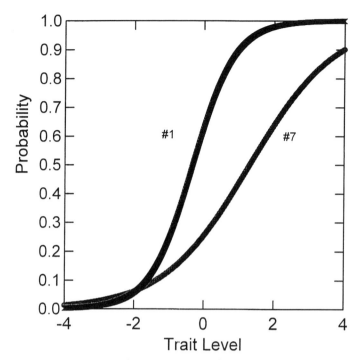

FIG. 10.1. Item Characteristic Curves for Items #1 and #7

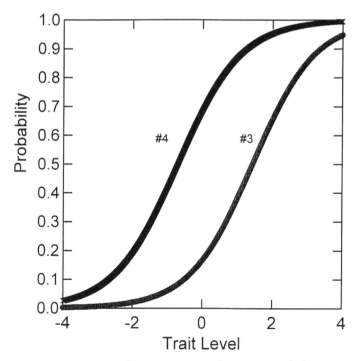

FIG. 10.2. Item Characteristic Curves for Items #3 and #4

terms of discrimination capacity; Item #3 has a discrimination of 1.13 and a difficulty of 1.43 and Item #4 has a discrimination of 1.11 and a difficulty of −0.71. Thus, Item #4 is much easier than Item #3 in the sense that any examinee who is −0.71 Θ units below the mean on this trait will be more likely to endorse this item than not, whereas for Item #3, only examinees who are high on the latent trait have a better than 50/50 chance of endorsing this item. A more expansive and detailed example of fitting the 2-parameter logistic test model to personality test data can be found in Reise and Waller (1990). These authors estimated 2-parameter logistic item parameters for each of the 11 trait scales on the MPQ (Tellegen, 1982).

The goal of fitting an IRT model, such as the 2-parameter logistic just described, is to estimate the α and β parameters for every item on a scale, and to estimate one Θ parameter for every examinee. This can be accomplished through one of several computer programs that are currently in the marketplace. Among the most popular programs are BILOG (Mislevy & Bock, 1990), XCALIBRE (Yoes, 1996), and MULTILOG (Thissen, 1991). These programs all make use of a marginal maximum likelihood (Bock & Aitken, 1981) estimation routine, and consequently, the number of subjects needed will be at least 200 for dichotomously scored items and will increase depending on the number of response categories (Reise & Yu, 1990). The first two programs only estimate item parameters for dichotomous IRT models, such as in a true/false test or in a multiple-choice test that is scored correct or incorrect. However, the MULTILOG program can estimate a wider variety of IRT models including models for both dichotomous and polytomous response test items.

Although only a single IRT model was described in this section, it is important to note that a variety of alternatives exist. For example, to analyze dichotomous test items there is the popular 1-parameter logistic model (Wright, 1977). In this model, the item discriminations are a constant across items. This is roughly equivalent to saying that the test items have equal loadings in a factor analytic sense. There is also a 3-parameter logistic (3PL) model for dichotomous item responses. In the 3PL a pseudo-guessing parameter is estimated, called c, that is the lower asymptote of the item characteristic curve. This model is important because with multiple-choice tests, examinees have a nonzero probability of responding correctly by chance regardless of how low on the trait scale they are, and thus there is a need for a nonzero lower asymptote.

IRT models also exist for representing polytomous item responses (e.g., Likert rating scales) such as are common on many personality questionnaires. For example, there is the graded response model (Samejima, 1969), which is simply a generalization of the 2PL model described in Equation 10.1. Although detailed description of the various polytomous IRT models is beyond the scope of this chapter, Table 10.1 provides a list of alternative

TABLE 10.1
Potential IRT Measurement Models

BINARY DATA

1-Parameter logistic (Wright, 1977)
 -Item difficulty only, slopes constant
2-Parameter logistic (Birnbaum, 1968)
 -Item difficulty and discrimination
3-Parameter logistic (Lord, 1980)
 -Item difficulty, discrimination, and guessing

POLYTOMOUS DATA

Partial credit model (Masters, 1982)
 -Polytomous generalization of Rasch model
Graded response model (Samejima, 1969)
 -Polytomous generalization of 2PL
Rating scale model (Andrich, 1978)
 -Scale location, item thresholds, slopes constant
Nominal response model (Bock, 1972)
 -For unordered response categories

---

models, a brief overview of each, and a citation to relevant articles that provide more details. Also, Thissen and Steinberg (1986) provided a taxonomy of various polytomous IRT models. Separate chapters describing each can be found in van der Linden and Hambleton (1996).

WHAT IRT MODELS CAN AND CANNOT DO TO IMPROVE PERSONALITY ASSESSMENT

The application of IRT measurement models affords several advantages over CTT-based psychometric procedures. Now that the 2-parameter logistic model has been briefly reviewed, which can be used to analyze dichotomously scored personality test data, in this section, I describe several advantages that are facilitated by IRT modeling as applied in personality assessment. The following discussion is limited to just four topics: (a) describing test and item properties, (b) identifying differential item functioning, (c) computerized adaptive testing, and (d) assessing person-fit. This is by no means a thorough review of advantages of, or differences between, IRT and traditional psychometric procedures. Interested readers should seek further reading such as Thissen (1993) or Embretson (1996), who describe and detail differences between modern and traditional measurement theory. Also, Table 10.2 provides an overview of basic differences between classical and modern psychometrics. Not all of these topics will be described, however, due to space limitations.

TABLE 10.2
Analyzing Psychometric Properties of Test and Items

Traditional	IRT
Strength of item judged by:	
ITEM–TEST CORRELATION	ITEM DISCRIMINATION
Appropriateness of item judged by:	
PROPORTION ENDORSED	ITEM DIFFICULTY
Precision of measurement judged by:	
COEFFICIENT ALPHA	TEST INFORMATION
Test properties are:	
SAMPLE DEPENDENT	SAMPLE FREE
Comparing examinees requires:	
PARALLEL TESTS	COMMON METRIC
Encourages the writing of:	
LONG TESTS	SHORT, TARGETED TESTS
Measurement theory is:	
NOT MODEL BASED	MODEL BASED
Encourages item formats that are:	
SAME ACROSS ITEMS	APPROPRIATE

Evaluating the Basic Psychometric Properties of Items and Tests

It is of fundamental importance to test users to know how a particular test works in measuring a particular construct in a given examinee population. In addressing this issue, three topics are paramount. These are: (a) what is the dimensionality of the test? (b) is the test too easy or too difficult? and (c) how precise is the measurement? In this section, IRT methods of addressing these basic questions about the psychometric properties of personality tests are described. These are: (a) full-information item factor analysis (Muraki & Engelhard, 1985), (b) inspection of IRT item parameters, and (c) the use of psychometric information.

As is well known, it is important to investigate the dimensionality of a personality measure. It is essential for researchers to investigate how many factors are influencing the observed item responses. The most common tool in personality assessment research used for addressing this issue is common linear factor analysis. Unfortunately, the linear factor analysis model is not appropriate for the analysis of dichotomous item responses (Bock, Gibbons, & Muraki, 1988). This is a problem and limitation in personality assessment because many popular scales have dichotomous (true or false) response formats. As pointed out by many researchers, traditional factor analysis assumes continuous ratings and normality, which are often violated in personality assessment leading to underestimates of factor loadings and overestimates of the number of significant dimensions (see Gibbons, Clark, Cavanaugh, & Davis, 1985).

However, the problems in linear factor analysis can be avoided by using IRT models to assess dimensionality. The reason is that IRT models are essentially equivalent to nonlinear factor models, or what are called full-information item factor analysis models (Muraki & Engelhard, 1985). Programs like TESTFACT (Wilson, Wood, & Gibbons, 1991) have been developed that allow researchers to assess the structure of their binary data by conducting statistical tests of the number of latent factors. Stated differently, IRT modeling with marginal maximum likelihood estimation is essentially the same thing as performing a full-information item factor analyses. Such an analysis provides researchers with an estimate of an item's discrimination (or factor loading) on multiple dimensions as well as an estimate of an item's threshold or difficulty.

Hendryx, Haviland, Gibbons, and Clark (1992) and Haviland and Reise (1996) used the TESTFACT program to fit a multidimensional IRT model to investigate the dimensionality of the Toronto Alexithymia Scale (TAS; Taylor, Bagby, & Parker, 1992). Treating the TAS responses dichotomously, the objective of these studies was to use IRT to investigate the feasibility of using a global TAS score as an index of alexithymia severity. Generally speaking, results of these studies indicated that the TAS is multidimensional and that the dimensions are not highly correlated with each other. Great caution should thus be used when interpreting global TAS scores. Beyond the topic of these specific personality assessment results, because personality researchers tend to understand factor analyses well but tend not to be familiar with IRT, the topic of full-information item factor analysis and the TESTFACT program can provide an excellent bridge for spanning the knowledge gap.

In traditional test analysis, two psychometric item properties play central roles in scale evaluation. First is the item–test correlation coefficient that is often used as an indicator of an item's strength as a trait indicator. Personality researchers often want item–test correlations to be as high as possible, but of course, this can lead to a lack of bandwidth of measurement. The second main traditional index is the item mean (or proportion endorsed with dichotomous items). Often personality researchers try to write or find dichotomously scored scale items that have proportions endorsed around 0.50. This increases test score variance and leads to higher internal consistency indices. It is important to note that both of these CTT-based item indices are sample dependent; that is, their values will be highly dependent on the distribution of the trait in the administered sample.

IRT offers analogues to the CTT item indices just described. Specifically, in the context of the 2PL model, personality scale items can be judged by their item difficulty and item discrimination parameters. Note that technically speaking, and assuming the model fits the data, neither of these IRT item indices is sample dependent and thus they provide less ambiguous interpretations than their classical test theory counterparts. As described earlier, in the 2PL model, the IRT item difficulty parameter is the trait level necessary to have a 50% probability of endorsing an item, and the item discrimination parameter is the slope of the item characteristic curve (i.e., how rapidly the endorsement probabilities change). Although the IRT and the traditional indices are roughly analogous, it could be argued that the IRT parameters offer some interpretative advantages over their CTT counterparts (see for example, Steinberg & Thissen, 1996).

Beyond the sample invariance property, the advantage of the IRT parameters over the traditional indices lies in the ability to conduct advanced analyses based on the IRT parameters. For example, in IRT the item difficulty is on the same scale as the latent trait variable, thus items can be selected and tests can more easily be designed to make discriminations among examinees fall in particular trait ranges. Also, as will be elaborated later this chapter, the IRT parameters facilitate, or allow for, the identification of item bias (called differential item functioning, or DIF), computerized adaptive testing, and the identification of person-fit—three advances in measurement that are all exceedingly difficult without IRT. Perhaps the chief advantage of the IRT item parameters and their corresponding item characteristic curve is their ability to be transformed into information curves as described next.

Traditionally, the precision of personality tests is judged by their internal consistency coefficients and all subjects receive the same standard error of measurement. Under an IRT framework, however, personality tests can be judged by the information they provide and by examinees at different trait levels receiving different standard errors. IRT-based psychometrics thus acknowledges that personality tests perform differently for examinees with different trait levels. To understand this, one needs to understand the concept of test information and its relationship to examinee errors of measurement.

With an IRT model, a researcher can use the parameters from an item characteristic curve to derive what is known as an item information curve (IIC). An IIC tells a researcher how much psychometric information (discrimination ability) a test item provides at each level of the latent trait. For the 2-parameter logistic model previously described, the formula for item information is shown in Equation 10.2.

$$\text{ITEM}_{\text{INFO}} \mid \Theta = \alpha^2 \times P \mid \Theta \times Q \mid \Theta \qquad (10.2)$$

Where,

$$Q \mid \Theta = 1 - P \mid \Theta$$

What may or may not be apparent in Equation 10.2 is that the amount of information an item provides toward reducing uncertainty about an examinee's trait level is determined by the item discrimination parameter (the higher, the more information) and where that information is located on the trait continuum is determined by the item difficulty parameter. Specifically, information is peaked at the item's difficulty.

To make this more concrete, the item information curves for the four Stress Reaction scale items shown previously are displayed in Figs. 10.3 and 10.4. To recap, the item discrimination and difficulty parameters for these items were: 0.82 and 1.31 for Item #7; 1.67 and −0.32 for Item #1; 1.13 and 1.43 for Item #3; and 1.11 and −0.71 for Item #4, respectively. Notice how in each of these figures the item information is peaked at the item difficulty and the amount of information (height of curve) is determined by the item discrimination. Intuitively, this makes sense because items that are more discriminating should provide for finer distinctions between examinees. In addition, difficult items (those with large positive β values) should differentiate (provide information) between high trait examinees and be worthless for differentiating among low trait level examinees. Conversely, easy items (those with large negative β values) should be able to differentiate among low trait level examinees but not high trait level examinees.

There are two important consequences regarding item information that are extremely useful to test developers and ultimately useful for test inter-

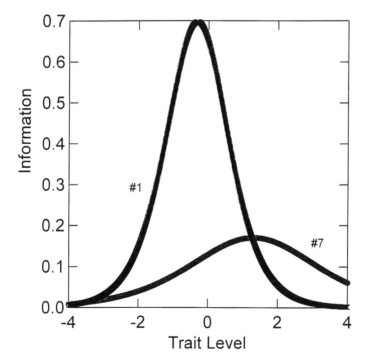

FIG. 10.3. Item Information Curves for Items #1 and #7

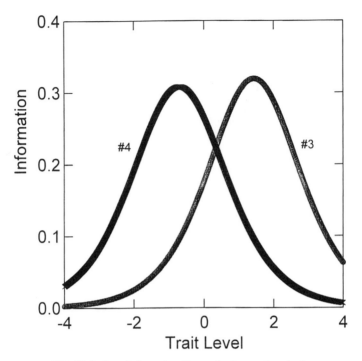

FIG. 10.4. Item Information Curves for Items #3 and #4

pretation. First, IICs are additive across items measuring the same latent variable. Thus, a researcher can tell how much information a test or subtest contains by adding together these curves. Such a test information curve indicates exactly where on the trait continuum the test provides maximal information or equivalently, the best discrimination among examinees. For example, in Fig. 10.5, the item information curves for the 4 example items have been added together in order to form a test information curve.

The second useful feature of item (or test) information is that it is inversely related to an examinee's error of measurement, as shown in Equation 10.3:

$$\text{Standard Error}\,|\,\Theta = 1\,/\,\text{SQRT}(\text{TEST}_{\text{INFO}}\,|\,\Theta) \qquad (10.3)$$

According to Equation 10.3, the more information a test provides at a particular trait level, the smaller the standard error for examinees who score in that range. In terms of Fig. 10.5, the test information curve for the four example Stress Reaction items shows that this subtest is best for differentiating among middle trait examinees. Appropriately, these examinees would have smaller errors of measurement associated with their scores than examinees at the extreme.

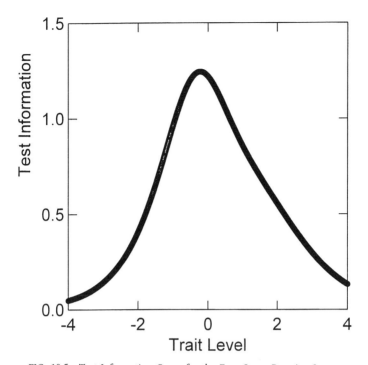

FIG. 10.5. Test Information Curve for the Four Stress Reaction Items

Based on the information provided in this section, it should be clear that IRT information analysis provides a different way of looking at personality scales than traditional psychometric techniques. For example, two competing scales would not necessarily be judged by their alpha coefficients, but rather by their test information curves. Two tests may have equal alpha coefficients but provide information in different ranges of the latent trait. Furthermore, in terms of test construction, IICs can be used to create scale that target a specific type of examinee. For example, perhaps a researcher may want to make fine discriminations between examinees who are greater than or less than 2 standard deviations above the mean on a given variable.

Testing for Differential Item Functioning

IRT models are useful in creating a common latent trait metric by which items from different tests, or items that have been given to different samples of examinees, may be compared. To understand this, assume we have two self-report measures of a similar construct. Using IRT procedures, it is possible to link the latent scales of these tests—that is, place the item characteristic curves on the same scale. This would allow researchers to compare the tests more readily. All a researcher would need to accomplish this objective is a subset of examinees that responded to several of the items (called an anchor set in IRT jargon) on both measures. Note that this metric linking would be difficult, but not impossible, to accomplish with CTT procedures. This ability to calibrate items onto a common metric with IRT has led to several interesting studies. For example, Steinberg (1994) used IRT methods to study item position effects in a personality assessment context.

Most important, the ability to place items onto a common metric in IRT greatly facilitates the study of differential item functioning (DIF) or item bias (Thissen, Steinberg, & Gerrard, 1986). In IRT terms, a test item displays DIF if examinees with the same trait level have different probabilities of responding to an item correctly. In other words, a personality item is biased if the ICCs are not the same across two or more groups of examinees. This is an important issue because in order for test scores to be comparable across groups, the items must work in the same way; that is, they must be measurement invariant.

Although the topic of DIF is important in psychological testing, especially for large-scale testing programs, little work has occurred in personality assessment. Traditionally, this issue has been dealt with by investigating the factorial invariance (i.e., equal loadings) of a measure across two or more groups using confirmatory factor analytic (CFA) methods. Reise, Widaman, and Pugh (1993) compared confirmatory factor analyses and IRT methods of testing measurement invariance in the context of a personality measure. Specifically, they investigated the invariance of a 5-item mood measure across samples of American and Chinese subjects. They concluded that the IRT and CFA analyses produced similar results. However, the IRT analysis facilitated the investigation of both whether items were more discriminating in one group versus another and whether an item was more or less difficult for one group versus another. Note that an IRT item-discrimination parameter is analogous to a factor loading and thus, when researchers test for factorial invariance with CFA this can be thought of as testing whether the items are equally discriminating in an IRT sense. However, although establishing the invariance of factor loadings or item discrimination parameters is important, differences between groups in item difficulty parameters can also be substantively interesting. Items can be equally discriminating across groups—indicating that the item works in both groups—but can have different item difficulties.

For example, Reise and Smith (1997) investigated differential item functioning between gender groups on the Stress Reaction scale of the MPQ (Tellegen, 1982). The BILOG–MG (Zimowski, Muraki, Mislevy, & Bock, 1996) program, which was specifically designed to study DIF, was then used. First, assuming that the items are equally discriminating across groups, the BILOG–MG program estimates a common set of item discrimination parameters for each group, but freely estimates separate item difficulties for each group.

For each item, separate item characteristic curves are estimated for each examinee group with the constraint that they have the same slope across groups.

Reise and Smith's (1997) findings indicated that there was significant DIF between gender groups on several Stress Reaction scale items. Interestingly, some items were relatively easier to endorse (required a lower trait level) for men and some of the items were relatively easier to endorse for women. Looking at the results as a whole, it appeared to Reise and Smith (1997) that the items that are easier to endorse for men tend to come from a group of items described as easily upset and irritable, whereas the items that are easier to endorse for women tend to come from a cluster of items characterized as sensitive or vulnerable.

Computerized Adaptive Testing

With tests designed under a CTT framework, examinees can only be compared if—and only if—they received the exact same item set or equated test forms. Unless the tests are parallel, scores across different versions of a measure cannot be directly compared. This is a severe limitation, especially because many items within a scale are a waste of examinee time. What does this mean? Consider intelligence testing as an example. For the upper 25% of examinees, the items designed to discriminate between low and average IQ are a waste because these examinees have a high probability of responding to such items correctly. For average examinees, all the very difficult and very easy items are a waste of time; that is, they provide no information for discriminating among people in the middle of the trait range. Finally, for low IQ examinees, average- and high-difficulty items have little value because they have such high probabilities of responding incorrectly. This problem of administering uninformative test items can be overcome through a process of IRT-based computerized adaptive testing. In turn, the ability to perform computerized adaptive testing is a direct result of the capacity of IRT models to scale examinees (and items) on a common latent trait metric, even if they have taken a completely different set of items.

Computerized adaptive testing (CAT; Wainer, 1990) is a process by which test items are selected, via a computer, to match an examinee's trait level. Consequently, different examinees take different versions of a test, yet their scores are absolutely comparable on the same measurement scale. How does this work? Although there are many variants of CAT, the basic process is as follows. First, a pool of items must exist for which item characteristic curves have been previously estimated. It is hoped this pool will contain items with good discrimination and a wide spread of item difficulty parameters.

Given the existence of the item pool, actual adaptive testing can begin. Before taking the first item, an examinee is assumed to have a trait level estimate of zero. They are then administered an item with a difficulty parameter around zero. In other words, they are administered an item that has the most psychometric information for their estimated trait level. On the basis of the examinee's item response (e.g., endorse/not endorse), their trait level is then re-estimated (note that technically speaking, this would require use of a prior distribution that is beyond the scope of the current discussion). Based on this new trait level estimate, they are administered an item with a difficulty parameter around their new trait level estimate. The process of re-estimating their trait level, and administering a new item with a difficulty value around that trait level estimate, is repeated until the examinee's error of measurement is below a certain value. As described, the examinee's error of measurement is computed by taking one over the square root of the test information. In turn, the test information is determined by adding together the item information curves for the administered items. The end result of this process is that the examinee always receives a test that is maximally efficient for a person of their trait level. Continuing with the IQ example, bright examinees would receive more difficult items until they began answering items wrong, and they would never receive (i.e., waste their time with) an easy item.

There is a large literature on IRT-based CAT relevant to ability assessment and programs for item banking and test administration are available (Assessment Systems Corp., 1988), yet few investigations of the procedure have occurred in personality testing. Waller and Reise (1989) used Monte Carlo and real data simulations to study computerized adaptive testing with the 34-item Absorption scale from Tellegen's (1982) MPQ. Among their findings was that when items were tailored to match examinee trait level, 50% of the items could be eliminated with little loss of information. Although such findings bode well for potential applications of CAT in personality assessment, there is a strong tradition of long personality tests that needs to be fought against. On the other hand, these long self-report inventories may serve as a nice item bank by which to assess important personality constructs, like the dimensions of the Big-Five Model (i.e., neuroticism, extroversion, conscientiousness, agreeableness, and openness).

As noted, IRT facilitates CAT because IRT models allow for examinee position on a latent trait continuum to be estimated from any subset of test items that have been calibrated onto the same scale. Related to this property is the fact that IRT models place few restrictions on item formatting (Thissen, 1993). Most personality measures consist of items of the same format. This is not a necessity of CTT, but most researchers desire to maintain similar variances across items lest some items affect the total score more than others. In IRT, there is no compelling reason to maintain similar item formats (except to avoid respondent confusion) because there is no need ever to produce a reliability coefficient. Therefore, in the future, IRT-based personality tests can be constructed with some true/false and some Likert ratings, and the Likert rating items may even have a different numbers of options.

The Study of Person-Fit

IRT-based person-fit assessment involves the evaluation of the consistency of an examinee's item response pattern with a set of estimated IRT model parameters. Many educational psychologists have discussed response factors that decrease the interpretability of examinees' scores (i.e., trait level (θ) estimates) on psychological measures. For example, an examinee may cheat or mismark an answer sheet due to carelessness. In personality assessment contexts, researchers have also suggested response factors that may diminish the ultimate interpretability of test scores (Zickar & Drasgow, 1996). For example, socially desirable responding, malingering, or a unique interpretation of item content may bias item responses. In fact, several researchers suggest that responses to personality measures may be inconsistent because the construct being assessed is not applicable to the individual examinee (see Baumeister & Tice, 1988; Tellegen, 1988). Reise and Flannery (1996) reviewed how person-fit indices may be used to identify such response factors in personality contexts (see also Reise & Waller, 1993).

Regardless of whether a researcher is working from an aptitude or personality assessment framework, response factors that ultimately invalidate psychological measurements manifest themselves in the inconsistency of an individual's item response pattern. By *consistency* is meant the degree to which a subject's response pattern is congruent with some model of normative item responding (i.e., valid responding). Because IRT models are formal (statistical) models, they lend themselves readily to the examination of the consistency of an individual's item response pattern with respect to a set of estimated IRT model parameters.

Person-fit statistics have gone by many names in the IRT literature. For example, they are sometimes referred to as test-score appropriateness indices because they indicate the applicability of a particular measurement for a given subject (Drasgow, Levine, & McLaughlin, 1987). They have also been termed responses consistency indices, scalability indices, or even as test-score caution indices because interpreting test scores associated with poorly fitting response patterns must be treated with great caution (Tatsuoka, 1984). In this chapter, the convention used by Meijer (1996) is used and all these indices are referred to as person-fit statistics.

Many person-fit statistics have been proposed (Drasgow, Levine, & Williams, 1985; Tatsuoka, 1984; Tatsuoka & Linn, 1983) and a sizable body of research pertains to how these indices function in educational testing contexts. A recent special issue *of Applied Measurement in Education* (Meijer, 1996) reviews much of the current research in IRT-based person-fit. Despite the different names and formulas, all person-fit indices operationalize the degree of consistency of an examinee's response pattern with some normative or expected pattern of item responding. Next, one commonly used person-fit statistic, called Z_L, is explained.

An index that has been much researched (e.g., Nering, 1995; Reise, 1995; Reise & Due, 1991) and used in several studies is the Z_L person-fit index developed by Drasgow, Levine, and Williams (1985). The Z_L statistic works as follows. Assume that a group of examinees has responded to a dichotomously scored test with J items. Also assume that the items have been fit to a 2PL (Equation 10.1) model and thus item discrimination and difficulty parameters have been estimated for all items. Then, define an examinee's response vector U to be composed of zero and one responses, u, where 0 = fails to endorse the item and 1 = endorses the item. The log-likelihood (LL) of each individual's response pattern is computed by Equation 10.4.

$$LL \mid \Theta_i = \Sigma(u_{ij} \times \ln(P_{ij} \mid \Theta_i)) + ((1 - u_{ij}) \times \ln(1 - P_{ij} \mid \Theta_i)) \qquad (10.4)$$

In Equation 10.4, the summation is performed over all administered test items (J). The values in Equation 10.4 yield the log-likelihood of the response pattern given the estimated model parameters. This value cannot be used as a person-fit index because, as pointed out by numerous researchers, the expected value of the log-likelihood is contingent on examinee trait level. To overcome this problem, Drasgow, Levine, and Williams (1985) proposed the computation of a conditionally standardized person-fit statistic. Specifically, the expected value of the log-likelihood is shown in Equation 10.5, and the conditional variance is shown in Equation 10.6:

$$E(LL \mid \Theta_i) = \Sigma\{P_{ij} \mid \Theta_i \ln(P_{ij} \mid \Theta_i) + (1 - P_{ij} \mid \Theta_i \ln(1 - P_{ij} \mid \Theta_i))\} \qquad (10.5)$$

$$V(LL \mid \Theta_i) = \Sigma(P_{ij} \mid \Theta_i)(1 - P_{ij} \mid \Theta_i)[\ln(P_{ij} \mid \Theta_i/(1 - P_{ij} \mid \Theta_i))]^2 \qquad (10.6)$$

$$Z_L \mid \Theta_i = [LL \mid \Theta_i - E(LL \mid \Theta_i)]/(V(LL \mid \Theta_i)^{1/2} \qquad (10.7)$$

Combining terms in Equations 10.4, 10.5, and 10.6 produces the Z_L person-fit statistic as shown in Equation 10.7. These Z_L values indicate the relative log-likelihood of an item response pattern given the estimated model parameters. That is, the observed log-likelihood is compared to what is expected under the hypothesis of model fit, and then this difference is divided by the standard error of the sampling distribution of log-likelihoods. Because of the central limit theorem, on long tests (e.g., 50 items), Z_L scores are expected to be normally distributed with a mean of 0.0 and variance equal to 1.0. A Z_L score of 0 is the expected value under the null hypothesis of model fit (i.e., the examinee is responding according to the estimated model parameters). A positive Z_L indicates that the pattern of response has a higher likelihood than expected under the model. This occurs when an examinee responds in a Guttman scalable manner—in perfect accordance with the item difficulties. Negative Z_L scores indicate poor person-fit or an aberrant (i.e., inconsistent) item response pattern. The test scores (i.e., θ estimates) associated with poor person-fit have limited interpretability because the examinee is not responding in accordance with the model used to interpret the measurement.

In regard to the Z_L index, extensions have been developed for polytomous item response formats (Drasgow, Levine, & Williams, 1985) and for tests that have multiple subscales (Drasgow, Levine, & McLaughlin, 1991). Note that person-fit indices such as Z_L ordinarily are computed within a measure of a single construct. Multitest extensions allow the examination of response consistency with respect to an entire inventory that may contain multiple subscales.

By way of example, Table 10.3 shows the response patterns for four hypothetical examinees who responded to a 6-item dichotomously scored test. The test items all have the same item discrimination parameters of α = 1.0, and the difficulties are β = −2, −1, −0.5, 0.5, 1.0 and 2.0, from left to right, respectively. All examinees have endorsed exactly two items and all have the same estimated trait level score of −0.96. Also shown are the Z_L scores for each of these response patterns. The first two examinees have poor person-fit, and it is clear why—they endorse items with difficulty parameters above their estimated trait level and they fail to endorse items with difficulties below their estimated trait level. This makes little sense. Thus, these response patterns are highly unlikely and the test scores for these two examinees should be treated with great caution. The last two examinees in Table 10.3 show good fitting response patterns in the sense that they tend to endorse items with difficulties below their estimated trait level and fail to endorse items with difficulties above their estimated trait level. In other words, they are responding consistently with the estimated model parameters. It should be noted that although person-fit indices such as Z_L may do

TABLE 10.3
Examples of Good and Poor Fitting Examinees

Response Pattern	Items						Θ	ZL
	1	2	3	4	5	6		
1	0	0	0	0	1	1	−0.96	−4.10
2	0	0	0	1	0	1	−0.96	−3.68
3	1	0	1	0	0	0	−0.96	0.53
4	1	1	0	0	0	0	−0.96	0.95

a good job at identifying model inconsistent response patterns, once such response patterns are identified, the source or cause of the poor person-fit remains to be determined.

Research in IRT-based person-fit has been conducted almost entirely in the context of educational assessment. Appropriately, this research has focused on the identification of response factors that mitigate the interpretability of test scores in educational context (Harnisch, 1983; Harnisch & Linn, 1981). For example, a main focus has been to identify examinees who get correct answers on multiple-choice tests by cheating. The results of these studies, however, are not easily extended to the study of person-fit under personality testing contexts. The main reason is that the factors that cause poor person-fit are different between these contexts (Reise & Flannery, 1996). For example, cheating is not a concern in personality measurement, although faking good or faking bad to create a more favorable impression of the self is clearly of major importance. Furthermore, in personality measurement, examinees may have poor person-fit because the indicators of the trait construct do not form a univocal structure for particular individuals (Reise & Waller, 1993). Stated differently, some examinees may have an unique personality trait structure (Tellegen, 1988). Finally, the IRT models used are different in the two assessment contexts—the 3PL being used in multiple-choice aptitude testing and the 2PL or graded response model (Samejima, 1969) used in personality measurement.

To my knowledge, only three studies have focused specifically on person-fit in typical performance assessment contexts. First, Zickar and Drasgow (1996) investigated the ability of a person-fit procedure to identify faking on personality instruments. Findings indicated that the person-fit index showed great promise relative to more traditional methods (e.g., social desirability scales). Second, Reise and Waller (1993) examined the ability of the Z_L statistic to identify poor person-fit on the 11 scales of the Multidimensional Personality Questionnaire (Tellegen, 1982). More specifically, they attempted to use person-fit statistics to show that, although the MPQ scales are univocal measures for most examinees, for some examinees the items did not hold together in a univocal manner. They showed that some examinees with poor person-fit were responding inconsistently to the scale items as a whole, but, when considered within specific facets of item content, responses made sense. Reise and Waller (1993) also established that person-fit scores are modestly correlated across different scales of the MPQ, suggesting that person misfit is a more general characteristic. When person-fit scores were aggregated across the 11 MPQ scales, the resulting aggregate was found to correlate with impulsivity and stress reaction as measured by the MPQ scales.

A third study offered some not so promising findings. Reise (1995) conducted a series of Monte Carlo studies that examined various psychometric properties of the Z_L index on three MPQ scales. Basic findings were that Z_L was not well standardized under these personality testing conditions. For example, after estimating item parameters for one of the MPQ scales, data were simulated to fit an IRT model under these conditions. When the Z_L statistic was computed, it did not have a normal distribution. This would be problematic if one were to use Z_L to conduct strict hypothesis tests of fit. Furthermore, in the Reise (1995) study, the effects of different scoring strategies (e.g., maximum likelihood, expected *a posteriori*) on the power of the Z_L statistic was explored. Findings indicated that power was low regardless of scoring strategy. This means that examinees who were simulated not to fit the IRT model were not identified with high accuracy as such by the Z_L statistic. Person-fit statistics have different power for different types of response deviance. In the Reise study, only one method was used to simulate poor-fitting examinees.

THE DISADVANTAGES OF IRT

Now that I have highlighted several key features of IRT that personality assessment researchers should be aware of, it is now time for the bad news. That is, discussion of the limitations or pratfalls of modern testing theory. First, IRT modeling can have the negative consequence of limiting the type of constructs assessed by personality psychologists. By this is not simply meant that the unidimensionality assumption required by most available IRT models is too restrictive, but rather that conceptually speaking, some of the constructs we wish to assess do not lend themselves to an IRT type of analysis.

Bollen and Lennox (1991) elaborated on an important distinction between emergent variable and latent variable measurement models. In a latent variable measurement model, the construct causes the indicators and thus explains the item covariances (analogous to a factor model), whereas in an emergent variable measurement model, the construct is defined by the indicators (analogous to a components model). IRT is clearly a latent variable measurement model and attempting to fit constructs that do not fit this mold is bound to lead to problems. It is easy to think of important personality variables and their associated measures that do not easily fit an IRT framework. For example, Gough's folk constructs as measured by the CPI would be problematic, as well as the concept of Antisocial Personality Disorder as defined by the DSM–IV manual. Simply stated, in personality assessment a wide variety of constructs exist that are on different theoretical levels (see Ozer & Reise, 1994) and not all of them are appropriately assessed by an IRT measurement framework.

A second broad criticism or problem is the technical and expensive nature of the IRT enterprise. This combined with the sparseness in graduate level courses on IRT can lead to: (a) little future IRT research on the part of personality assessment researchers, and (b) poor or improper applications of the technique. From a technical standpoint, there are some features of IRT modeling that detract from its application. For example, all IRT researchers talk about unidimensionality, and the commonly applied IRT models assume this. However, personality researchers may not be particularly interested in the type of construct and associated measurement instrument that is strictly—mathematically—unidimensional. Consider the broad construct of locus of control. Some researchers have argued that this is a multifaceted construct and the facets such as health locus of control, achievement locus of control, and so on, need to be distinguished. As the homogeneity of the items increases within these facet scales, IRT models become more appropriate. However, the scales themselves may become less substantively interesting. Multidimensional IRT models offer promise in this type of assessment situation but are just now starting to emerge.

Another technical problem in IRT is scoring. Estimating someone's position on a latent trait continuum using their pattern of item responses requires advanced numeric methods and is nowhere near as easy as adding up raw item responses. In addition, it is unclear at this time the extent to which the added complexity is worth the trouble in terms of test validity. Furthermore, the issue of model-fit is a concern in IRT, whereas researchers typically do not consider the issue of model fit under traditional testing theory. At this time, there is no trustworthy gold-standard set of methods for assessing IRT model fit, and furthermore, it is not clear what the effects of violating model assumptions are. Finally, from a practical standpoint, although computer programs are available for estimating IRT parameters, they can be expensive and are generally orientated toward researchers who are very familiar with IRT techniques.

CONCLUSIONS

IRT modeling definitely offers advantages over traditional procedures but it is clearly not the solution to all measurement problems in personality assessment. The chief strengths of IRT, in terms of personality assessment, appear to lie in the capacity to address interesting psychometric and substantive issues that would otherwise be very difficult with traditional procedures. In particular, the study of item positioning effects (Steinberg, 1994), the study of differential item functioning, and the analysis of person-fit are prime examples of IRT's advantages. Furthermore, IRT is also valuable as an alternative way of studying the psychometric characteristics of a test and ultimately for interpreting test score. On the other hand, some of the advantages of IRT may ultimately be of little interest to personality assessment researchers. For example, the ability to link metrics, or even computerized adaptive testing, seems perhaps more crucial to large-scale testing programs like ETS and ACT than to the basic personality researcher. I look forward to seeing future creative applications of IRT in the personality assessment domain, especially applications of IRT to the study of personality change and development and the study of differences between self-reports and observer evaluations of personality.

REFERENCES

Andrich, D. (1978). A rating formulation for ordered response categories. *Psychometrika, 3,* 561–573.

Assessment Systems Corporation (1988). *MICROCAT 3.0* [computer program]. St. Paul, MN: Assessment Systems Corporation.

Baumeister, R. F., & Tice, D. M. (1988). Metatraits. *Journal of Personality, 56,* 571–598.

Birnbaum, A. (1968). Some latent trait models and their use in inferring an examinee's ability. In F. M. Lord & M. R. Novick (Eds.), *Statistical theories of mental test scores* (pp. 397–479). Reading, MA: Addison-Wesley.

Bock, R. D. (1972). Estimating item parameters and latent ability when the responses are scored in two or more nominal categories. *Psychometrika, 37,* 29–51.

Bock, R. D., & Aitken, M. (1981). Marginal maximum likelihood estimation of item parameters: An application of the EM algorithm. *Psychometrika, 46,* 443–459.

Bock, R. D., Gibbons, R., & Muraki, E. (1988). Full information item factor analysis. *Applied Psychological Measurement, 12,* 261–280.

Bollen, K., & Lennox, R. (1991). Conventional wisdom on measurement: A structural equation perspective. *Psychological Bulletin, 110,* 305–314.

Drasgow, F., Levine, M. V., & McLaughlin, M. E. (1987). Detecting inappropriate test scores with optimal and practical appropriateness indices. *Applied Psychological Measurement, 11,* 59–79.

Drasgow, F., Levine, M. V., & McLaughlin, M. E. (1991). Appropriateness measurement for some multidimensional test batteries. *Applied Psychological Measurement, 15,* 171–191.

Drasgow, F., Levine, M. V., & Williams, E. A. (1985). Appropriateness measurement with polychotomous item response models and standardized indices. *British Journal of Mathematical and Statistical Psychology, 38,* 67–86.

Embretson, S. E. (1996). The new rules of measurement. *Psychological Assessment, 8,* 341–349.

Gibbons, R. D., Clark, D. C., Cavanaugh, S. V., & Davis, J. M. (1985). Application of modern psychometric theory in psychiatric research. *Journal of Psychiatric Research, 19,* 43–55.

Hambleton, R. K., Swaminathan, H., & Rogers, H. J. (1991). *Fundamentals of item response theory.* Newbury Park, CA: Sage.

Harnisch, D. L. (1983). Item response patterns: Applications for educational practice. *Journal of Educational Measurement, 20,* 191–206.

Harnisch, D. L., & Linn, R. L. (1981). Analysis of item response patterns: Questionable test data and dissimilar curriculum practices. *Journal of Educational Measurement, 18,* 133–146.

Haviland, M. G., & Reise, S. P. (1996). Structure of the twenty item Toronto alexithymia scale. *Journal of Personality Assessment, 66,* 116–125.

Hendryx, M. S., Haviland, M. G., Gibbons, R. D., & Clark, D. C. (1992). An application of item response theory to alexithymia assessment among abstinent alcoholics. *Journal of Personality Assessment, 58,* 506–515.

Lord, F. M. (1980). *Applications of item respone theory to practical testing problems.* Hillsdale, NJ: Lawrence Erlbaum Associates.

Masters, G. N. (1982). A Rasch model for partial credit scoring. *Psychometrika, 47,* 149–174.

Meijer, R. R. (1996). Person-fit research: An introduction. *Applied Measurement in Education, 9,* 3–8.

Mislevy, R. J., & Bock, R. D. (1990). BILOG-3: Item analysis and test scoring with binary logistic models [Computer software]. Mooresville, IN: Scientific Software.

Muraki, E., & Engelhard, G. (1985). Full information item factor analysis: Application of EAP scores. *Applied Psychological Measurement, 9,* 417–430.

Nering, M. L. (1995). The distribution of person fit using true and estimated person parameters. *Applied Psychological Measurement, 19,* 121–130.

Ozer, D. J., & Reise, S. P. (1994). Personality assessment. *Annual Review of Psychology, 45,* 357–388.

Reise, S. P. (1995). Socring method and the detection of response aberrancy in a personality assessment context. *Applied Psychological Measurement, 19,* 213–229.

Reise, S. P., & Due, A. M. (1991). The influence of test characteristics on the detection of aberrant response patterns. *Applied Psychological Measurement, 15,* 217–226.

Reise, S. P., & Flannery, W. P. (1996). Assessing person-fit on measures of typical performance. *Applied Measurement in Education, 9,* 9–26.

Reise, S. P., & Smith, L. L. (1997, March). *Using IRT to detect item bias in personality assessment instruments.* Poster presented at Society for Personality Assessment, San Diego, CA.

Reise, S. P., & Waller, N. G. (1990). Fitting the two-parameter model to personality data: The parameterization of the Multidimensional Personality Questionnaire. *Applied Psychological Measurement, 14,* 45–58.

Reise, S. P., & Waller, N. G. (1993). Traitedness and the assessment of response pattern scalability. *Journal of Personality and Social Psychology, 65,* 143–151.

Reise, S. P., Widaman, K. F., & Pugh, R. H. (1993). Confirmatory factor analysis and item response theory: Two approaches for exploring measurement invariance. *Psychological Bulletin, 114,* 352–566.

Reise, S. P., & Yu, J. (1990). Parameter recovery in the graded response model using MULTILOG. *Journal of Educational Measurement, 27,* 133–144.

Samejima, F. (1969). Estimation of latent ability using a response pattern of graded scores. *Psychometrika Monograph,* No. 17.

Steinberg, L. (1994). Context and serial order effects in personality measurement: Limits on the generality of "measuring changes the measure." *Journal of Personality and Social Psychology, 66,* 341–349.

Steinberg, L., & Thissen, D. (1995). Item reponse theory in personality research. In P. E. Shrout & S. T. Fiske (Eds.), *Personality research, methods, and theory: A festschrift honoring Donald W. Fiske* (pp. 161–181). Hillsdale, NJ: Lawrence Erlbaum Associates.

Steinberg, L., & Thissen, D. (1996). Uses of item response theory and the testlet concept in the measurement of psychopathology. *Psychological Methods, 1,* 81–97.

Tatsuoka, K. K. (1984). Caution indices based on item response theory. *Psychometrika, 49,* 95–110.

Tatsuoka, K. K., & Linn, R. L. (1983). Indices for detecting unusual patterns: Links between two general approaches and potential applications. *Applied Psychological Methods, 7,* 81–96.

Taylor, G. J., Bagby, R. M., & Parker, J. D. A (1992). The revised Toronto Alexithymia Scale: Some reliability, validity, and normative data. *Psychotherapy and Psychosomatics, 57,* 34–41.

Tellegen, A. (1982). *Brief manual for the Multidimensional Personality Questionnaire.* Unpublished manuscript, University of Minnesota, Minneapolis, MN.

Tellegen, A. (1988). The analysis of consistency in personality assessment. *Journal of Personality, 56,* 621–663.

Thissen, D. (1991). *MULTILOG: Multiple, categorical item analysis and test scoring using item response theory (Version 6).* Chicago: Scientific Software.

Thissen, D. (1993). Repealing rules that no longer apply to psychological measurement. In N. Frederiksen, R. J. Mislevy, & I. Bejar (Eds.), *Test theory for a new generation of tests* (pp. 79–97). Hillsdale, NJ: Lawrence Erlbaum Associates.

Thissen, D., & Steinberg, L. (1986). A taxonomy of item response models. *Psychometrika, 51,* 567–577.

Thissen, D., Steinberg, L., & Gerrard, M. (1986). Beyond group mean differences: The concept of item bias. *Psychological Bulletin, 99,* 118–128.

van der Linden, W. J., & Hambleton, R. K. (1996). *Handbook of modern item response theory.* New York: Springer-Verlag.

Wainer, H. (1990). *Computerized adaptive testing: A primer.* Hillsdale, NJ: Lawrence Erlbaum Associates.

Waller, N. G., & Reise, S. P. (1989). Computerized adaptive personality assessment: An illustration with the absorption scale. *Journal of Personality and Social Psychology, 57,* 1051–1058.

Wilson, D. T., Wood, R., & Gibbons, R. (1991). *TESTFACT: Test scoring, item statistics, and item factor analysis.* Chicago: Scientific Software.

Wright, B. D. (1977). Solving measurement problems with the Rasch model. *Journal of Educational Measurement, 14,* 219–226.

Yoes, M. E. (1996). *User's manual for the XCALIBRE marginal maximum-likelihood estimation program.* St. Paul, MN: Assessment Systems Corp.

Zickar, M. J., & Drasgow, F. (1996). Detecting faking on a personality instrument using appropirateness measurement. *Applied Psychological Measurment, 20,* 71–88.

Zimowski, M. F., Muraki, E., Mislevy, R., & Bock, R. D. (1996). *BILOG-MG: Multiple-group IRT analysis and test maintenance for binary items.* Chicago: Scientific Software.

CHAPTER ELEVEN

Summary and Future of Psychometric Methods in Testing

Susan E. Embretson
University of Kansas

Scott L. Hershberger
California State University—Long Beach

The goal of this book is to explicate some aspects of measurement that are routinely neglected in measurement and testing textbooks. We believed that insufficient coverage of several topics has led to training test professionals who are unfamiliar with some important principles behind many current tests. To organize this volume, we constructed an ideal list of topics and authors. Apparently, our concerns about the coverage of measurement topics were shared by many psychometricians. Not only were the intended authors willing and able to cover the suggested topics, but, in fact, they seemed enthusiastic about the project.

In this final chapter, we recommend some new directions for topics in basic measurement and testing courses. To accomplish this goal, we summarize issues that cut across chapters. Although many issues developed much as we had anticipated, some interesting new issues emerged as well. Furthermore, the topics covered in the chapters extend beyond their initial classification into cognitive and personality measurement.

Two chapters, by their nature, concerned general issues in measurement. Although these chapters were included in the cognitive measurement section for convenience, the issues raised by Wright (chap. 4) and by Marcoulides (chap. 6) do not depend on specific content areas. Wright is primarily concerned with objective measurement principles and how the Rasch measurement model may be applied to accomplish them. Marcoulides is primarily concerned with how generalizability theory may be applied to systematize results on test measurement error. These topics apply equally well both to cognitive measurement and to personality measurement.

The three other chapters in the cognitive measurement section, written by Thorndike (chap. 2), Daniel (chap. 3), and Woodcock (chap. 5), concern issues that are typically associated with the area. In cognitive measurement, high psychometric standards have been relatively easy to obtain. Cognitive constructs are much better defined than personality constructs. Thus, construct validity issues are not as overwhelming as for personality measurement. Cognitive measurement is characterized more by refinements of basic principles. However, many issues revealed in the chapters can also extend to personality measurement.

Three chapters concerned mainly personality measurement. As noted in the preface to these chapters, fundamental issues in construct validity, the nature of individual differences (trait dimensions vs. taxonomies), and the applicability of traits to specific individuals continue to be debated. The chapters by Exner (chap. 8), Waller (chap. 9), and Reise (chap. 10) address these issues. However, the issues raised in their chapters do extend to cognitive measurement as well. All three issues are appearing in new guises in the rapidly changing context for cognitive measurement, such as computerized item presentation.

ITEM RESPONSE THEORY AS THE PSYCHOMETRIC BASIS FOR TESTING

Several chapters in this volume (chaps. 2, 3, 4, 5, 9, & 10) highlight the advantages of item response theory (IRT) as the psychometric basis for measurement. Issues in both cognitive and personality measurement that were only partially resolvable in classical test theory (CTT) become easily manageable with IRT. These issues include test equating, individual reliability assessment, missing data, adaptive testing, person misfit, and much more. Thus, these six chapters constitute substantial endorsement for IRT.

However, as to whether IRT should replace CTT, the authors do not agree. Thorndike, Wright, and Woodcock, as well as one co-editor (Embretson), support IRT over CTT. In fact, although CTT principles may be derived as special cases from IRT (see Lord & Novick, 1968), IRT principles do not follow from CTT. Woodcock has implemented his preference for IRT into practice. He has developed many tests based on the Rasch model. Daniel and Reise are more cautious in their support for IRT. Daniel has incorporated IRT measurement principles into some major contemporary tests. However, Daniel points out that test users are still largely unfamiliar with IRT. Thus, he has developed many concepts that bridge the gap between CTT and IRT. For example, because test users are familiar with the CTT reliability concept, Daniel's concept of local reliability allows the test user to easily understand the IRT indices for measurement errors at particular score levels. Reise notes that using unidimensional IRT models as the standard may limit the type of constructs that can be measured, particularly in personality research. Therefore, Reise would argue for a broader set of measurement principles, although it is not clear that CTT would contribute to them. Furthermore, like Daniel, Reise worries about the technical expertise required to implement the models, given the current level of IRT expertise among testing professionals.

Marcoulides, in contrast, views a continuing role for CTT. Generalizability theory, an extension of CTT, assesses many other sources of measurement error that are not usually considered in IRT. In IRT, the standard error of measurement indicates only the informativeness of the items about the person's standing on the latent trait. The IRT standard error of measurement depends on both item difficulty and item discrimination. Item difficulty contributes to measurement error because if few items are appropriate for a particular trait level (i.e., the items are much too easy or much too hard), then persons at that level cannot be accurately assessed. Item discrimination contributes to measurement error in IRT in a manner analogous to CTT, by impact on internal consistency.

Marcoulides notes that differing judges, times, or functions are sources of measurement error that are ignored by IRT. Marcoulides shows how IRT information, as well as other information, may be placed into a generalizability design to estimate variance components. Interestingly, Marcoulides notes that IRT models also can be extended to handle more diverse contributions to error. IRT models can estimate other error sources by including parameters to represent the conditions that influence test performance. However, IRT models are rarely applied this way, and, furthermore, the extended IRT models do not always yield the same results as the generalizability theory analysis. Marcoulides views generalizability theory as more comprehensive because information is provided for designing, assessing, and improving the dependability of measurement.

Considering all these viewpoints, one might argue that a comprehensive approach to measurement and testing would consider various psychometric issues in the context of both IRT and CTT. In some cases, IRT and CTT would be alternative representations of similar information about the tests. In other cases, however, the methods are not comparable, due to different concerns or to different results. Such a comprehensive approach may have some interesting side effects, as well. For example, the shortcomings of typical IRT applications in representing some sources of measurement error may become more salient; thus, inspiring more routine inclusion of parameters to represent these error sources.

WHICH IRT MODEL IS BEST?

The authors disagree about which IRT model is most appropriate. Wright strongly favors the Rasch IRT model as defining objective measurement. The Rasch model contains only one item parameter; namely, item difficulty. The

Rasch model is also sometimes known as the one parameter logistic (1PL) model because a single item parameter is included in a logistic model of item responses. Woodcock, as well as Daniel, have developed several tests based on the Rasch model. Two alternative IRT models, the two parameter logistic (2PL) and the three parameter logistic (3PL) models, are also quite popular in aptitude testing, however. The 2PL model contains parameters to represent item differences in both difficulty and discrimination, whereas the 3PL model adds a third parameter to represent guessing. Thorndike is neutral about which model should be applied. Reise and Waller, however, routinely apply the 2PL model.

Which model is best? This topic has been debated with great passion for nearly three decades. And the fires burn as brightly as ever. We suspect that this debate will never be resolved. At issue are two opposing measurement guidelines. The relative value that a psychometrician places on these guidelines leads to qualitatively different approaches to measurement data and, consequently, to selecting different IRT models. First, a model should be empirically appropriate for the data. The more complex models, such as 2PL and 3PL, will fit a greater variety of test data than the simple Rasch model. Thus, psychometricians who value fitting observed test data are more likely to prefer the 2PL or 3PL models. Second, the principle of parsimony dictates that measurement data should be fit by simple models. Both the 2PL and 3PL model contain more item parameters than the Rasch model. Furthermore, even scoring trait level is more complicated in the 2PL and 3PL models; that is, items are weighted by their discrimination. In the Rasch model, total score is a sufficient statistic for estimating trait level. Psychometricians who value parsimony would choose the Rasch model. Even if the Rasch model is not appropriate for a test initially, fit often can be obtained by further effort in defining constructs and eliminating poor items. Items that represent more than one trait are particularly amendable to deletion or revision.

However, refining constructs and selecting items will not always yield a test that fits the more simple IRT models. In the cognitive measurement, one impact of cognitive psychology is to provide a strong rationale for viewing items as inherently multidimensional. Solving complex aptitude items involves several separate aspects of cognitive processing, each of which could define a latent trait. In the personality domain, item responses often depend on confounding dimensions. For example, social desirability (see Jackson, 1973) is often a salient process behind persons' item endorsements on self-report inventories. Thus, different item discriminations may be essential to construct definition in some personality traits. Adding the item discrimination parameter in the 2PL and 3PL models assures that the predominant dimension is measured most efficiently.

But, this is only one solution. An alternative approach to adding item discrimination parameters is to measure several two or more traits simultaneously. Multidimensional Rasch models have been developed (Adams & Wilson, 1996; Embretson, 1991, 1997) for this purpose. Therefore, shifting to a multidimensional perspective does not end the debate. Rather, it shifts to a new level.

INTERPRETING SCORE MEANING

It is axiomatic in measurement that raw test scores have no meaning. Norm-referenced scoring has become so routine that many testing professionals believe that it is ludicrous to even question their utility. However, the usefulness of norm-referenced score interpretations clearly emerged as an issue from the chapters. Thorndike (chap. 2) shows that in the early development of measurement methods, item-referenced score interpretations were seriously considered. Thurstone (1928) and E. L. Thorndike and collaborators (Thorndike, Bregman, Cobb, & Woodyard, 1926) both envisioned an item-referenced method for interpreting scores. Thorndike (chap. 2) notes several developments that undermined the development of item-referenced scoring. E. L. Thorndike's evoluntary scaling of intelligence, for example, fell into disregard quickly, whereas Stern's (1914) method to standardize mental age (for CA) was retained.

Wright elaborates an example that shows how norm-referenced scoring does not yield useful score interpretations. Wright applied the Rasch model to a behavioral rating scale for PECS Lifestyles, a measure of everyday living skills. In this rating scale, living skills such as Knows Medications, Safety Awareness, and Urinary Program are rated for persons with problems in everyday living skills, such as elderly persons. To utilize this scale as an assessment instrument, several questions are pertinent. First, are the behaviors scalable as a continuum? Are functions lost progressively? Is the loss of a particular function regularly preceded by the loss of other functions? Wright shows that scalability is met for PECS Lifestyles. Further, the distances between the behaviors varies substantially as well. Urinary Program and Skin Care Program are close in the scale, whereas Knows Medications is much higher. Second, once scalability is established, scores may be interpreted directly on the scale. Thus, if the person has lost a low-level function, we know that the higher-level functions are quite unlikely. Importantly, the person's position on the scale yields diagnostic information about which skills may be a viable target for remediation. Skills that are just at the person's level are the best candidate because the person is as likely to pass as to fail them. Third, the item-referenced scaling also can have direct meaning for prognosis in different living situations. What is the maximum degree of loss associated with effective living in environments with varying degrees of assistance? Therefore, various placements could be located for minimal required skill levels on the item-referenced scale.

Notice, in contrast, how little meaning a norm-referenced interpretation of the PECS Lifestyles would have. Comparing a particular 92-year-old person's score to a norm group (e.g., other 90-year-olds) tells us nothing about what the person can do.

Woodcock (chap. 5) outlines several different types of scores that utilize item-referenced information. Although Woodcock's tests provide the traditional norm-referenced information, several additional indices are available. For example, the Woodcock Language Proficiency Battery (Woodcock, 1991) provides several criterion-referenced indices that are derived from the Rasch scaling of items. Indices such as the Relative Proficiency Index and the Developmental Zone index assesses the person's quality of performance on reference language tasks. Thus, like the PECS Lifestyles, Woodcock's task-referenced indices provide information about what the person can do.

These chapters clearly suggest that alternatives to norm-referenced score meaning are now available. The examples provided show that item-based interpretations not only enhance score meaning, but that sometimes norm-referenced interpretations compare very poorly with item-based interpretations. Furthermore, the alternatives are not limited to educational domains, such as criterion-referenced test interpretations.

APPROACHES TO CONSTRUCT VALIDITY

In the chapters on personality measurement, methods to enhance construct validity were predominant. Projective tests provide a good example of tests with basic problems in construct validity. In fact, projective tests are often so beret of problems that they are sometimes designed as techniques rather than tests (see Anastasi & Urbina, 1997). However, Exner's Comprehensive System for scoring the Rorshach has provided new life for this classic projective test.

First, and importantly, Exner has not only systematized the scoring system, he has also shifted the construct. Rather than emphasize the diagnosis of psychopathological syndromes, such as DSM–IV, the Rorschach indices are now regarded as more traitlike. Thus, more meaningful validity data are behavior ratings and person perception judgments. For example, peer nominations for traits, observed interpersonal interaction styles, prosocial behaviors and more, are viewed by Exner as providing more appropriate validity data. In this sense, a goal for the Rorschach is to predict what the clinician cannot see outside the therapy session; namely, how the person interacts with and is perceived by others. Second, Exner is actively revising the scoring system for constructs that are poorly operationalized. For example, Exner has more recently changed the Special Scores. The various cognitive slippage scales, such as Deviant Verbalization and Incongruous Combinations, had promising validity in diagnosing schizophrenia in early studies in the 1970s. However, later studies showed problems in discriminating between diagnostic categories. Furthermore, children often scored very highly on the indices. More recently, by adding an additional scoring factor (level) to each scale, Exner again gets promising validity for distinguishing schizophrenics from other diagnostic categories and from children.

Waller examines a traditional issue in construct validity; namely, the dimensional structure of test items. Waller shows how traditional item factor analysis leads to spurious factors on a major instrument for assessing psychopathology, the Minnesota Multiphasic Personality Inventory (MMPI). By applying an appropriate factor analytic method to MMPI item responses for a very large sample, Waller identifies a meaningful hierarchial structure. Sixteen lower-order factors, as well as three higher-order factors, generalized across subgroups. Furthermore, Waller shows how IRT models can be effectively applied to the lower-order factors.

Interestingly, construct validity is again a significant issue in cognitive measurement. First, the impact of cognitive psychology on testing has created challenges to the construct validity concept itself. New views of the type of relevant data (Embretson, 1983, 1995) and the role of test design to maximize validity (Embretson, in press-a) may lead to major changes in the construct validation paradigm. Second, the rapid switch to computerized item presentation is also creating some new problems for the construct validity of ability tests. Although cognitive measurement has been stable for decades, computerized item presentation not only requires redesigning some item types (e.g., long reading passages cannot be read on a single screen) but has made some interesting new item types now feasible (see Bennett & Sebrechts, 1997). Thus, the construct validity of the redesigned and new item types must be addressed.

In summary, new issues in construct validation have salience in both personality and cognitive measurement. The chapters in this volume have focused on increasing construct validity by approaches to validation research for existing tests (i.e., the Rorschach and the MMPI). Certainly the results to date have enhanced the construct validity of these tests. Another direction, however, is maximizing construct validity initially by applying design principles to developing test items. In ability measurement, for example, cognitive psychology principles are increasingly applied and consequently, the types of measures are changing (see Embretson, in press-b, for a summary). Similarly, research following Jackson's (1973) item development principles could enhance the construct validity of personality measurements.

THE NATURE OF INDIVIDUAL DIFFERENCES

Ability measurement has a long and successful history for measuring dimensions. The standard IRT models assume that a latent trait dimension underlies item responses. The chapters that emphasize applications to ability tests (e.g., Daniel and Woodcock) show successful applications of IRT models. This is not surprising because literally decades of research have been devoted to defining and refining dimensional models of ability. Carroll (1993) summarized the factor-analytic research on cognitive ability factors. Carroll reanalyzed hundreds of studies with published correlation matrices with common methods of factor rotation. Carroll's (1993) stratum theory, which is headed by a general intelligence factor similar to Spearman's g, unifies and organizes his results.

As noted previously (Hershberger, chap. 7), the use of dimensions versus taxonomies is debated frequently in personality and psychopathology research. The Rorschach has some history for diagnosing discrete types of psychopathology (see Exner, chap. 8). Similarly, the MMPI was developed initially to classify persons into a psychiatric category. The items on the clinical scales were selected to distinguish various clinical groups from a normal control group. The clinical scales, although revised, still appear on the current revision of the MMPI. Methodologists such as Waller (chap. 9) have developed algorithms to extract taxonomic structure from item relationships.

Perhaps it is surprising that the chapters in this volume represent movements toward applying dimensional structures to personality and psychopathology. For example, the items on the MMPI clinical scales are well known to be heterogeneous. Attempts to apply dimensional psychometric models to the MMPI, by and large, have failed. Waller notes that IRT has not been feasible for this scales, due to their failure to fit the models. Furthermore, Waller also notes that factor analysis of the MMPI scales have not led to consistent and meaningful results, either. The items overlap between many clinical scales. In addition, the heterogeneity of the scales themselves lead to confounded patterns of score correlations. Interesting, however, Waller has successfully extracted a hierarchial factor structure from the MMPI, using the item correlations rather than scale correlations. The structure seems not only readily interpretable, but also yields clusters of items with sufficient homogeneity to be appropriate for IRT scaling.

But perhaps equally surprising, and mentioned in passing in one chapter (see Daniel, chap. 3), is a trend in cognitive measurement to incorporate taxonomies. Although traits have been the mainstay of cognitive measurement, powerful new IRT-based models that assess qualitative differences in the basis of item responses are now available. Models that combine IRT with latent class analysis (e.g., Rost, 1990) can identify groups of persons who apply different strategies or knowledge structures in item solving. The rule space methodology (Tatsuoka, 1983, 1985) uses misfit indices like those mentioned by Reise (chap. 10) to diagnose individual differences in knowledge states or strategies among people with the same ability level.

The new developments suggest, paradoxically, that personality and psychopathology research is moving toward dimensional structures, whereas ability measurement is incorporating aspects of taxonomies! Although measurement textbooks typically do not consider methods appropriate for assessing taxonomies, the importance of taxonomies is by no means a moribund issue. It appears the debate of dimensionality versus taxonomies is appearing in new guise.

QUALITATIVE DIFFERENCES IN TRAIT MEANING

Reise (chap. 9) shows how IRT is useful for resolving and assessing certain issues in personality measurement. For example, differential item functioning (DIF) occurs when response endorsement probabilities are not related to the latent construct in the same way in different groups of people. Historically, group factors such gender, race, age, and so forth are often described as influencing self-report personality test items. DIF can be evaluated by examining the empirical fit of a single set of IRT item parameters across groups. To give an example, gender differences in self-reporting of depressive behaviors and attitudes can be assessed by DIF.

Although not mentioned in these chapters, DIF is a major research area in cognitive measurement. Ability tests that are used for selection and classification, such as the GRE and SAT, are routinely checked for DIF. Items that function in the same way across groups, such as gender or racial–ethnic groups, are preferred over biased items.

Sometimes, however, biased items must be retained. DIF may be so prevalent, as in some personality measures, or some items regarded as so crucial that they must be included on the test. Two solutions are possible. First, the biased items can be balanced by items showing the opposite pattern of DIF. This strategy has sometimes been employed on achievement measures, for example, by including items that are biased toward each group. Second, IRT has some potential to circumvent the problems of biased items. The biased item can be included on the test, but with different item parameters depending on the group membership of the examinee.

The fit of an individual person's response pattern to the trait model was examined in several chapters. Person fit indices assess the typicality of the person's item response pattern. At the same trait level, for example, different persons may endorse quite different items. An atypical pattern may indicate that the construct being assessed is not relevant to the person. Reise (chap. 9) reviews person misfit in personality as an indicator of traitedness. Similarly,

Wright (chap. 4) also examines the implications of person fit for scale interpretations. For example, he routinely applies a misfit index to examine the idiosyncracies of a patient's status on the PECS Lifestyles scale. In conjunction with a strong scaling model, such as the Rasch model, the individual pattern deviations can be quite revealing (see Wright, chap. 4, Fig. 4.4). Daniel (chap. 3) suggests that person-fit indices in cognitive measurement can signal errors in test conditions or in the appropriateness of the test for an examinee. For the latter, Daniel notes that physical handicaps, as well as language and cultural differences, can lead to atypical response pattern, which in turns leads one to question the score that was received.

Thus, the appropriateness of a measurement scale for particular individuals or for particular groups of individuals remains an important issue. Advances in IRT models and in the assessment of DIF have made quantification of test appropriateness now feasible.

CONCLUSION

How should general measurement textbooks be changed to reflect the new rules of measurement? We recommend the following changes:

1. IRT and CTT approaches should be integrated in a comprehensive approach to measurement issues. Often, textbooks consider IRT in an isolated chapter and thus the reader does not understand how IRT and CTT results compare. The chapters in this book suggest that IRT and CTT are sometimes alternative representations of similar information about the tests. Other times, however, they do not yield comparable results. A comprehensive approach to psychometric models would lead to new insights about both methods.

2. General criteria for choosing an IRT model for a particular measure should be elaborated. Individuals who strongly prefer particular IRT models place different values on two fundamental issues; empirical fit of test data to a model versus designing a test to fit a justifiable measurement model. In one case, the data is considered fundamental, whereas in the other, the model is considered more fundamental. Further guidelines about the implications of model choice are clearly needed.

3. Alternative systems for anchoring scores should be elaborated. Several chapters in this volume suggest that item-based score anchors are often more meaningful than norm-referenced anchors. Measurement and testing textbooks should describe the conditions under which the alternative anchoring systems are most useful. Furthermore, because the item-based score anchors are relatively uncommon, elaborated examples are needed to promote their usage.

4. The methods by which construct validity can be evaluated and maximized should be more fully elaborated. Most textbooks contain a general list of data that support construct validity, such as factor analysis and contrasted groups. However, these guidelines need to be tempered with some additional issues for certain tests. Inappropriate applications of factor analysis on the clinical scales of the MMPI and inappropriate applications of the contrasted group criterion on the Rorschach indices have not led to support for construct validity. Furthermore, although fully elaborating how construct validity can be evaluated is very important, material on how to design tests so that construct validity will be maximized is noticeably absent in most textbooks. This area clearly needs to be considered more fully.

5. Different types of models for individual differences should be elaborated. Although dimensional models have been successful in both cognitive measurement and personality measurement, taxonomic structures remain interesting in both areas. Although empirical methods to construct tests to identify taxonomies have been available (i.e., empirically keyed tests), justifiable psychometric models were not available. New developments in identifying taxonomies and in estimating a person's membership in a latent class render taxonomic structures increasingly feasible. These should be included in measurement textbooks.

6. Methods for assessing qualitative differences in the meaning of a trait should be elaborated. Test scores may have different meanings for some individuals or for persons with diverse backgrounds (e.g., racial–ethnic group, handicapped groups, etc.). Recent advances in psychometric methods make assessment of qualitative differences in trait meaning now feasible. These methods should be routinely covered in measurement textbooks.

In summary, advances in psychometric methods have changed both the aspects of individual differences that can be measured and the methods by which tests are constructed. The new rules of measurement allow greater freedom for test developers and test users alike. The cost, however, is greater technical sophistication. Future textbooks not only should present the technological material in a more fundamental manner, but also should ground the technology in basic testing issues. It is evident that some effort is required to elaborate the suggested changes, but the new rules of measurement present an exciting future for psychometric methods.

REFERENCES

Adams, R. A., & Wilson, M. (1996). Formulating the Rasch model as a mixed coefficients multinomial logit. In G. Engelhard & M. Wilson (Eds.), *Objective measurement III: Theory into practice* (pp. 143–166). Norwood, NJ: Ablex.

Anastasi, A., & Urbina, S. (1997). *Psychological testing.* Upper Saddle River, NJ: Prentice Hall.

Bennett, R. E., & Sebrechts, M. M. (1997). A computer-based tasks for measuring the representational component of quantitative proficiency. *Journal of Educational Measurement, 34,* 211–219.

Carroll, J. B. (1993). *Human cognitive abilities: A survey of factor-analytic studies.* New York: Cambridge University Press.

Embretson, S. E. (1983). Construct validity: Construct representation versus nomothetic span. *Psychological Bulletin, 93,* 179–197.

Embretson, S. E. (1991). A multidimensional latent trait model for measuring learning and change. *Psychometrika, 56,* 495–516.

Embretson, S. E. (1995). Developments toward a cognitive design system for psychological tests. In D. Lupinsky & R. Dawis (Eds.), *Assessing individual differences in human behavior* (pp. 17–48). Palo Alto, CA: Davies-Black Publishing Company.

Embretson, S. E. (1997). Structured ability models in tests designed from cognitive theory. In M. Wilson, G. Engelhard, & K. Draney (Eds.), *Objective Measurement III* (pp. 223–236). Norwood, NJ: Ablex.

Embretson, S. E. (in press-a). A cognitive design system approach to generating valid tests: Application to abstract reasoning. *Psychological Methods.*

Embretson, S. E. (in press-b). Cognitive psychology applied to testing. In F. Durso (Ed.), *Handbook of applied cognitive psychology.* London: Wiley.

Jackson, D. N. (1973). Structured personality assessment. In B. B. Wolman (Ed.), *Handbook of general psychology* (pp. 775–792). Englewood Cliffs, NJ: Prentice-Hall.

Lord, F. N., & Novick, M. (1968). *Statistical theories of mental tests.* New York: Addison-Wesley.

Rost, J. (1990). Rasch models in latent classes: An integration of two approaches to item analysis. *Applied Psychological Measurement, 3,* 271–282.

Stern, W. (1914). *The psychological method of testing intelligence* (G. M. Whipple, Trans.). Baltimore: Warwick & York. (Original work published 1912)

Tatsuoka, K. K. (1983). Rule space: An approach for dealing with misconceptions based on item response theory. *Journal of Educational Measurement, 20,* 34–38.

Tatsuoka, K. K. (1985). A probabilistic model for diagnosing misconceptions in the pattern classification approach. *Journal of Educational Statistics, 12,* 55–73.

Thorndike, E. L., Bregman, E. O., Cobb, M. V., & Woodyard, E. (1926). *The measurement of intelligence.* New York: Teachers College Bureau of Publications.

Thurstone, L. L. (1928). The absolute zero in the measurement of intelligence. *Psychological Review, 38,* 406–427.

Woodcock, R. W. (1991). *Woodcock Language Proficiency Battery—Revised: Examiner's manual.* Chicago, IL: Riverside.

Author Index

Subject Index